IMAGES
of America

BARNEGAT LIGHT

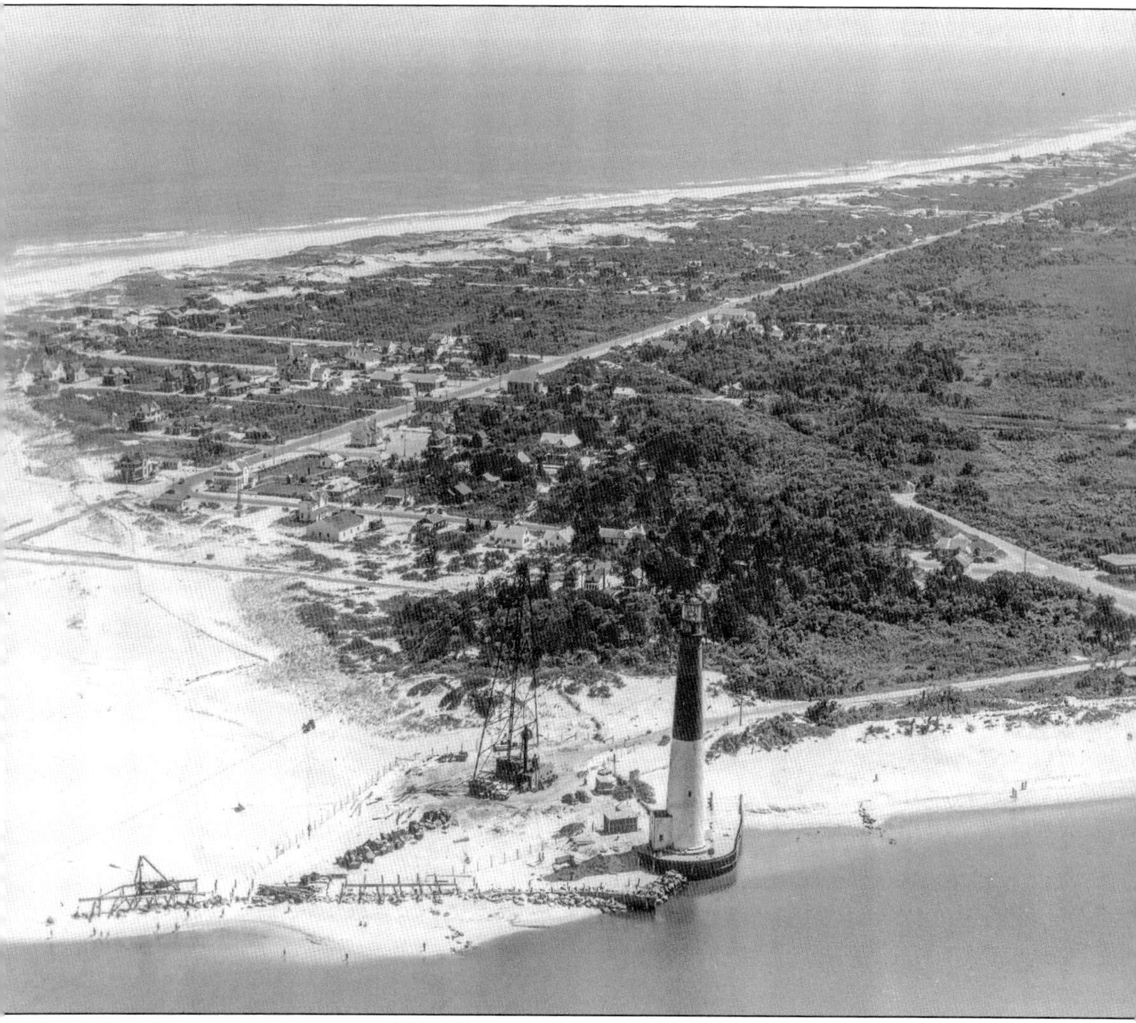

This 1939 aerial view of Barnegat City shows the little fishing town before the post–World War II development boom. Less than 200 called the town home then, only growing to just under 600 today in spite of the annual swell of summer vacationers. Vast stretches of pines, bushes, meadows, and dunes dwarfed the occasional unpaved street and cottages that dotted the still virginal landscape. (Courtesy Hagley Museum & Library.)

On the Cover: Barnegat City resident John Sculthorp sits in his boat with a friend on Barnegat Bay in this c. 1915 photograph. The safe haven inside Barnegat Inlet has enjoyed a long history of commercial and pleasure boats. Tall ships dropped anchor here to weather storms and resupply. Those out to sail would tack about the waterway on yachts. Some lived on the protected waters in houseboats. (Courtesy Barnegat Light Historical Society & Museum.)

IMAGES
of America

BARNEGAT LIGHT

Reilly Platten Sharp for the
Barnegat Light Historical Society & Museum

ARCADIA
PUBLISHING

ISBN 978-1-4671-0326-8

Published by Arcadia Publishing
Charleston, South Carolina

Printed in the United States of America

Library of Congress Control Number: 2018962855

For all general information, please contact Arcadia Publishing:
Telephone 843-853-2070
Fax 843-853-0044
E-mail sales@arcadiapublishing.com

Visit us on the Internet at www.arcadiapublishing.com

To my grandparents Jack and Barbara Platten, who found heaven on earth at Barnegat Light and shared it with the rest of us.

Contents

ACKNOWLEDGMENTS

This book would not be possible without the dedicated service of the past and present members of the Barnegat Light Historical Society & Museum (BLHS&M). They are the storytellers and documentarians who help preserve our history for future generations. Unless noted otherwise, all images are courtesy of the BLHS&M archive.

I wish everyone who generously contributed to the archive could be acknowledged, but much was given anonymously. To those who are known, my thanks: Anna Lisa Olsen Ray; Carol Inman Niemiec; Frednia Brodbeck; the family of Chief Earl Hussey; the National Archives; Capt. Jerry Mason, US Navy (Ret.), and Charla Mason of uboatarchive.net; Ronald Marr and the Long Beach Island Museum; Surf City Fire Department chief Emil Tum Suden (Ret.); the Yale Center for British Art's Paul Mellon Collection; Fred Thornes; Anna J. Mason; Tomm Robinson; Minnie D. Kelly; A. Jerome Walnutt; Richard Plunkett; Jack Lamping; Bowen & Co. engravers; and the family of Edith Duff Gwinn.

My gratitude goes to the Library of Congress for sharing some of its immense collection. The Hagley Museum & Library of Wilmington, Delaware, and its staff were most helpful in locating photographs from its invaluable archive. The Library Company of Philadelphia and staff were equally generous with its rarities.

Historians owe a debt to the team from the Coastal and Hydraulics Laboratory Engineer Research and Development Center for finding and saving remarkable aerial photographs of our coast spanning the 20th century.

Appreciation must be given to those authors who sought out and recorded varied portions of Long Beach Island's history that have collectively contributed to the whole of our knowledge of where our beloved island communities come from. These include the works of Bayard Randolph Kraft, John Brinckmann, Mary Montgomery Karch, Thomas Jay France, Ronald Spisso, John Bailey Lloyd, and Margaret Thomas Buchholz. We who tell the tales after them are standing on the shoulders of giants.

Special thanks to Poochy Buchholz for her unyielding encouragement and advice and for sharing some of her photo collection. You're a treasure.

I am grateful to BLHS president Karen Larson for her leadership and warm friendship. You are a true example to emulate.

Last but not least, to Arcadia Publishing and its excellent staff, I could not have done this without your guidance. Erin Vosgien, your encouragement was a big boost. And to my editor, Angel Hisnanick, great thanks for shepherding this project across the finish line.

Introduction

Wild, wild the storm, and the sea high running;
Steady the roar of the gale, with incessant undertone muttering;
Shouts of demoniac laughter fitfully piercing and pealing;
Waves, air, midnight, their savagest trinity lashing;
Out in the shadows there milk-white combs careering;
On beachy slush and sand spirts of snow fierce slanting—
Where through the murk the easterly death-wind breasting,
Through cutting swirl and spray watchful and firm advancing
(That in the distance! is that a wreck? is the red signal flaring?),
Slush and sand of the beach tireless till daylight wending,
Steadily, slowly, through hoarse roar never remitting,
Along the midnight edge by those milk-white combs careering,
A group of dim, weird forms, struggling, the night confronting,
That savage trinity warily watching.

—Walt Whitman, "Patrolling Barnegat," 1881

From the vast, sandy, acidic pine barrens to the swampy expanses along the edge of the Atlantic, the southern coast of New Jersey is unwelcoming to any but the hardiest flora and fauna. The people of the Lenape tribe were the first humans to settle the area and flourished in spite of the challenges. In the summers, they would leave the barrens and hunting grounds for the coast, settling along the bays, including the western shore of Barnegat Bay that separated the mainland and the 18-mile barrier island to the east known today as Long Beach Island. Canoes were employed to cross over "long land lake," as they called the bay behind the island covered with tall pine forests. Fishing and oystering provided sustenance all season. When the weather turned cold, the summer residents would leave the coast and head back to their villages far inland.

It is not known for certain when Europeans first sighted Long Beach Island and Barnegat Inlet. Circumstantial evidence suggests it could have been Leif Eriksson of Iceland nearly 1,000 years ago. Some historians make a case for Italian explorer Sebastiano Caboto in 1508 or Giovanni Verrazzano in 1523. Whatever the case may be, it was Englishman Henry Hudson, employed by the Dutch East India Company to find a northwest passage to India aboard the *Halve Maen*, who first recorded the island and its infamous inlet, anchoring within sight of the beach on Labor Day weekend 1609. Others followed in his footsteps along the shore. Dutch sailors described the inlet in their journals as "*barende-gat*." Depending on the context in which it was used and who is doing the translation to English, it could mean "opening at the end of the barrens" or "flowing hole," among other variations. In either case, it stood as a warning to their brethren to be watchful when they approached this tidal mouth with its protruding breakers and powerful tidal forces.

In the ensuing decades, the description became synonymous with the place, becoming a name all but officially. Colloquialisms, though, gave rise to variations: Barendegat, Barnde-gat, Barne Gat, Brandende Gat, Barndegat, Barnigat, Barnigate, Barnagat, and Barnegat. The last became the norm by the mid-17th century, especially when the Dutch lost control of the region, known then as New Netherlands, to the British after the second Anglo-Dutch War (1665–1667).

Like the Lenape before them, the 17th century saw European settlers migrating to the mainland coast behind the protection of what was then called Long Beach. The town of Tuckerton flourished, becoming one of the ports of entry to the American colonies. To the north, Barnegat grew as a small but important fishing town and access point to the gateway to the Atlantic about six miles east of town. During the Revolutionary War, naval battles took place inside and outside old Barende-gat Inlet. Skirmishes from the beach to the far inland pine barrens raged as loyalists and patriots fought for the future of the United States. One of the most infamous incidents featured a massacre over cargo from a salvaged British vessel aground on the treacherous Barnegat shoals lining the approaches to the inlet. While patriots who had recovered the sloop's treasure slept in the dunes near the present-day Barnegat Lighthouse one night in 1782, opportunistic plunderers who happened to be loyalists, led by John Bacon, caught wind of what had happened. They crept up on the dozen or so men and executed most on that desolate beach. A manhunt led to the Battle of Cedar Bridge soon after, followed by another battle a few months later in Tuckerton, where Bacon was killed. This local legacy and reputation lingered well into the 1800s. Stories of the "Barnegat Pirates" became national, and international, news in a time when so much depended on marine transportation. To be sure, some men salvaged wrecks at the point of a sword or the muzzle of a musket. Rumors had it that a despicable few lured vessels onto the shoals with misleading signal fires from the beaches near the inlet. Most of the "Pirates," though, were opportunistic locals who were experienced at lifesaving, vessel salvage, and the laws of the sea. Often, wayward mariners gladly offered portions of their cargo as compensation for hospitable rescue during the deadliest storms.

After the war, whaling attracted mainlanders more regularly across the bay to Long Beach. Small cottages were built in various places up and down the island. By the early 19th century, peacetime meant that pleasure was a permissible pursuit, giving rise to boardinghouses along the Jersey shore for fishermen, duck hunters, and those who would enjoy the sea air. One of the first was built on the north end of Long Beach, a mostly deserted area locals called Barnegat Beach. Bornt Slaght's lodging house there soon gained a neighbor when, in 1834, a 40-foot-tall lighthouse was built to warn ships away from the shoals. By this time, the coast of New Jersey near Long Beach had become a well-trafficked point of entry for ships arriving from Europe. Tall ships would approach either this coast or the Long Island coast, then chart a course into New York harbor. The dangers of the ever-shifting shoals caused by the immense force of waters emptying and entering Barnegat Inlet gave rise to the area's reputation as a "graveyard of the Atlantic," with untold commercial losses and a growing human cost.

By the 1850s, the establishment of so-called resorts on the Jersey shore and their explosive growth crystallized in nearby Atlantic City. Developers in Philadelphia and the then-booming industrial town of Camden, New Jersey, saw opportunities for mass commercial entertainment in the barren sands of Long Beach. What followed would transform Barnegat Beach from a small but important site of historical drama to a planned city yearning for crowds that would take generations, not years, to finally come. In the intervening years, what grew out of such ambitions was what had endured all along—settler families deepening their roots, new arrivals setting down theirs, and slowly but steadily increasing throngs of summer visitors who would return again and again to old Barende-gat. This is their story, one that is inseparable from old "long land lake." What lured the Lenape, the Dutch, the settlers, and the developers continues to lure today as potently as ever. The rhythm of the sea speaks in a language everyone understands, and none can forget at Barnegat Light.

One

Old Barende-Gat

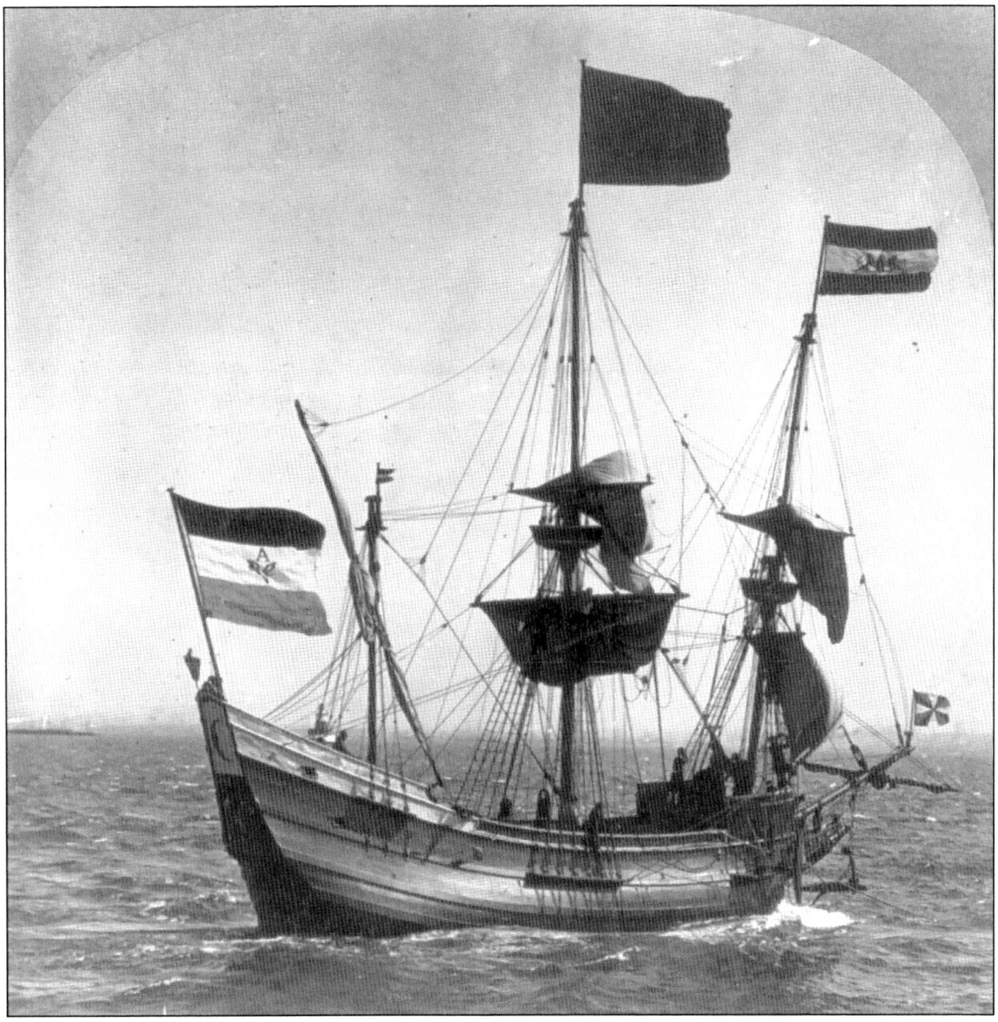

When the *Halve Maen* (*Half Moon*), a reproduction of which is seen here, brought English explorer Henry Hudson up Long Beach Island in early September 1609, he noted the foaming waves far out from a northern break in the barrier island and dropped anchor for the night, away from the inlet's tidal grasp. (Courtesy of the Library of Congress, Prints and Photographs Division.)

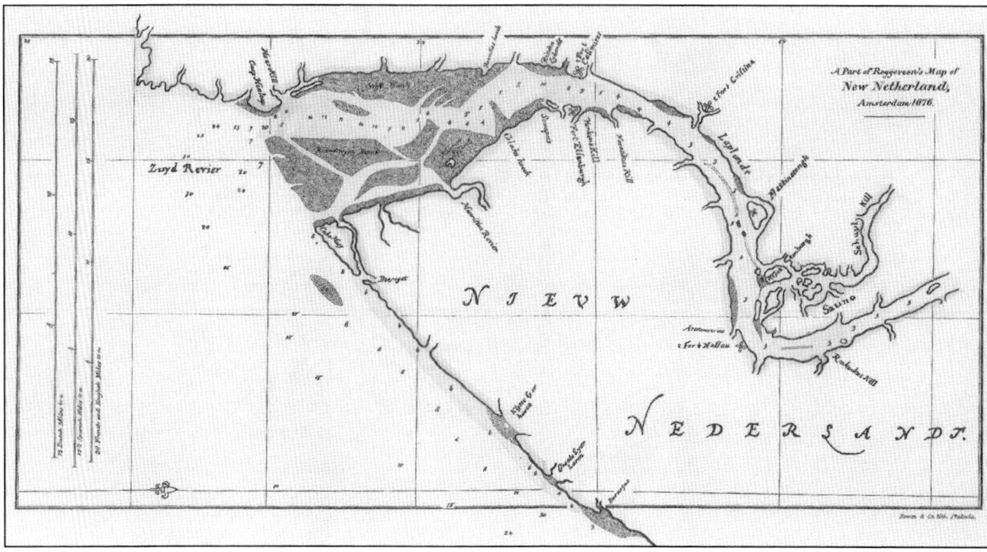

This 1876 anniversary reprinting of a well-known 1676 map, wherein southwest is up and northeast is down, shows how a portion of the New World appeared to settlers in its earliest years. Remnants of Swedish colonization are still plain to see along the Delaware River over 25 years after Dutch conquest. Along the coast, note the Dutch mapping and naming of inlets and banks, including "Barnagat" and its vast shoals.

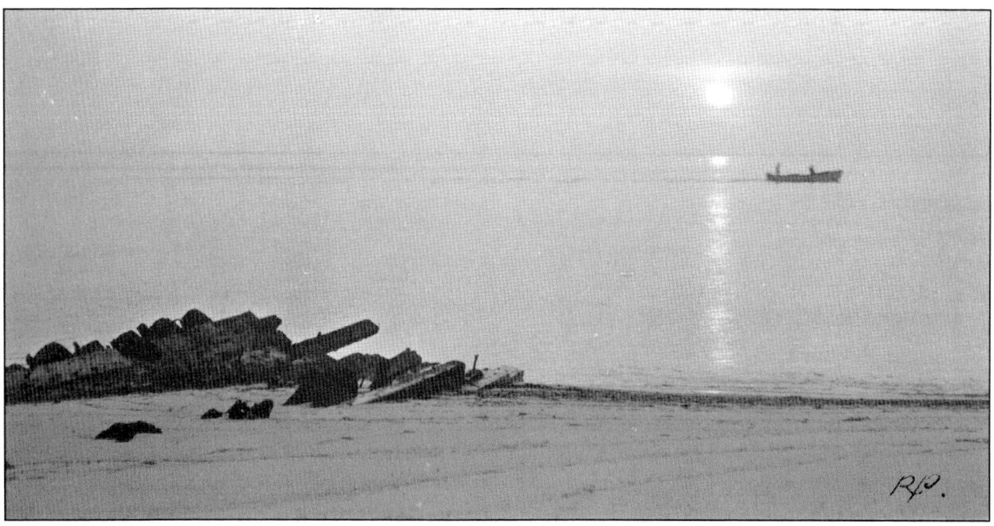

The scene pictured here was typical of Barnegat Light for much of its settled history. Barnegat Inlet would be passed by vessels of all sizes and manner of propulsion, carefully navigating by or through the channel. Many wrecked on the beaches or shoals, lingering for months as painfully visible skeletal reminders that a deadly toll would be paid in return for these waters' bounties.

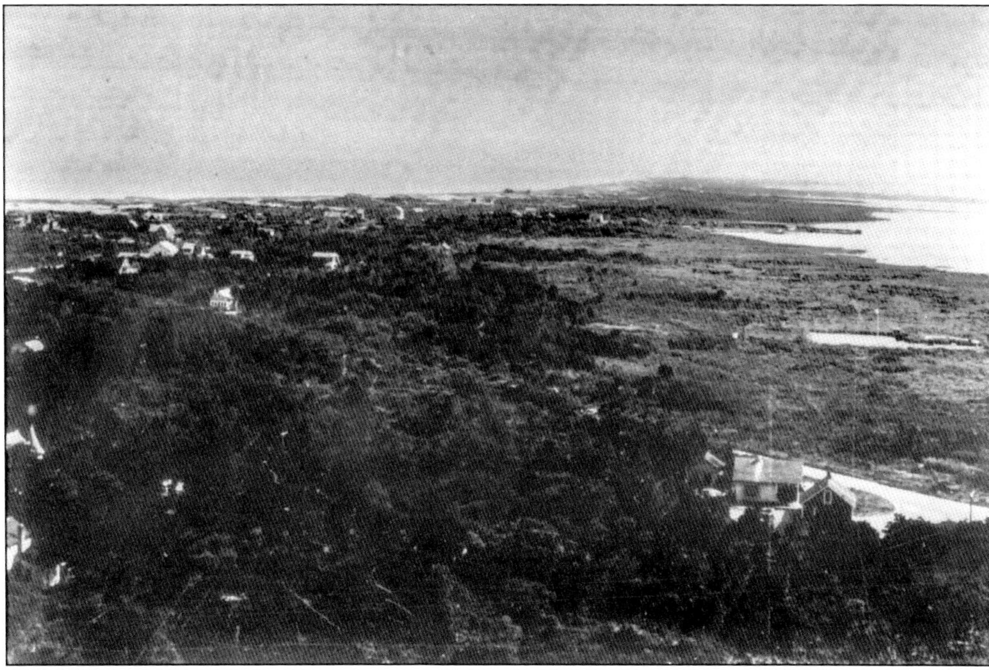

Barnegat Light began as a wilderness of pines, bushes, and meadows. Far from a barren and sandy spit of land, the lush north end, pictured here still mostly untouched around 1910, hosted many species of wildlife, from flocks of migratory birds to foxes and even deer. In the winter, the sometimes-frozen bay allowed larger animals to freely cross the four miles of water from the mainland to the island.

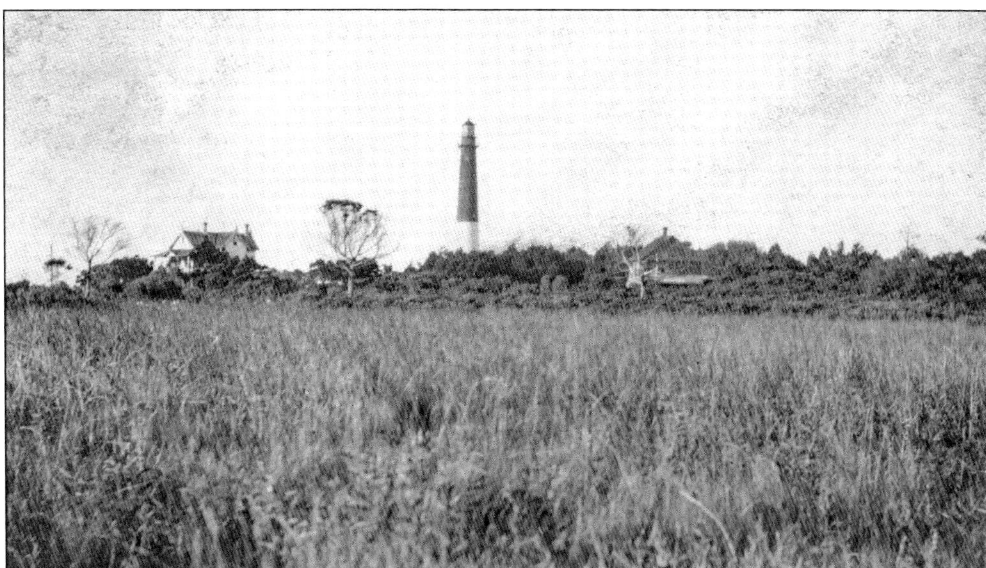

It was no simple task when the construction of cottages began. Tall forests dominated the high ground, while soggy, reed-filled meadows made the vast lowlands on the bayside a messy situation. This 1909 photograph taken from the present West Sixth Street canal looks across one such meadow toward the towering pines of West Fourth Street with an 1880s cottage (left) and Butterworth's General Store (right) nestled among them.

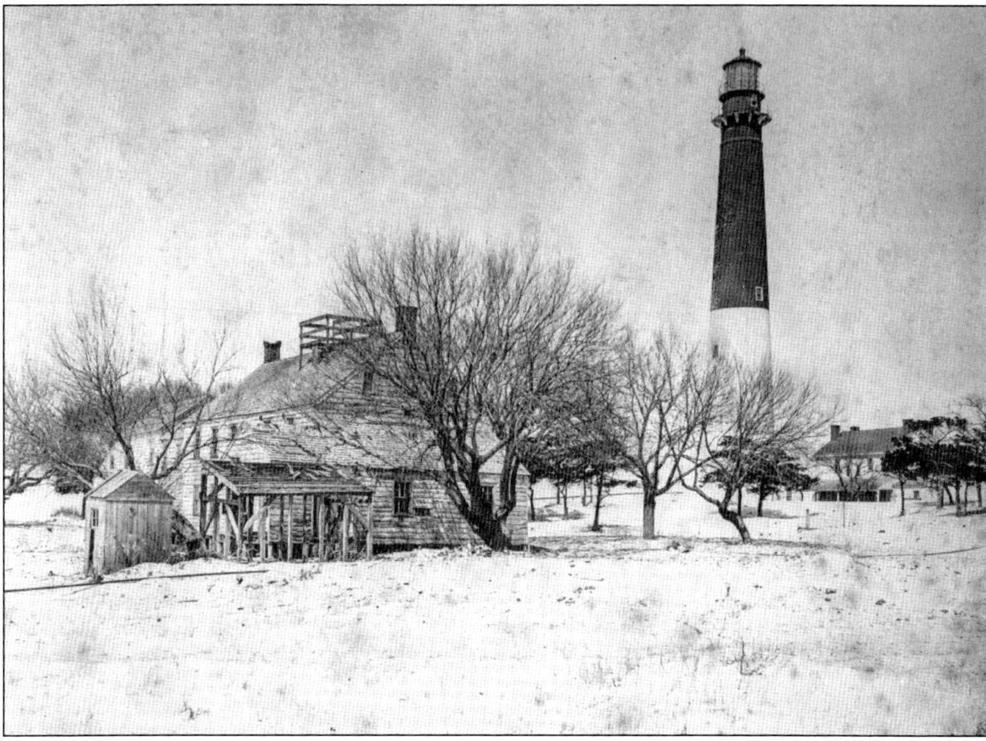

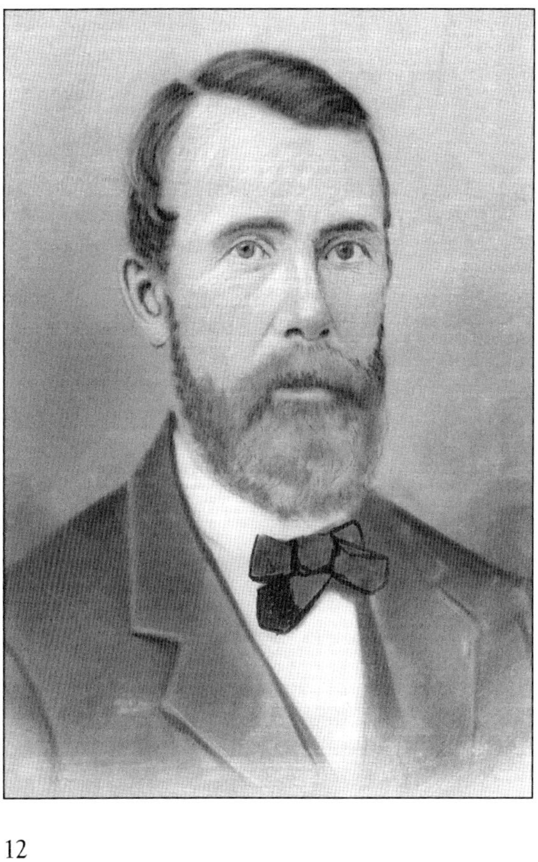

One of the first structures built was this boardinghouse for up to 100 guests, seen here around 1880. Bornt Slaght of Barnegat started construction around the same time as Surf City's Mansion of Health and Cape May's Congress Hall, collectively the first American shore resort hotels. Opened in 1822, it endured through fits and starts while its brethren enjoyed more success. (Courtesy of the Ocean County Historical Society.)

By the mid-1850s, Slaght's house was a creaky old haunt. That changed when a Manasquan wrecker, John Maxon Brown, bought it and much of the land around the inlet. He renamed it the Ashley House and put his children in charge, including John Ashley Brown, pictured here. The Brown family sold all their holdings in Barnegat Light after Ashley Brown died at sea in 1874.

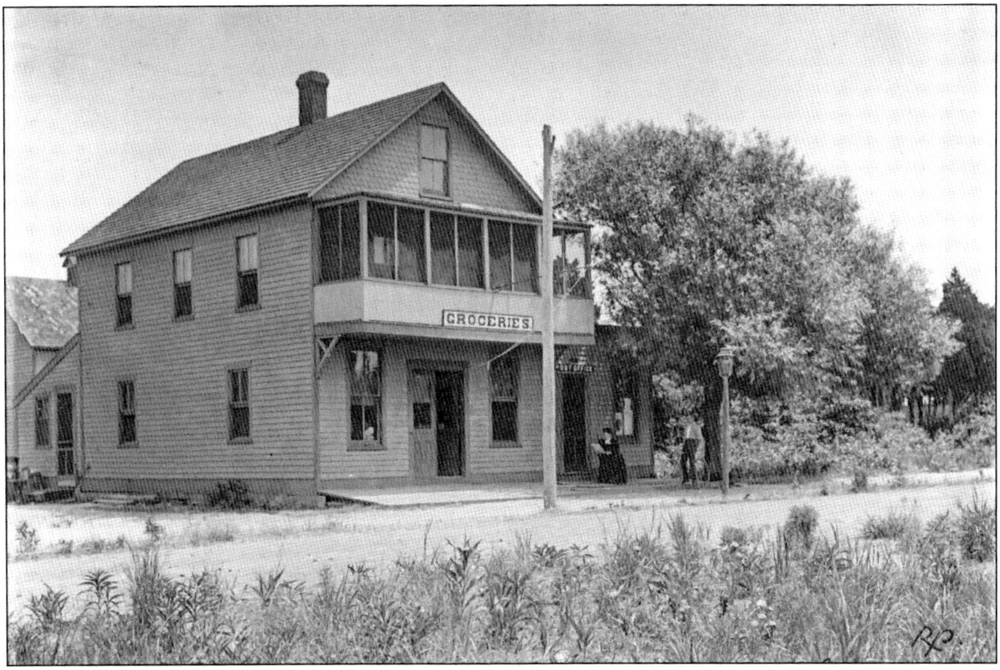

In this undated postcard, the Butterworth store and post office are seen on a typical day along West Fourth Street. Run by Lloyd and Lucretia Butterworth for 25 years, the store was built in 1882 and has changed hands only a few times. Lucretia is seen here sitting with a boy from the Applegate family.

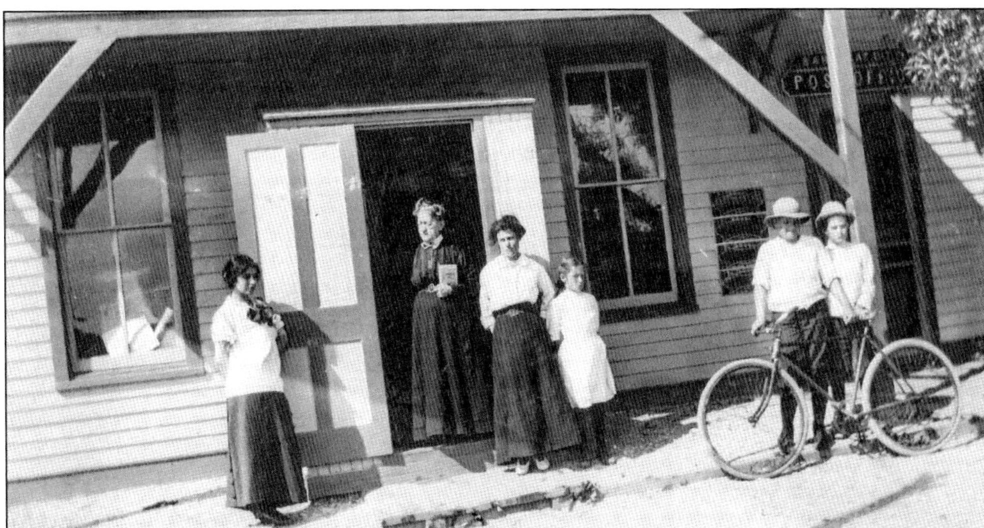

After Lloyd Butterworth died in 1905, Lucretia Butterworth, his wife, carried on with her duties at the store alone. As Barnegat Light grew, so did the number of customers, especially children. This c. 1915 photograph features, from left to right, Amelia ?, Lucretia Butterworth, Minnie Peckworth, unidentified, Bob Applegate, and ? Johnson. The tradition of the store as a gathering spot has continued ever since

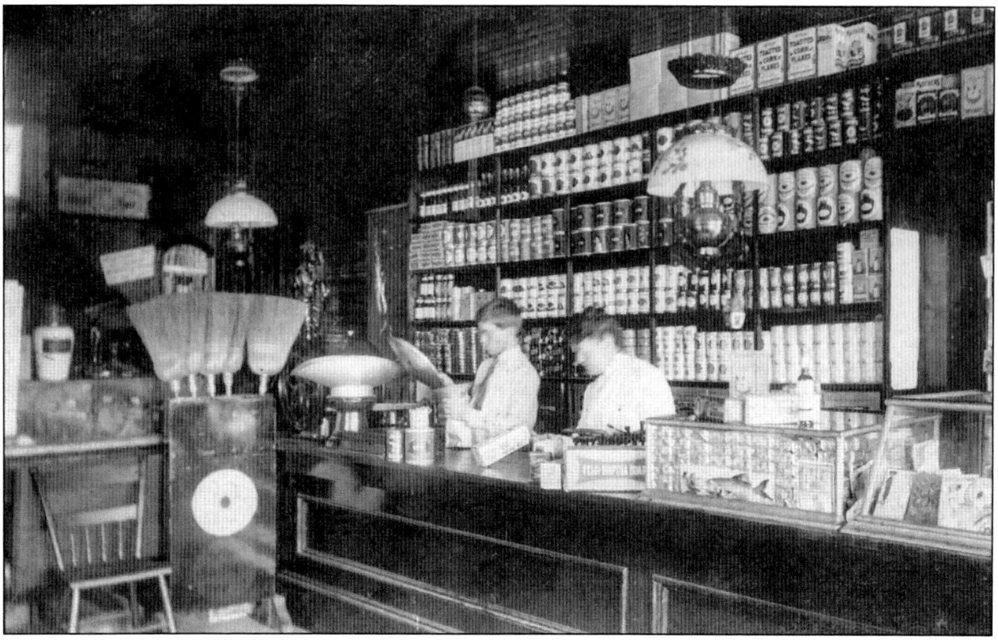

This c. 1920 photograph of the inside of the store, with a stock boy and Bertha Applegate, shows how it appeared for generations. Anyone who needed anything came to Butterworth's, later known as Applegate's Store, and the Inlet Deli. It served as the post office until 1950. Around that time, White's Market was established on the corner of West Sixteenth Street and Central Avenue and remains in business today.

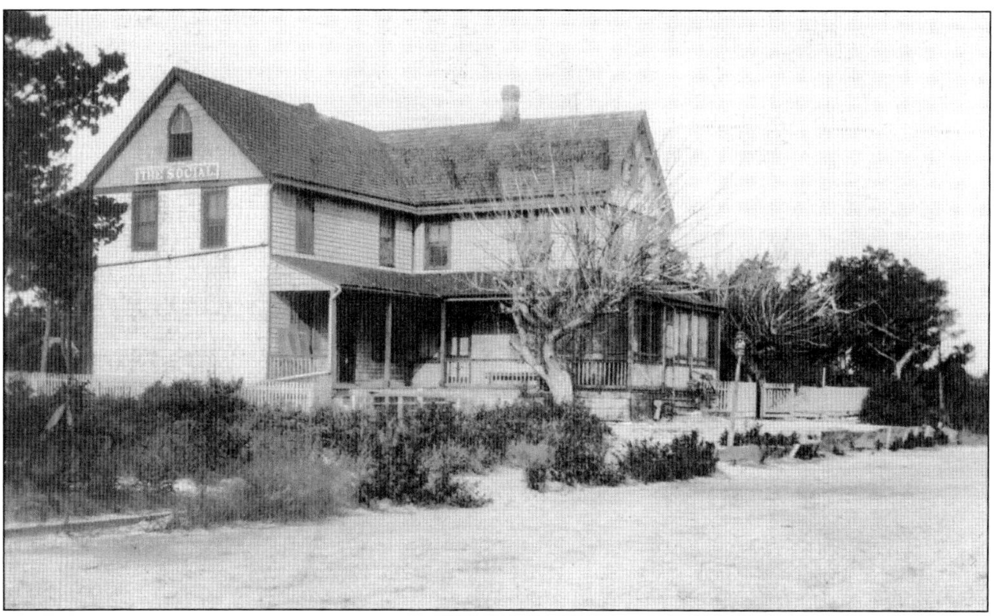

Pictured around 1920, the Social Hotel on West Fifth Street was a popular spot for the seasonal crowds of duck hunters who came for the area's famous bird migrations. Built c. 1883, the hotel was frequented until the 1950s, after which it was run as a bed-and-breakfast known as the Inlet of the Breakers. It eventually closed in the late 1980s and was torn down in 1994.

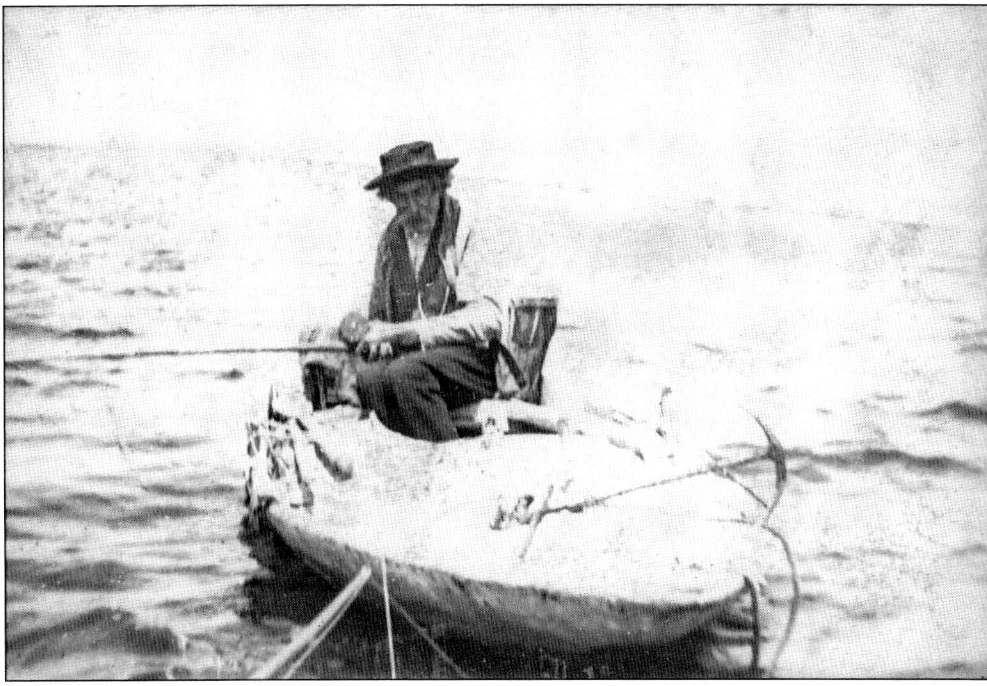

Caleb Parker, seen here in 1900, was one of the most storied locals. He was erroneously promoted by hoteliers down the island as "the last Barnegat Pirate" due to his Parker roots and their alleged involvement in the forcible salvage of wrecked ships years prior. Parker was better known for his fishing prowess, often seen headed out into the inlet in his boat. If there was a record catch, it was usually his.

Longtime lightkeeper Clarence Hazelton Cranmer, posing atop the lighthouse with the inlet at his back, owed his life to Caleb "Dad" Parker. In 1870, nine-year-old Cranmer fell out of a boat in sight of Parker and was swept out into the inlet. Parker dove in after him, kept his head above water through the rough current, and saved the boy from drowning.

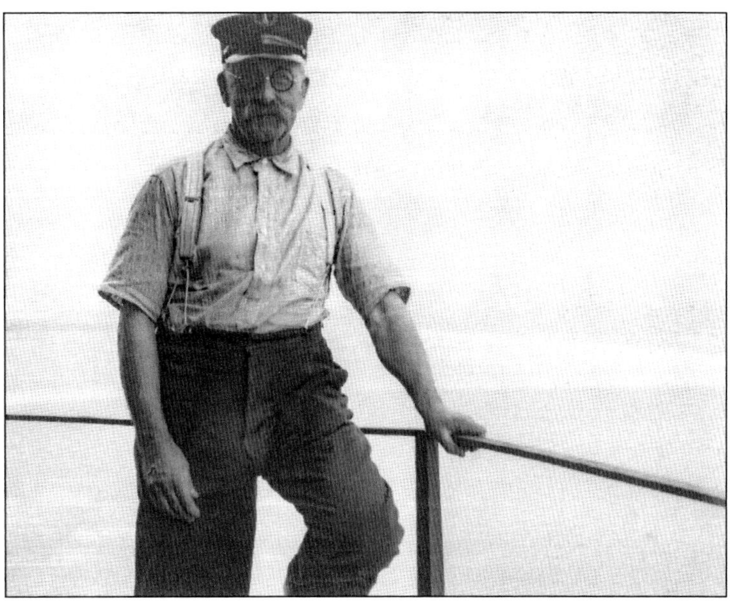

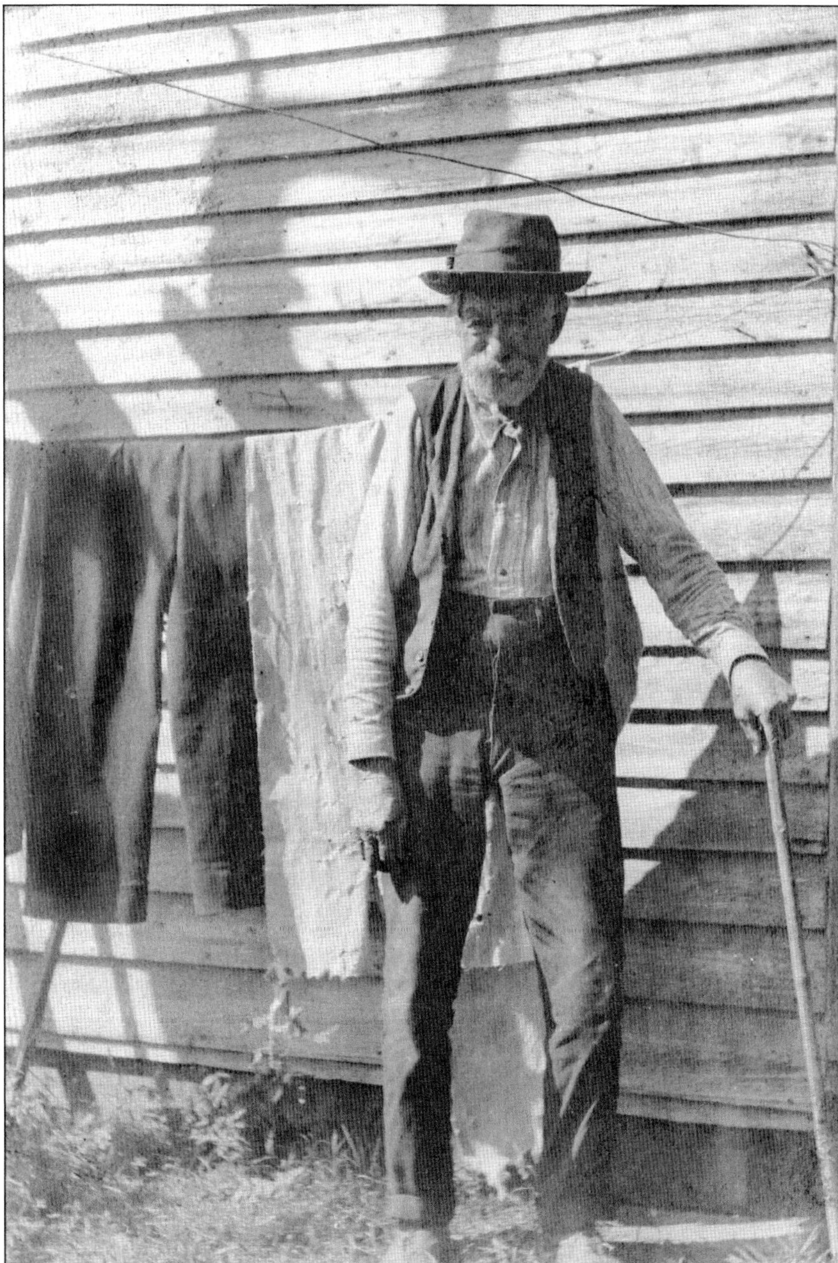

After the rescue, Clarence Cranmer's father, Captain Nathan Cranmer, and all the townspeople of Barnegat Beach and its mainland sister city, Barnegat, got together to hold a party in Caleb Parker's honor. The celebration included a presentation of an inscribed medal acknowledging his heroism. From then on, Parker earned a new nickname: "Uncle Cale." Once, Parker took in a bundle of Manx cats that washed up in a wreck, which gave rise to nationwide stories about old man Parker and his Manx cats. In his elder years, pictured here around 1905, everyone in town took turns housing and caring for "Uncle" Parker. In about 1904, locals built him a new house to live out his days. When he died in 1907, the outpouring of grief was enough to generate newspaper headlines around the county and state. With his death, the connection to a storied era passed into history.

Two

THE BARNEGAT LIGHTS

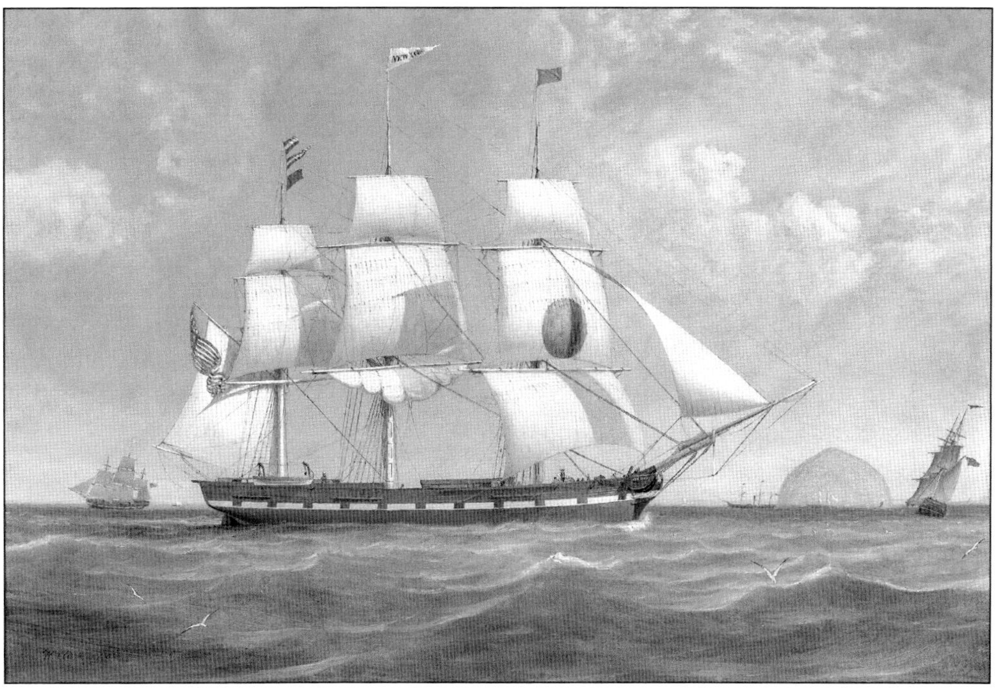

The first Barnegat lighthouse was a 40-foot tower designed by Winslow Lewis and built in 1834. The packet ship *New-York*, seen in this painting by William Clark, was its most famous casualty. In 1856, the ship grounded, unsure if the light was a lighthouse or a pilot boat, and sat for days during a blizzard with over 300 Irish immigrants aboard. (Courtesy of the Yale Center for British Art, Paul Mellon Collection.)

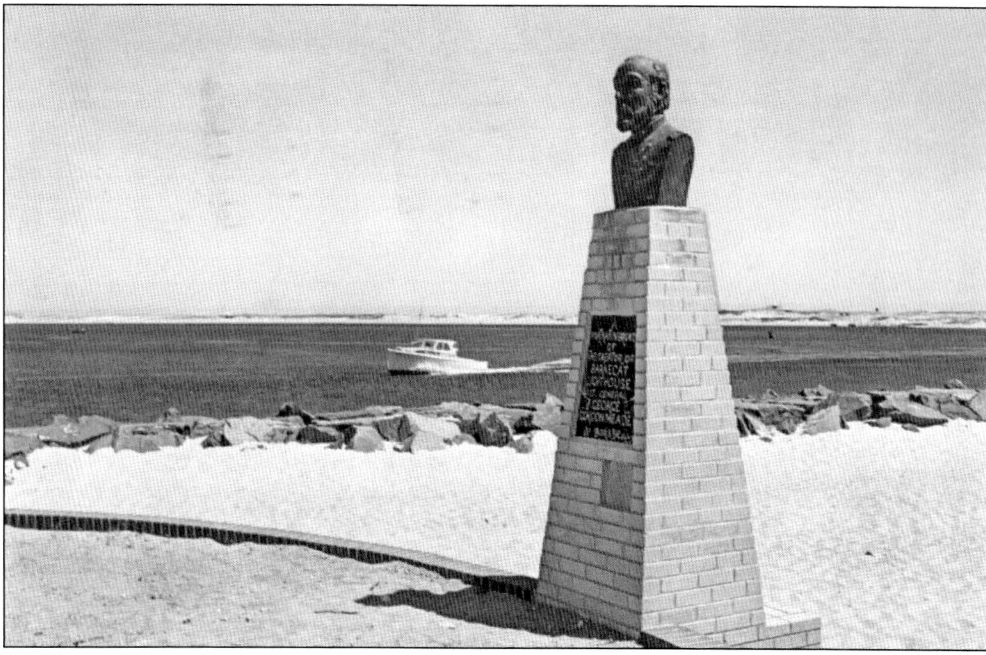

While the first lighthouse was causing trouble and in danger of collapse due to erosion and poor construction, US Army Corps of Engineers captain George Meade was busy designing new first-class lighthouses up and down New Jersey, including at Barnegat Inlet. A monument to his efforts was erected in the 1960s near the lighthouse, featuring a sculpture by renowned local and international artist Boris Blai, as seen in this postcard.

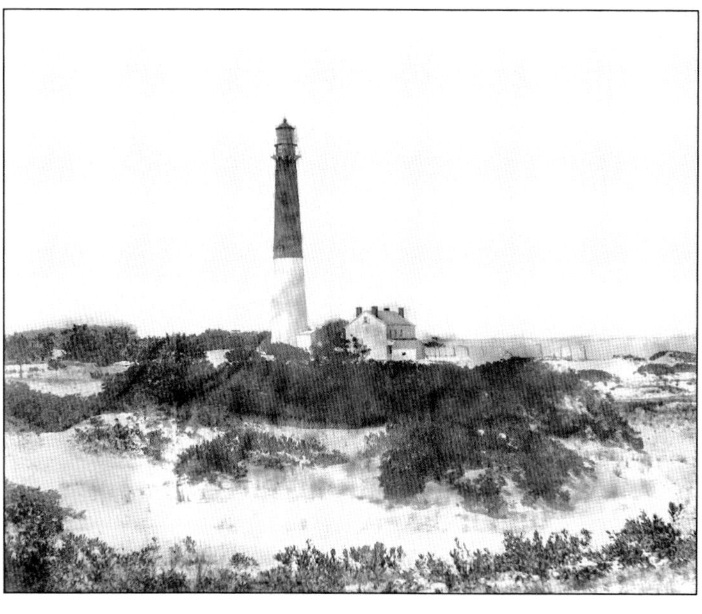

After design, construction began in 1857 of a 168-foot tower painted red on top and white on bottom, a daymark that allowed daytime identification by passing ships. A first-order Fresnel lens allowed the light to reach over 20 miles out at sea. First activated in 1859, the grounds included a modest keeper's house as seen in this c. 1887 image. (Courtesy of the Library Company of Philadelphia, edited by the author.)

In order to accommodate assistant keepers in support of the head keeper, the house was expanded in 1893 to the structure pictured here. No longer did the assistant need to live in a small dwelling on site, similar to the building on the right. The two men and their families now had a proper home to share.

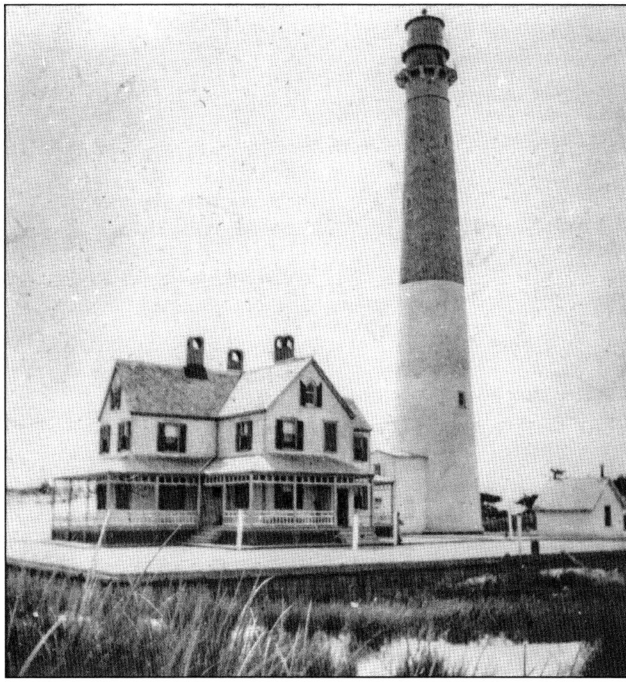

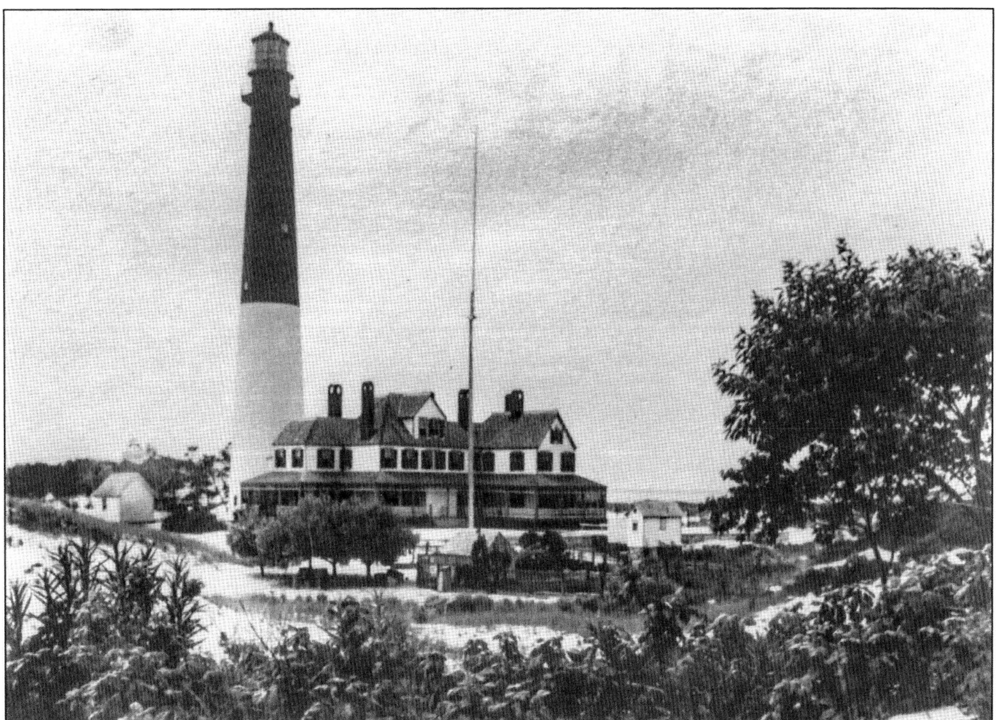

The keeper's house was expanded again in 1898. Pictured here are the vast grounds, including added outbuildings for storing wick oils and other supplies. By then, the role of keeper had expanded enough to allow for a third assistant. Twenty rooms now allowed for semi-comfortable living and the raising of families beneath the tower.

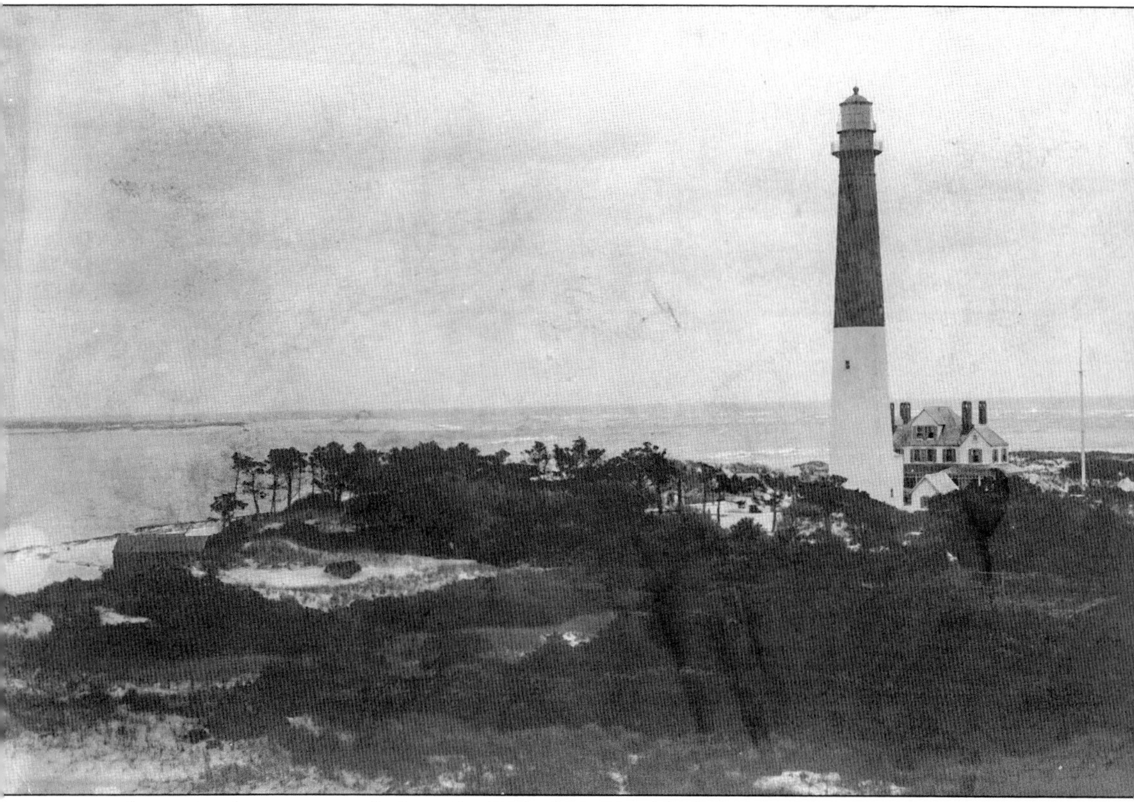

This c. 1910 image reveals how far back the second lighthouse once was from the inlet. The southward march of the channel from the 1820s was relentless. The location of the first lighthouse is about 1,000 feet north of the current one, which was itself about 300 feet from the inlet of 1834. To construct the second light, given the pace of erosion, the government had to buy a large tract of private property to allow for a wide buffer of land. It bought the property from none other than John Maxon Brown, whose Ashley House was only a stone's throw from the proposed site of the new light. Today's maritime forest near the lighthouse would be dwarfed by the tall trees that once made the grounds such a distinctive sight to passing mariners, as well as other forests that formerly populated the island.

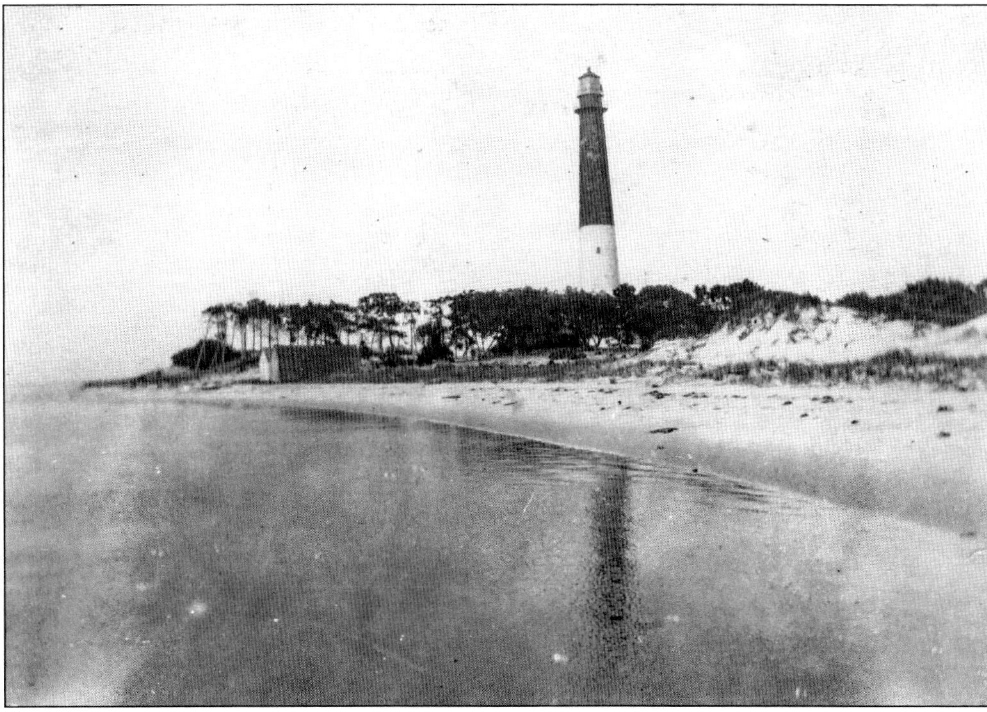

Immediately inside the inlet entrance, a tree-lined peninsula that once existed behind the lighthouse offered a sheltered stretch of beach. The two buildings near the water in this undated photograph were used by the crew of the nearby lifesaving station. They would launch boats into the relatively calm shallows here and train. Bathers, too, would come here to sit and swim as the boats went by.

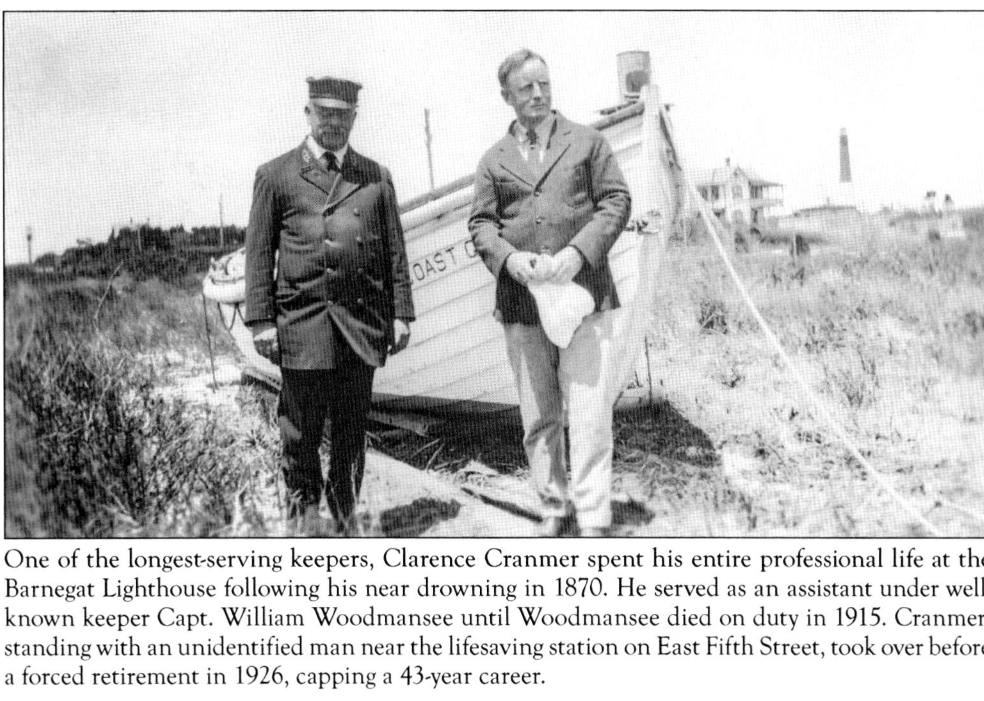

One of the longest-serving keepers, Clarence Cranmer spent his entire professional life at the Barnegat Lighthouse following his near drowning in 1870. He served as an assistant under well-known keeper Capt. William Woodmansee until Woodmansee died on duty in 1915. Cranmer, standing with an unidentified man near the lifesaving station on East Fifth Street, took over before a forced retirement in 1926, capping a 43-year career.

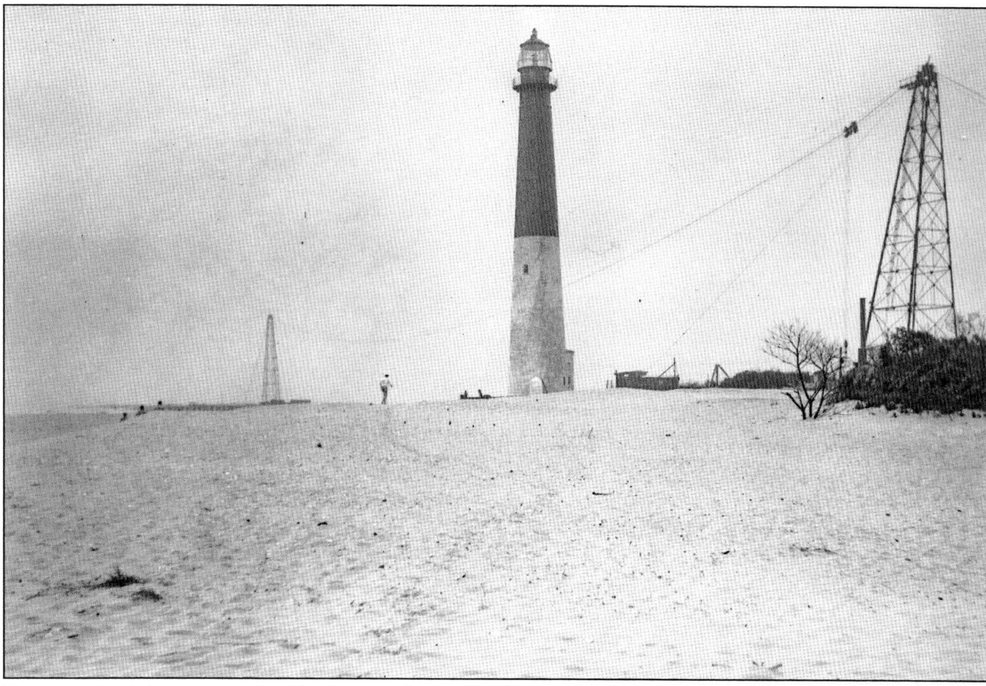

Barnegat Lighthouse was finally shuttered in 1927 due to the threat of erosion and a push to establish lightships. This began decades of state and local attempts to save the storied landmark. In 1939, the Army Corps of Engineers was back working on a jetty for the north side of the inlet using a cable system between towers, as seen here. (Courtesy of the Ocean County Historical Society.)

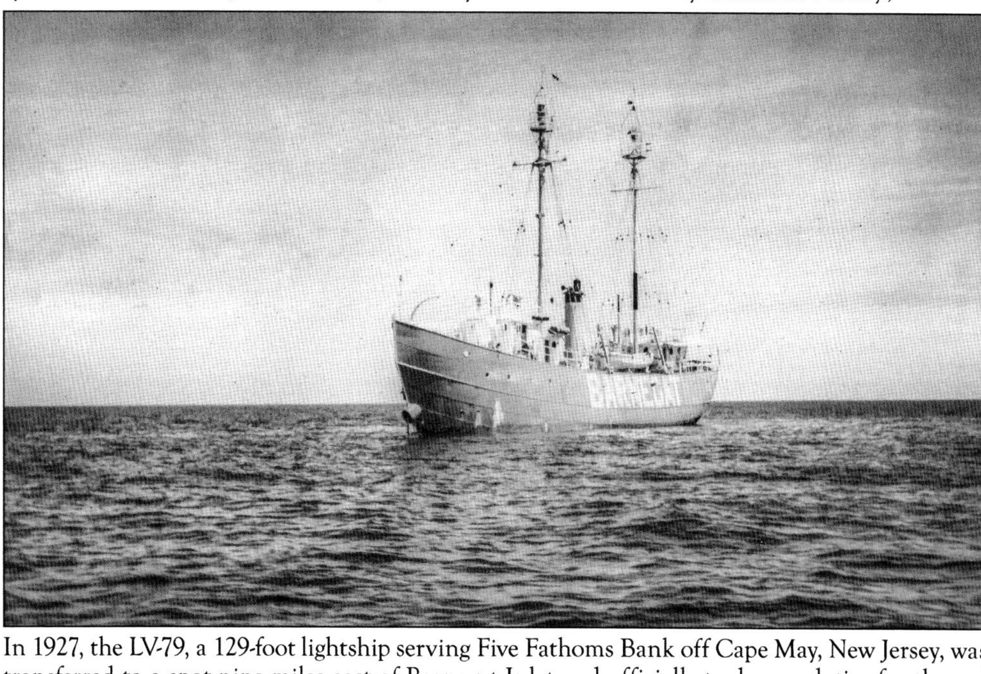

In 1927, the LV-79, a 129-foot lightship serving Five Fathoms Bank off Cape May, New Jersey, was transferred to a spot nine miles east of Barnegat Inlet and officially took over duties for the red and white tower. The rechristened lightship *Barnegat*, pictured here, was anchored to maintain its position along with another 35 similar vessels along the East Coast.

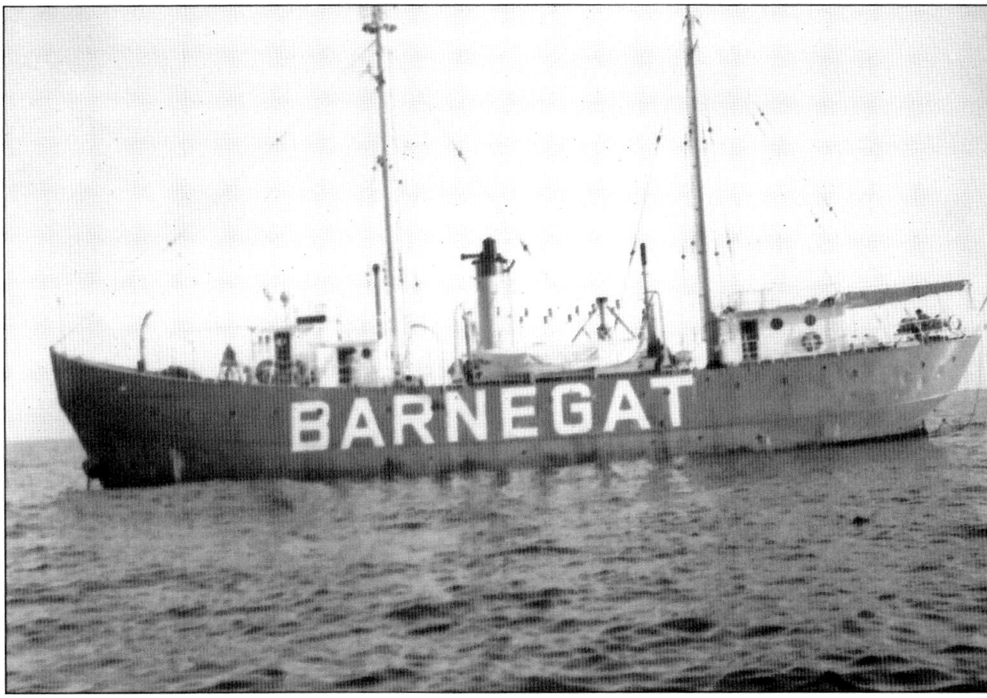

LV-79 remained active for 40 years, moving a few miles east in later years, with the exception of World War II. The threat from German U-boats forced the fleet of ocean-borne light stations to port from 1942 until after the war. (Courtesy of Margaret Thomas Buchholz.)

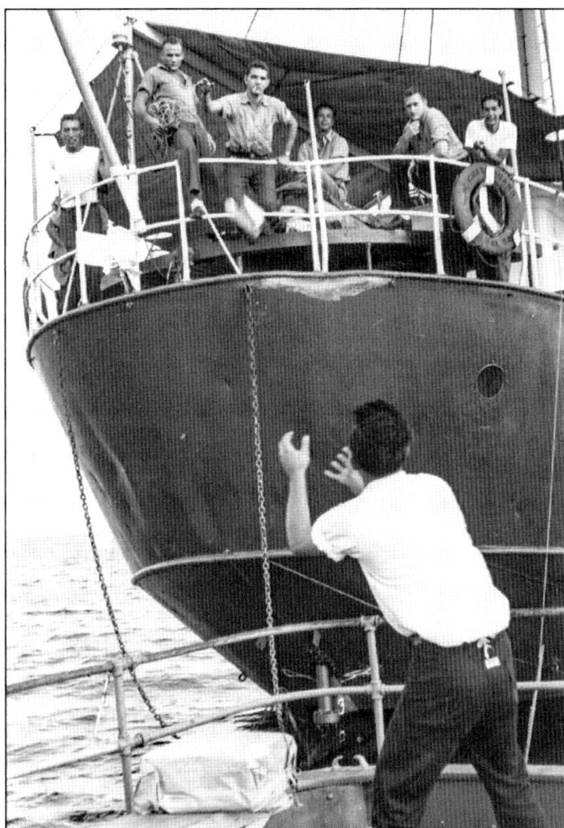

A 14-man crew, pictured swapping supplies with local fishermen, maintained the *Barnegat*, serving two weeks on and two weeks off. Onboard, jobs included cleaning the lamps, servicing the engines and fog horn, keeping the radio beacon active, and being able to cook good meals in the mess. Due to the isolation, troublemakers in the Coast Guard often found themselves on lightship duty. (Courtesy of Margaret Thomas Buchholz.)

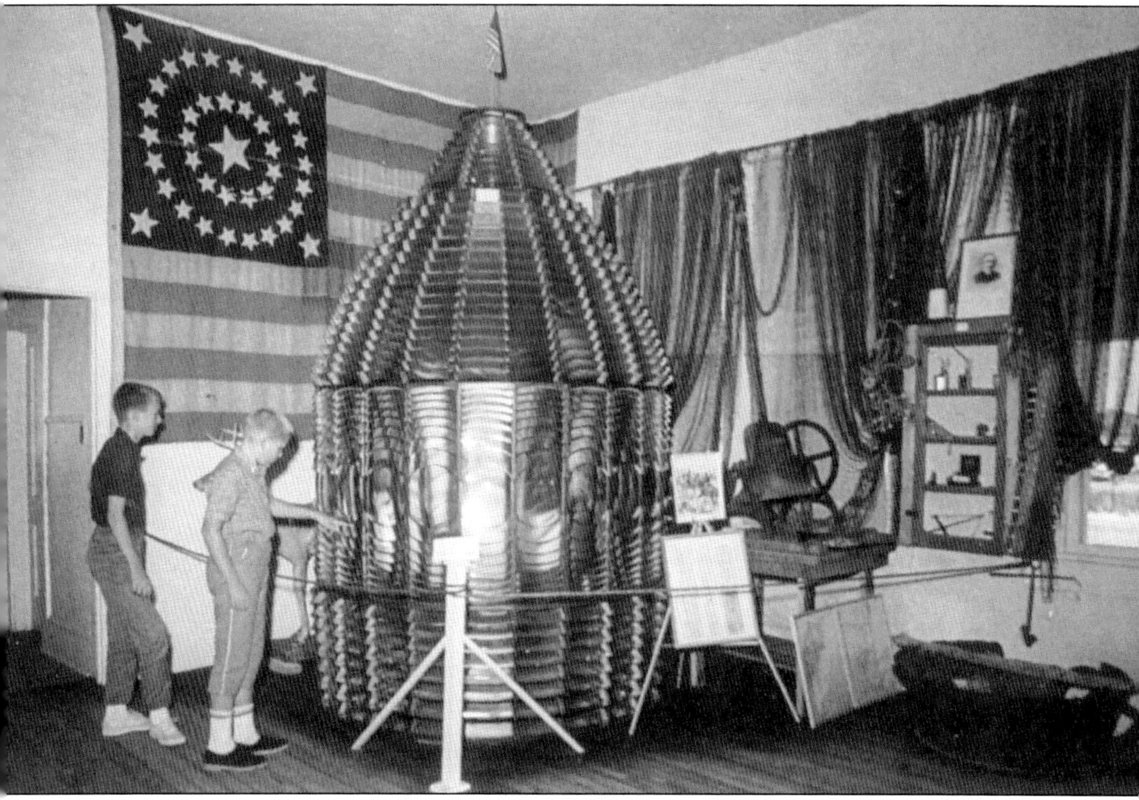

The critical component of the second Barnegat Lighthouse was its Fresnel lens. French engineer Augustin-Jean Fresnel advanced theories on how light travels and developed catadioptric lenses to improve upon France's lighthouse system in the 1820s. The lens worked by redirecting light passing through the glass horizontally instead of in all directions. This meant that the brightness would be increased dramatically, and the light would reach farther out to sea. When Capt. George Meade was designing lighthouses for the United States in the 1850s, the Fresnel lens was chosen. Each lens manufactured for US lighthouses was unique so mariners could tell one from another. Barnegat's had 24 thick bullseyes, showed a white light, and rotated to flash the light for 10 seconds every four minutes. Once Barnegat's first order lens was removed in 1927, it took 30 years before it returned to its home. Plans to reassemble the two-ton, 1,008-piece lens up in the tower were deemed impractical. It was placed in the Barnegat Light Museum, as seen here, where it remains to this day.

Three

The Brave Men of Life-Saving Station No. 17

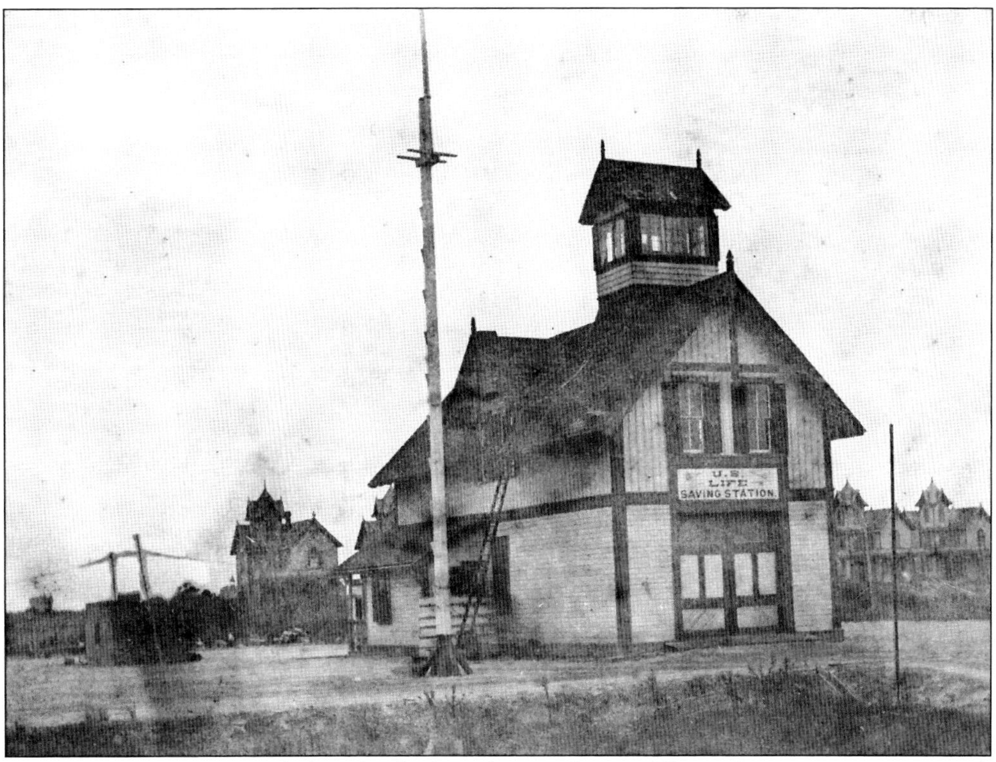

Before the US Coast Guard, the job of aiding ships in distress fell to volunteers. On Long Beach Island, organized groups of seamen risked, and lost, life and limb as early as the 1780s. The US Life-Saving Service was formalized in 1848; Barnegat's first small station was built in 1855. Barnegat Life-Saving Station No. 17, pictured here in the Red House style on East Fifth Street, was built in 1872.

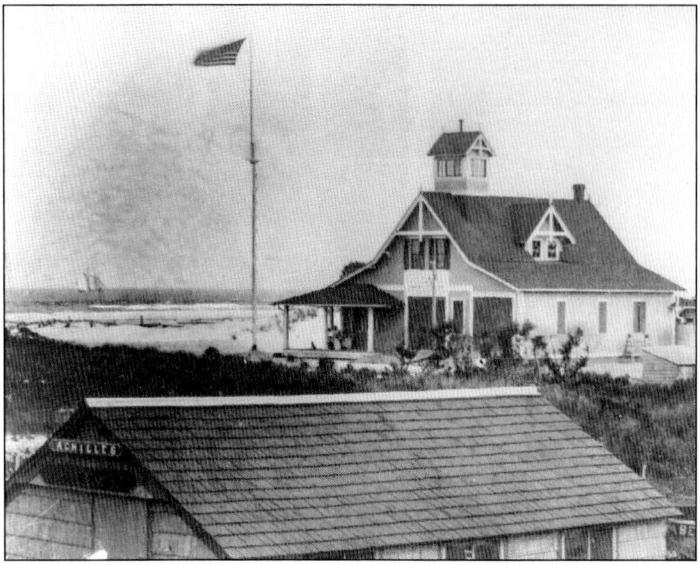

Located at the edge of the beach, the lifesaving station at Barnegat Inlet was well situated to render immediate aid, which it did many times over. These stations were so successful that federal funding was increased, allowing for expansions such as the one seen here, completed in 1884. The earliest boat houses were often ill-equipped and unoccupied; the job of lifesaving was considered only a seasonal one in those days.

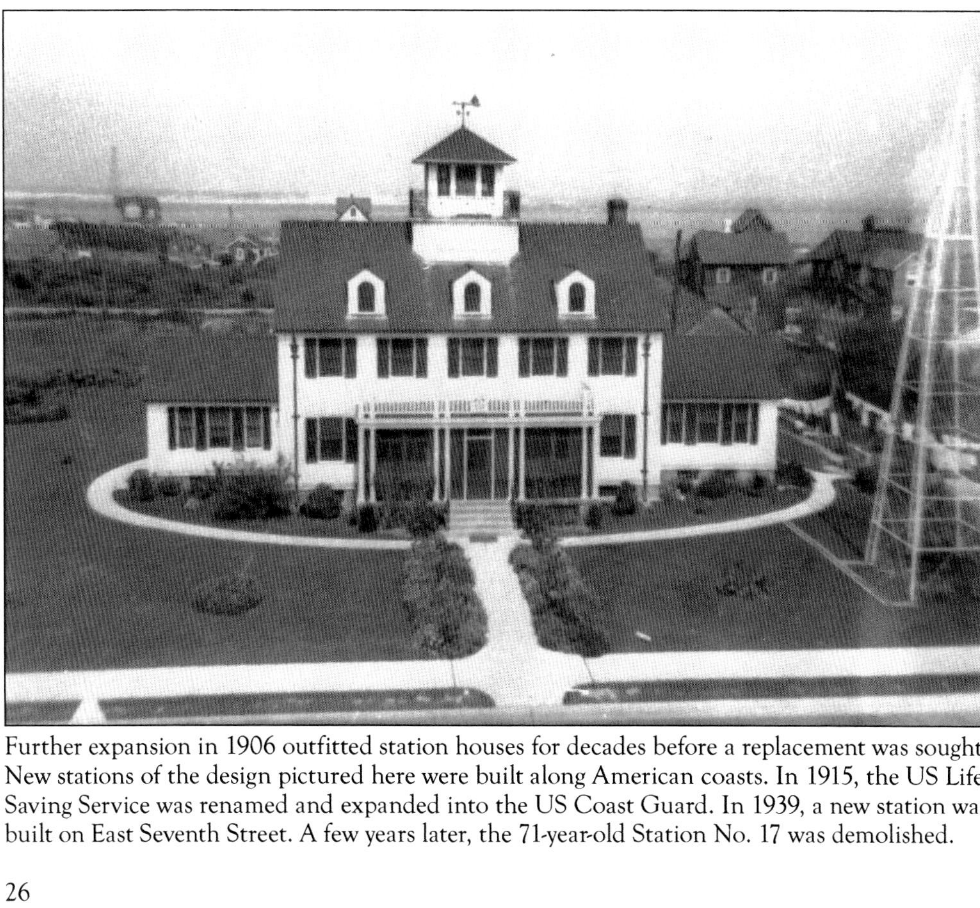

Further expansion in 1906 outfitted station houses for decades before a replacement was sought. New stations of the design pictured here were built along American coasts. In 1915, the US Life-Saving Service was renamed and expanded into the US Coast Guard. In 1939, a new station was built on East Seventh Street. A few years later, the 71-year-old Station No. 17 was demolished.

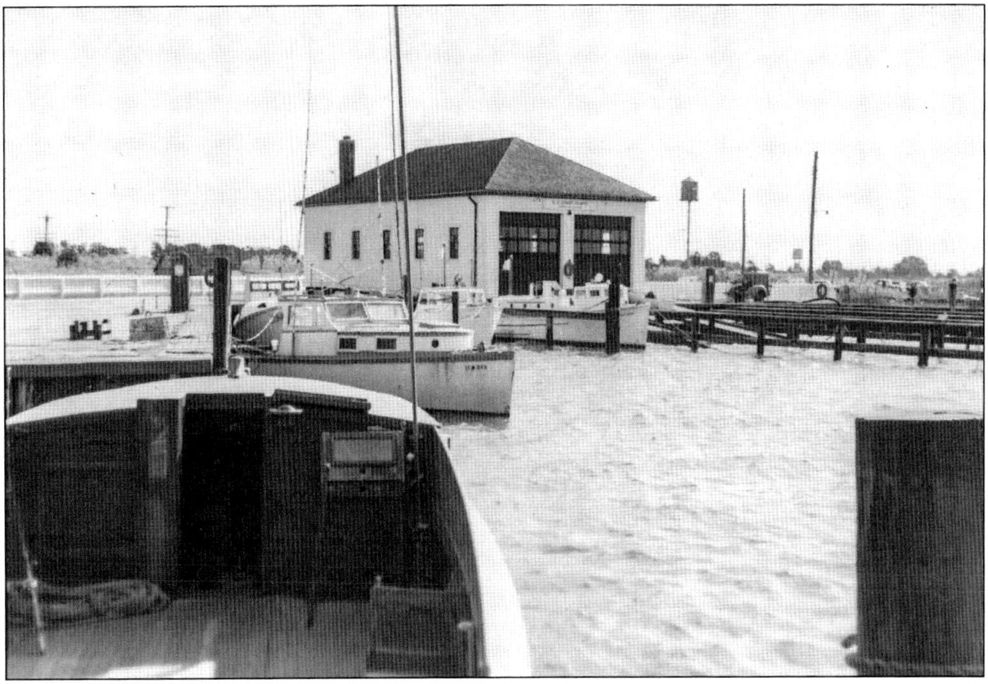

Modernization meant increased efficiencies and new logistics. After construction of the 1939 station, which was no longer used as a boathouse, a standalone structure was built on the bay at West Seventh Street. From here, larger powerboats capable of roaring around the island and through the inlet were now used.

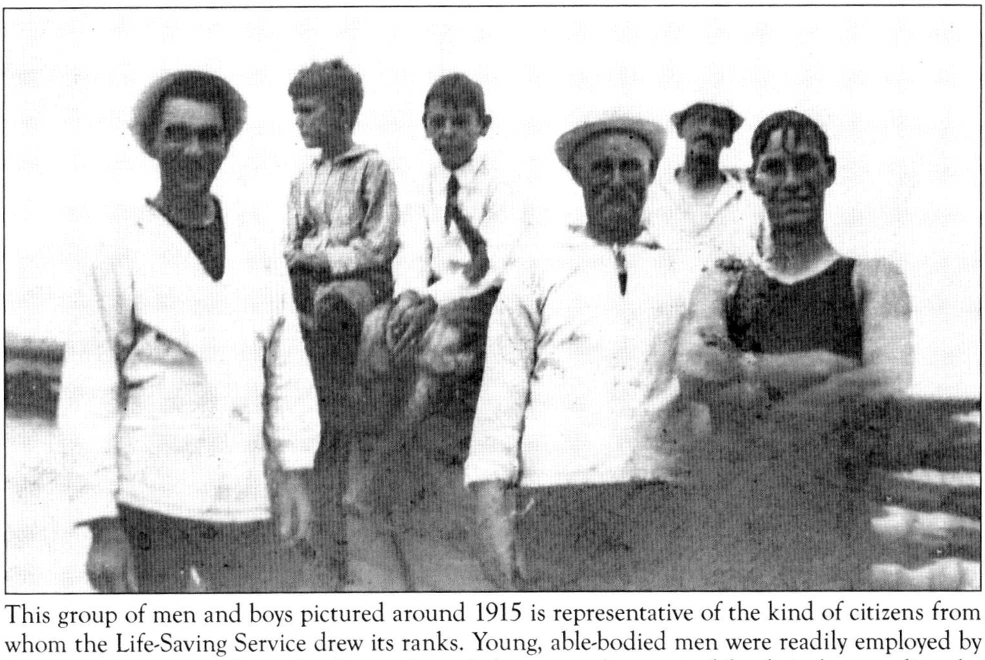

This group of men and boys pictured around 1915 is representative of the kind of citizens from whom the Life-Saving Service drew its ranks. Young, able-bodied men were readily employed by the station's captain, often a family member, while younger boys waited for their day guarding the coasts. Pictured here in Barnegat Light, from left to right are Bill and Bob Applegate, Bill Frick, Billie Falkinburg, Henry Brown, and Howard Falkinburg.

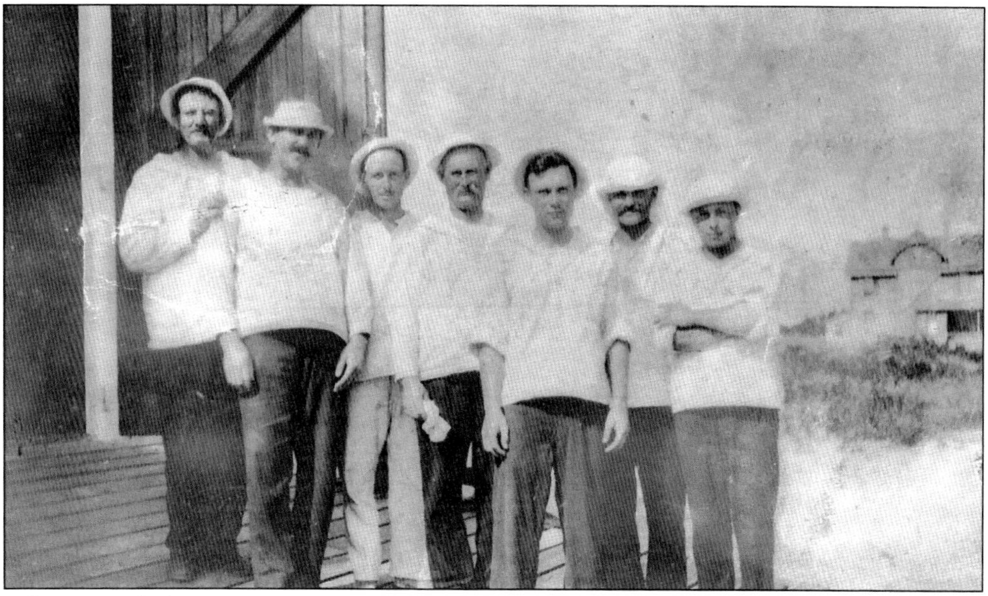

When trained, the station crew at Barnegat Inlet was among the best on the coast. At the end of the day, the men were family in a town of fewer than 150. Every rescue attempt was feared, and every fatality was deeply felt by the town. Pictured from left to right next to the station are Cornelius Thompson, Presgrove Kelly, ? Burnett, two unidentified, Bill Rutter, and ? Penn.

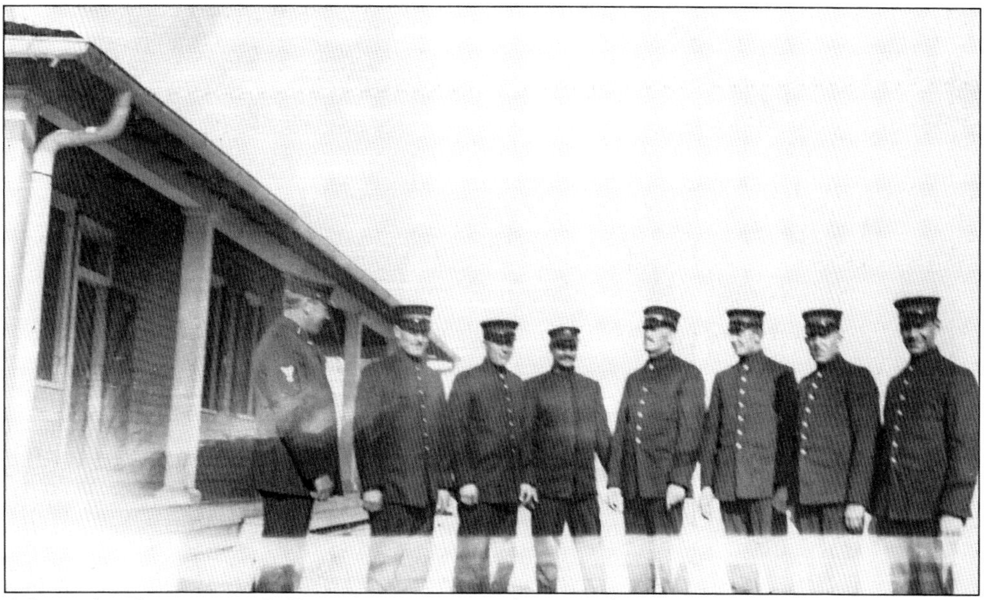

Often, a brother or son of a Barnegat service member served at the Harvey Cedars station, while another served at Loveladies station. Many fathers are seen in this image; from left to right are Presgrove Kelly, Percy Bennett, Bill Rutter, Lewis Mitchell, Henry Brown, Bill Neuendorf, Lloyd Camburn, and Howard Falkinburg.

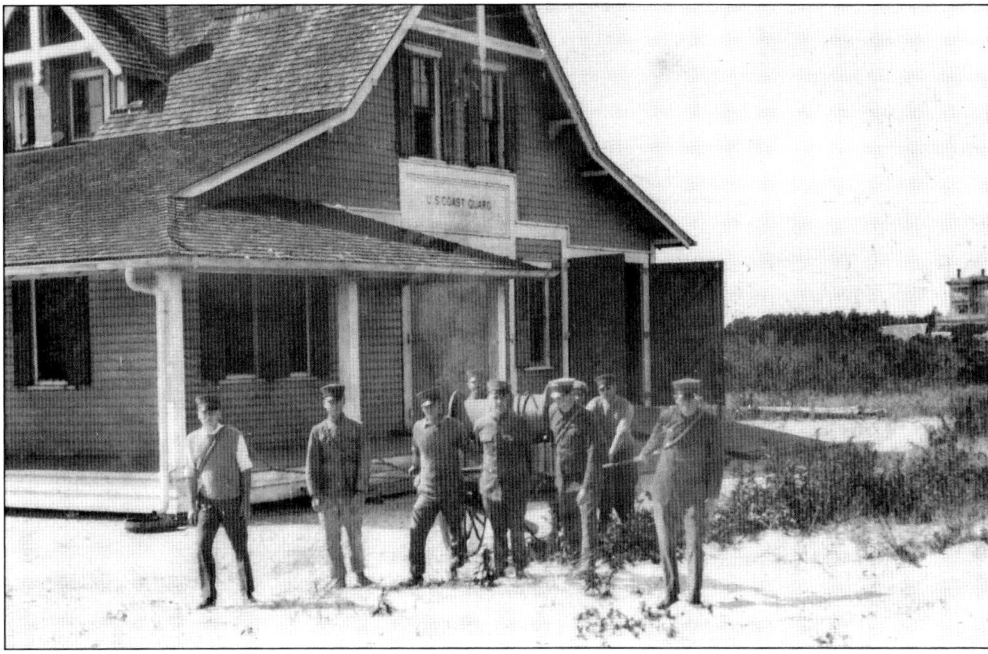

The work of a lifesaver could be back-breaking—and sometimes deadly. The men, though, were close to home, as seen here, with houses only a block away. Breaks in service gave time for families and for fishing jobs that, sadly, paid more than the federal government could give the brave men of the US Life-Saving Service.

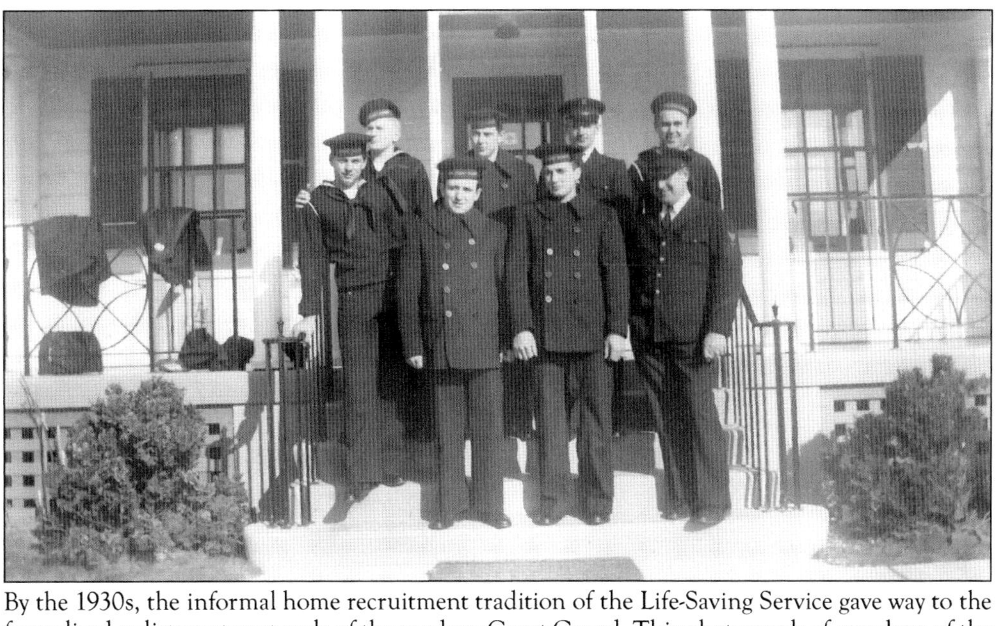

By the 1930s, the informal home recruitment tradition of the Life-Saving Service gave way to the formalized enlistment protocols of the modern Coast Guard. This photograph of members of the Barnegat City Coast Guard Station during World War II illustrates the point. These men came from as far away as Texas and as nearby as New York. None, however, came from Long Beach Island.

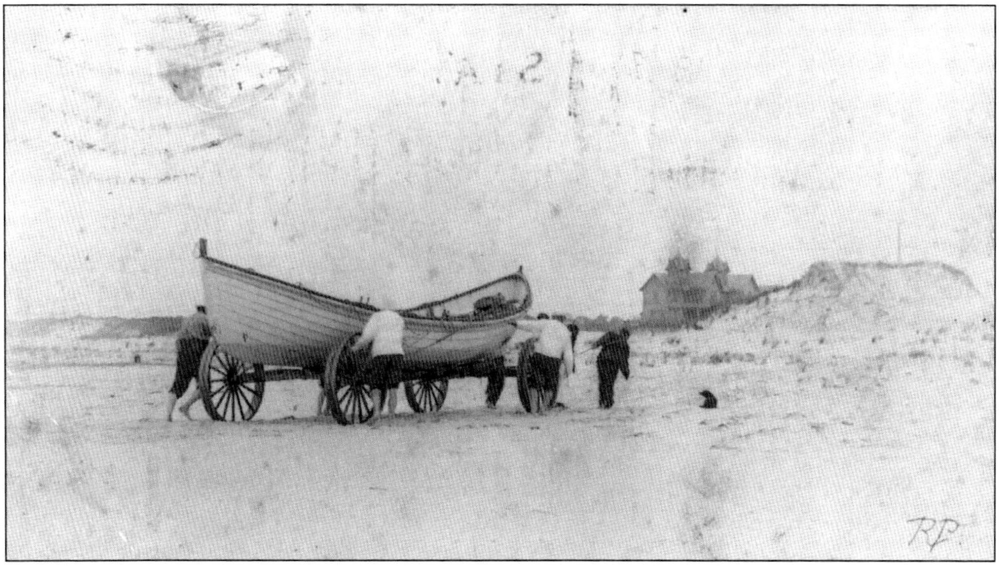

The duties of members of a lifesaving station changed over the years. The first and foremost responsibility was rescuing passengers and crew off stranded ships. As seen here, the job relied upon the lifeboats, which took many men to move. If available, horses could be used to aid in the job.

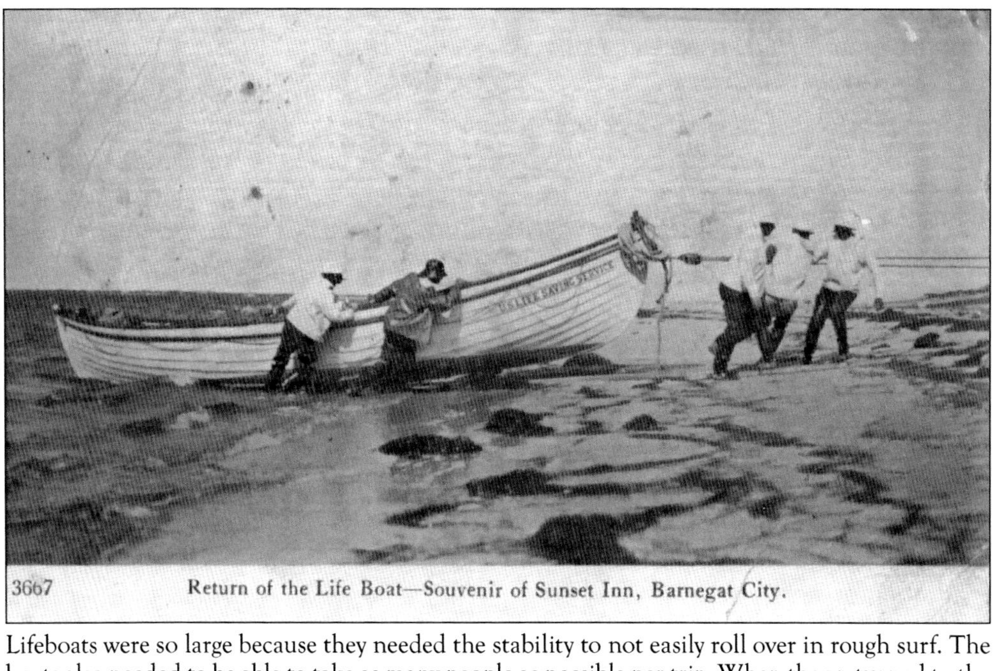

Lifeboats were so large because they needed the stability to not easily roll over in rough surf. The boats also needed to be able to take as many people as possible per trip. When they returned to the beach to unload survivors, the crews turned and headed back into the storm to continue the rescue.

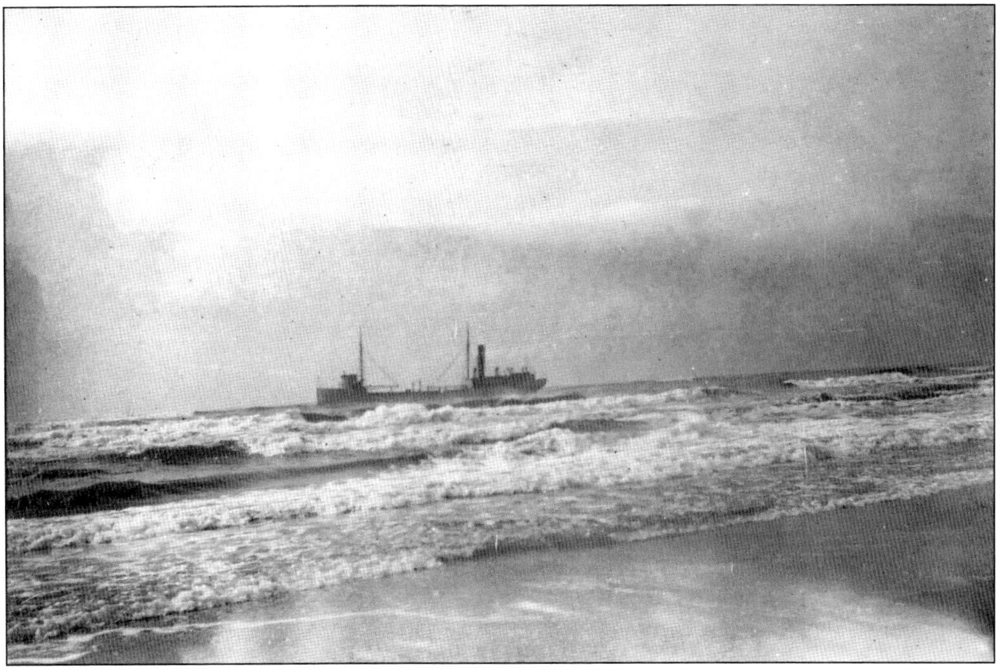

Whether due to mechanical failure, negligence, or a shifted shoal, the sight of a vessel stuck beyond Barnegat Light's breakers, as seen here around 1915, was common. In normal conditions, rendering assistance was still dangerous. The job of attempting to offload beside large ships amidst rolling swells led to numerous fatalities over the years among the lifesaving stations of Long Beach Island.

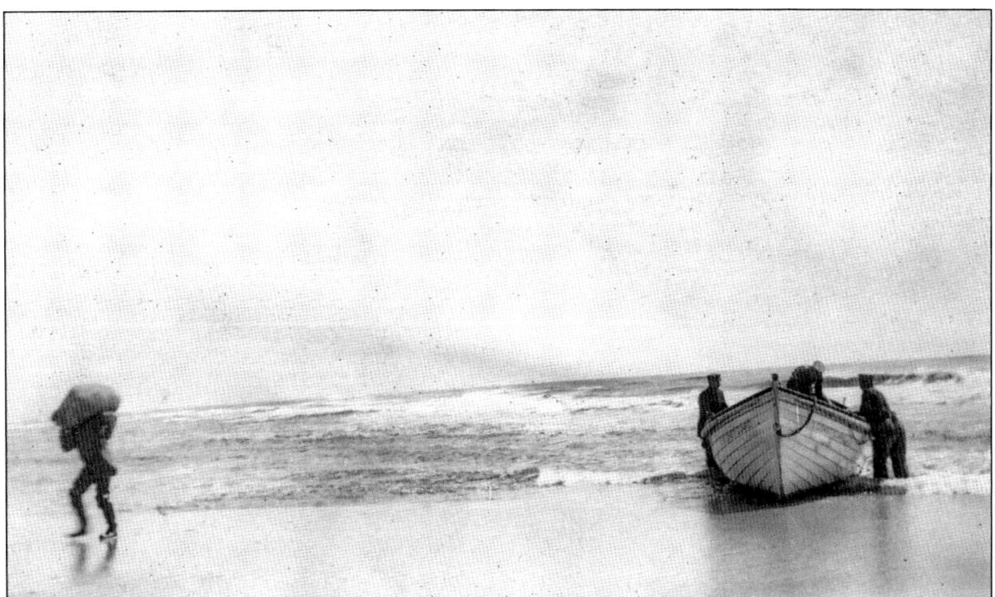

This c. 1915 photograph shows that sometimes, if conditions are right, the job of rescue could also include salvage, especially if the ship is deemed a likely loss. On this day, the crew of the Barnegat City station got lucky and brought ashore coffee beans, a precious resource that was often in limited supply from government sources and not available in large quantities locally.

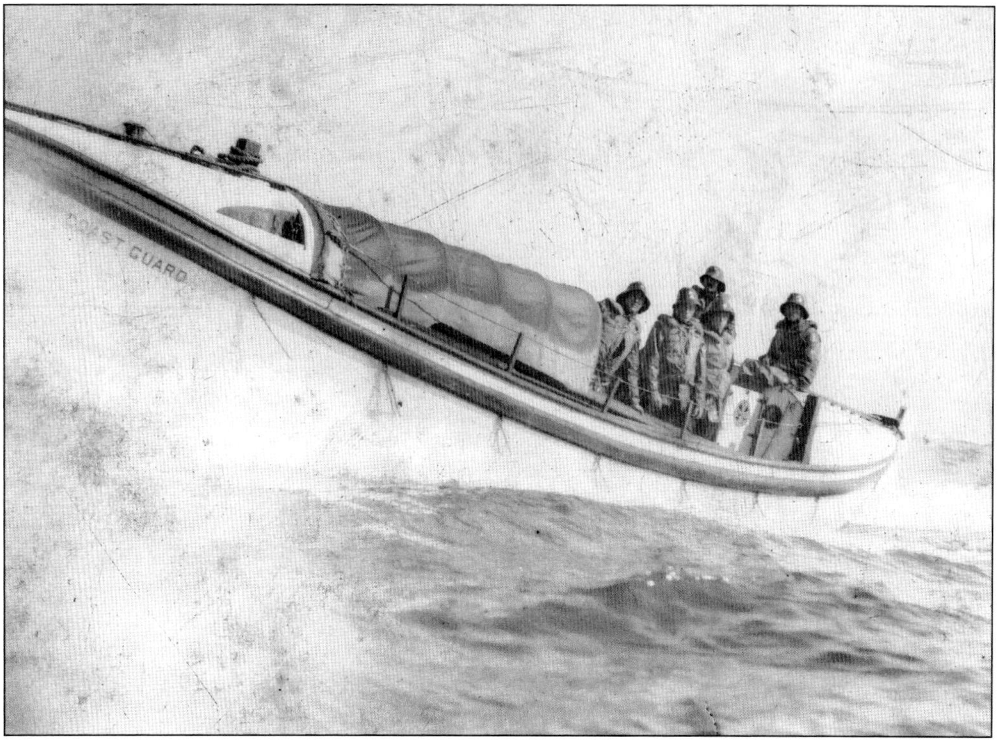

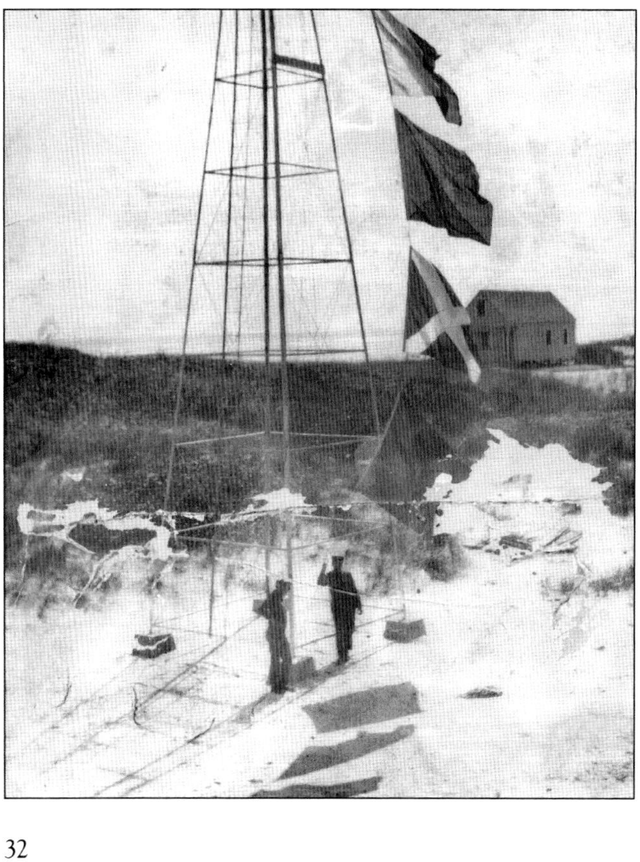

The 1920s brought electric horsepower to the Coast Guard stations. Pictured here around 1930 is Barnegat City station's type-T lifeboat. Some of its variations were 36 feet long, capable of reaching ships within 200 miles of port, and could achieve over 8 knots. Some of its most important features were its ability to self-right if it rolled over and to self-bail if swamped.

Communicating ship to shore before radio involved a system of signal flags. This undated photograph of the signal tower near Barnegat City's lifesaving station shows the crew practicing this old skill. Raising the flags on the towers enabled each station to issue warnings and send messages to passing marine traffic about local dangers or to make requests for communication.

The men in this photograph are practicing the semaphore signaling system. By moving the flags up and down, messages could be sent using a code that was commonly known among mariners.

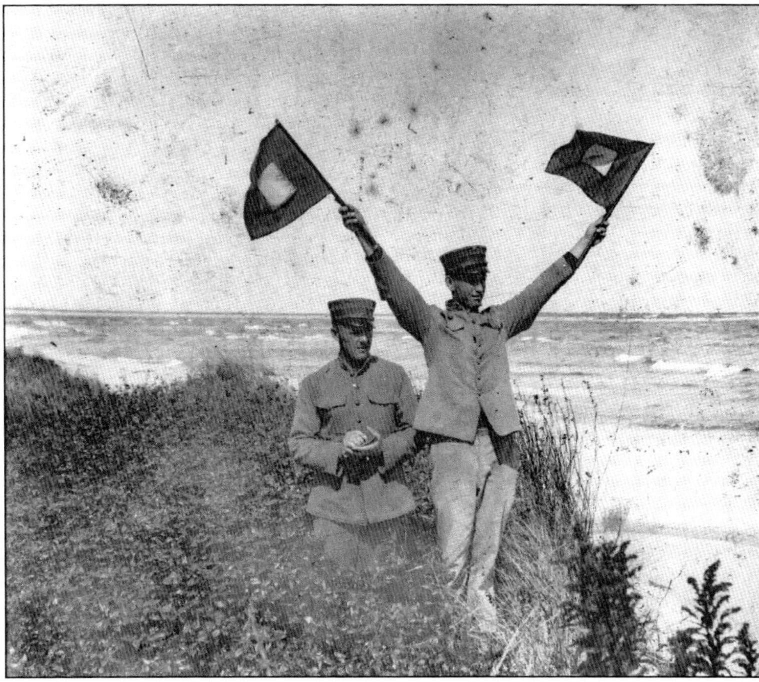

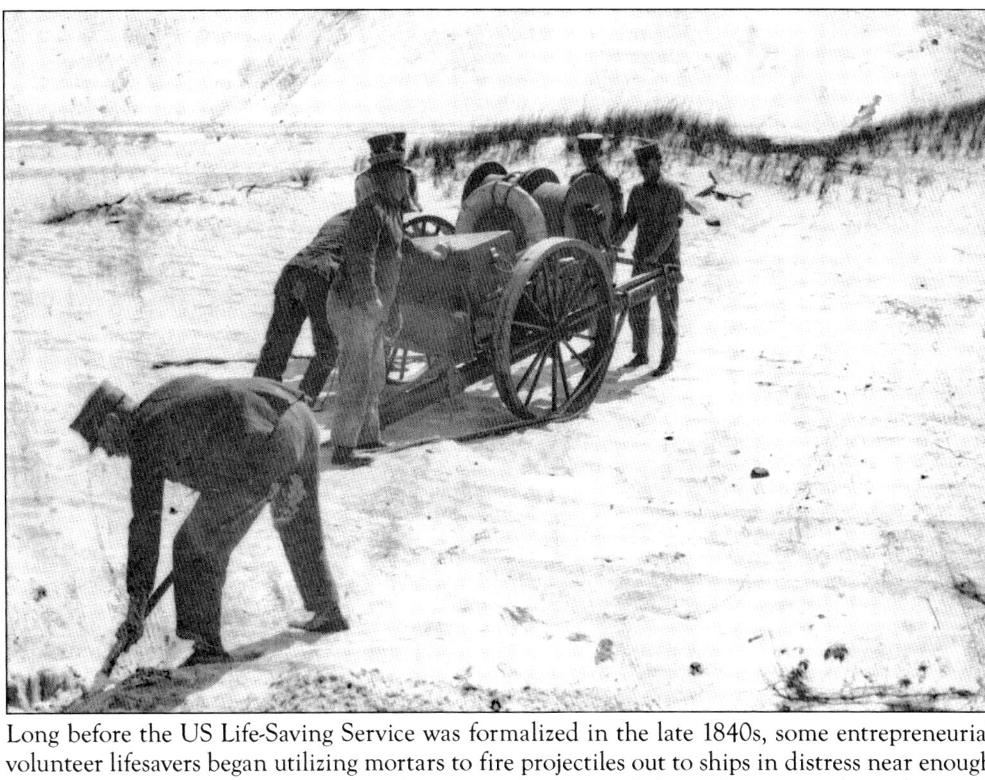

Long before the US Life-Saving Service was formalized in the late 1840s, some entrepreneurial volunteer lifesavers began utilizing mortars to fire projectiles out to ships in distress near enough the beach. British captain George William Manby pioneered this technique in the early 1800s. They attached very long lengths of rope, seen here in boxes and on spools, to the projectile, then fired the line over the ship's rigging.

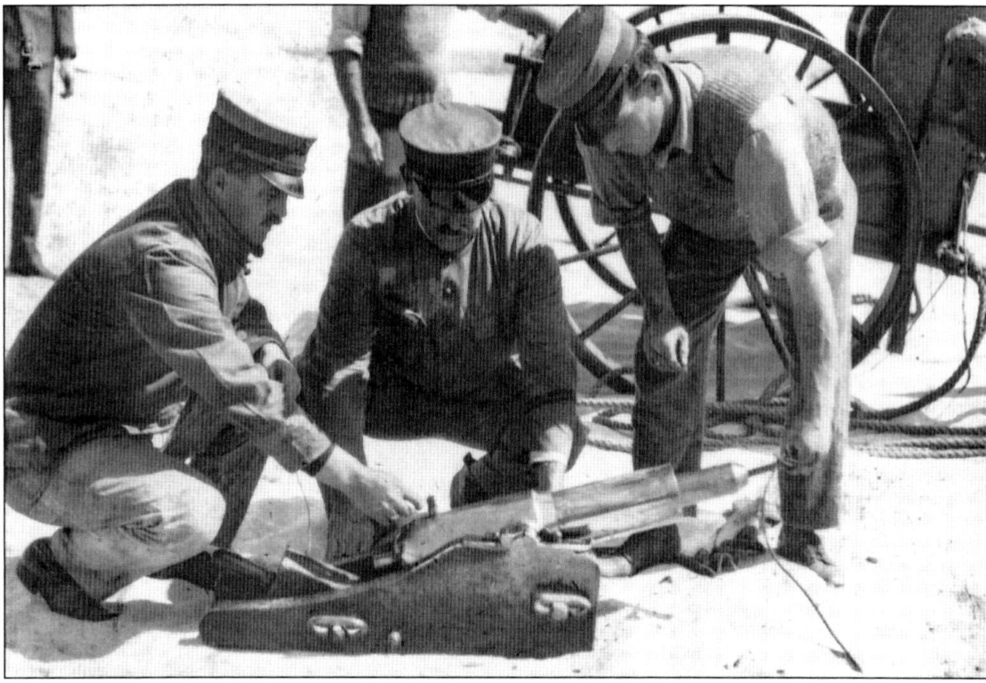

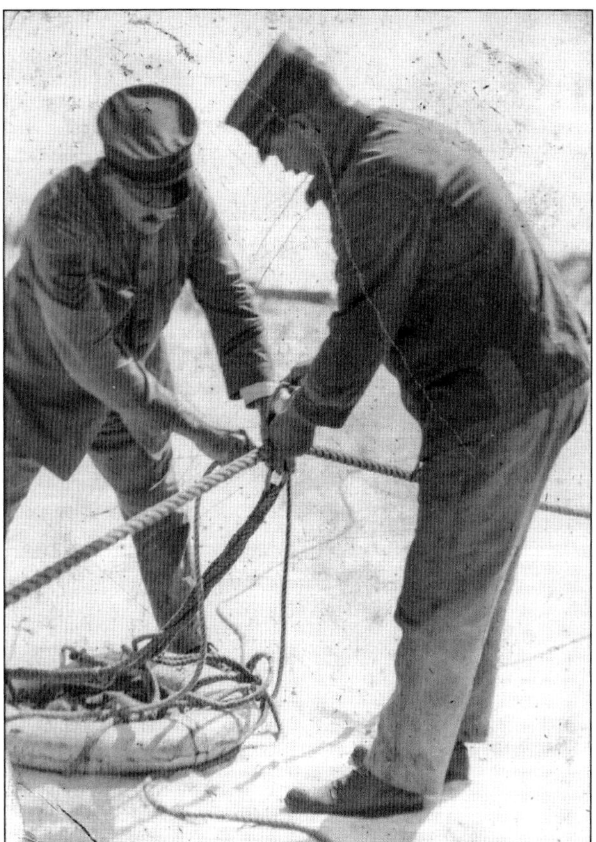

The earlier Manby Mortars were later replaced by Lyle guns, as pictured here being loaded by the crew of Barnegat City station. These line-throwing guns fired 18-pound projectiles up to 700 yards from shore. Long lines of rope were coiled among pegs in faking boxes that would ensure no tangles or snares once the pegged half was slid off and the end of the line tied to the projectile.

After the line was secured to a ship in distress, the breeches buoy system was deployed. The men pictured here are tying a harness rigged to a life ring and saddle to the line that would support one person at a time. This meant a slow evacuation, but it was safer than using a lifeboat in the breakers when the ship was within range of the gun.

Successfully employing the system required teamwork from the ship and the shore. After the first shot line was in place, an additional line with a pulley would have to be unspooled and reeled in by the crew of the vessel. A lifesaving crew would then raise the shot line with 12-foot shear legs and ratchet up the tension so survivors could ride down over the waves.

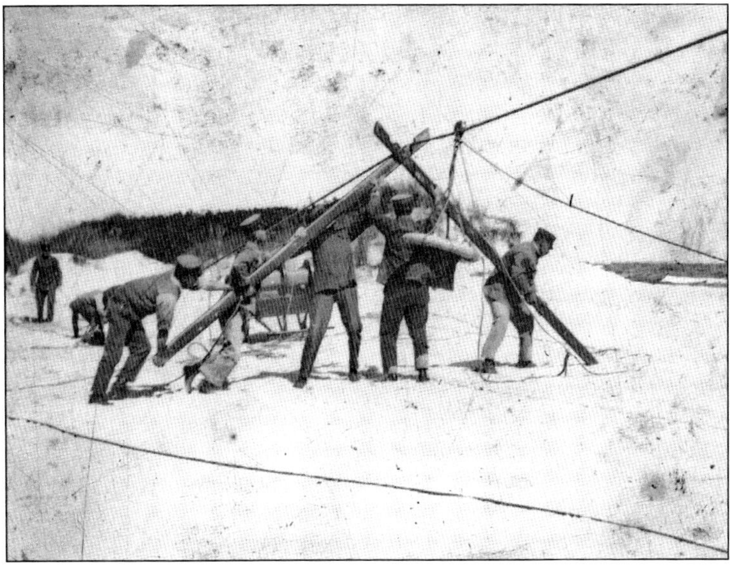

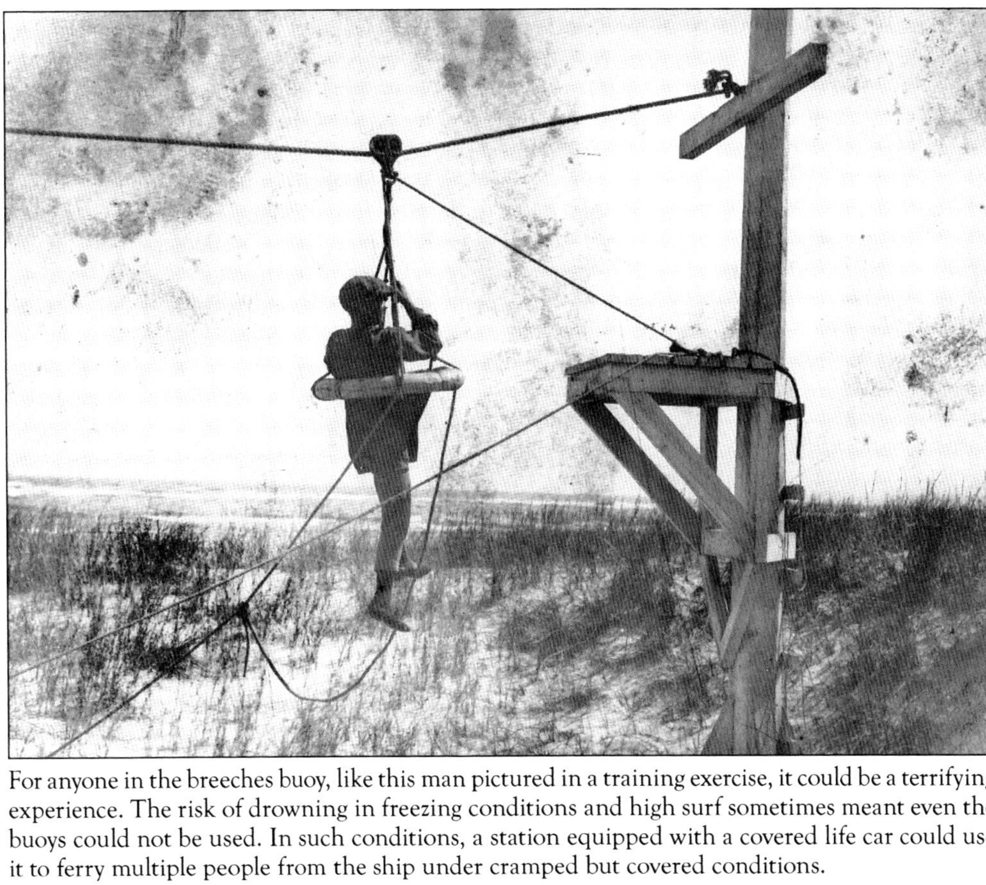

For anyone in the breeches buoy, like this man pictured in a training exercise, it could be a terrifying experience. The risk of drowning in freezing conditions and high surf sometimes meant even the buoys could not be used. In such conditions, a station equipped with a covered life car could use it to ferry multiple people from the ship under cramped but covered conditions.

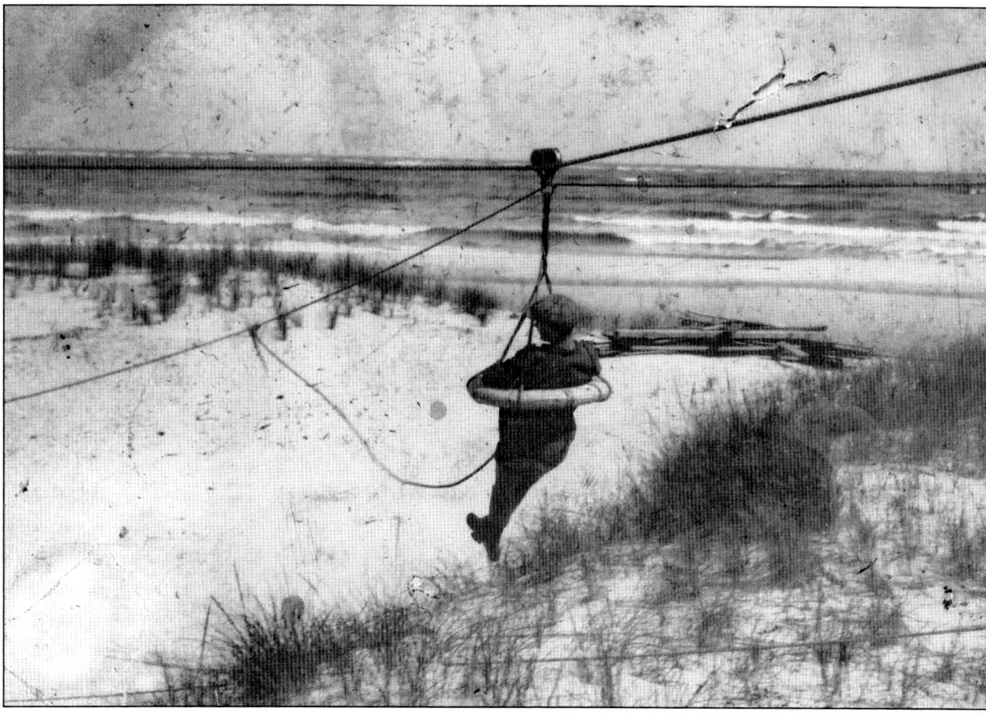

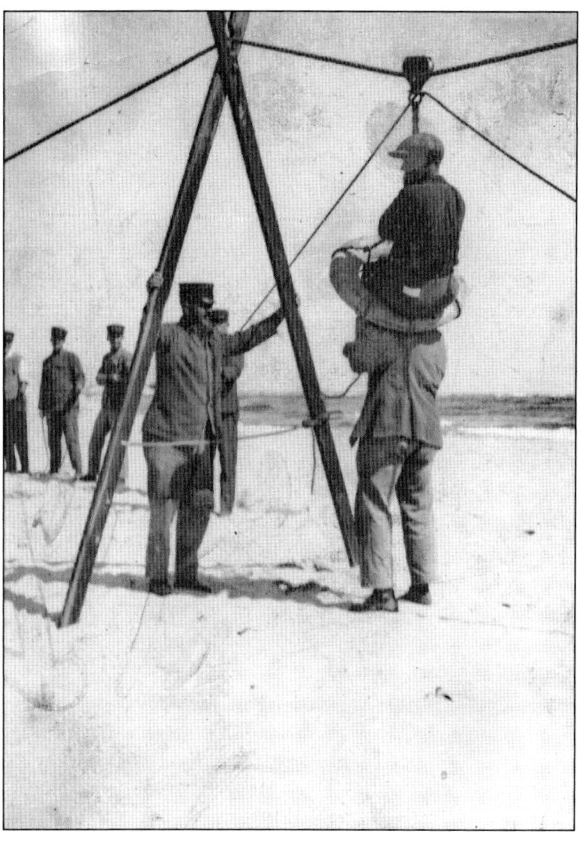

When riding the shot line, a person in the harness would be hauled along by the crew on the beach pulling the second line, pictured here. Multiple attempts would sometimes be needed to establish the lines. The crew on some vessels, especially foreign, were not trained in this manner of rescue, which is why written instructions would always be sent out with the second line and breeches buoy.

It was standard procedure for lifesaving station crews, like Barnegat City's assembled on the beach in this photograph, to practice these rescues every week. Even after the dangers of the weather and the inexperience factor of some ship crews, mistakes made by the lifesavers could prove fatal. Time, too, was of the essence. Regular training allowed their efforts to be as fast and efficient as possible when it counted most.

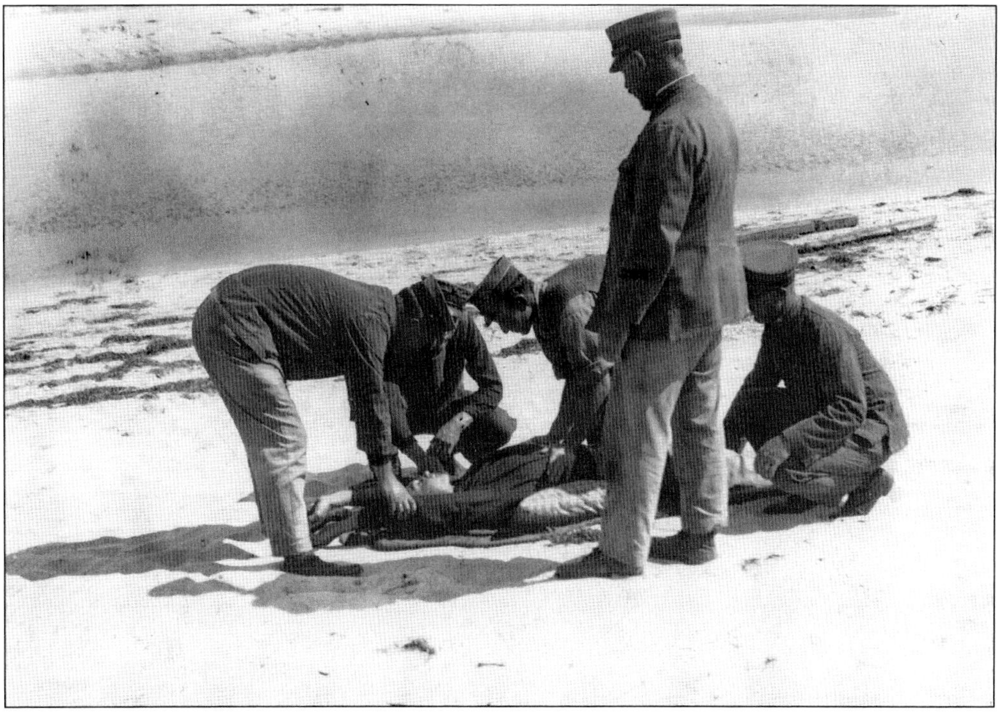

Other procedures the Barnegat City station crew practiced included the crude but effective treatment seen here for victims of drowning called "restoring the apparently drowned." Predating modern CPR, this technique was similar in that the stretching, tilting of the head, and arm movements helped open the airways and used natural compressive movements to encourage breathing and ejection of water from the lungs.

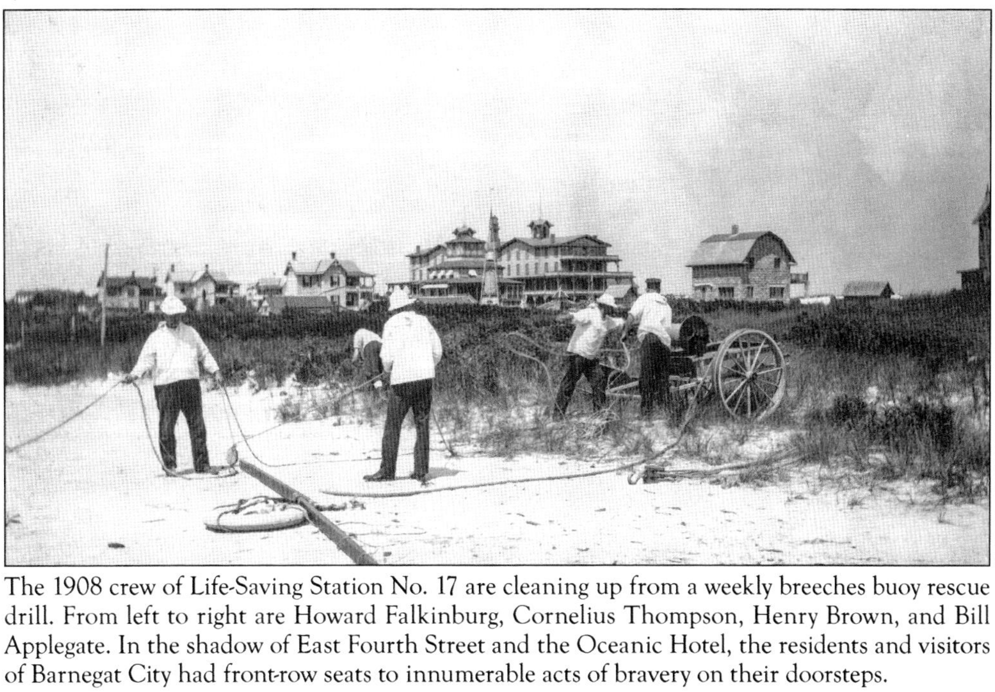

The 1908 crew of Life-Saving Station No. 17 are cleaning up from a weekly breeches buoy rescue drill. From left to right are Howard Falkinburg, Cornelius Thompson, Henry Brown, and Bill Applegate. In the shadow of East Fourth Street and the Oceanic Hotel, the residents and visitors of Barnegat City had front-row seats to innumerable acts of bravery on their doorsteps.

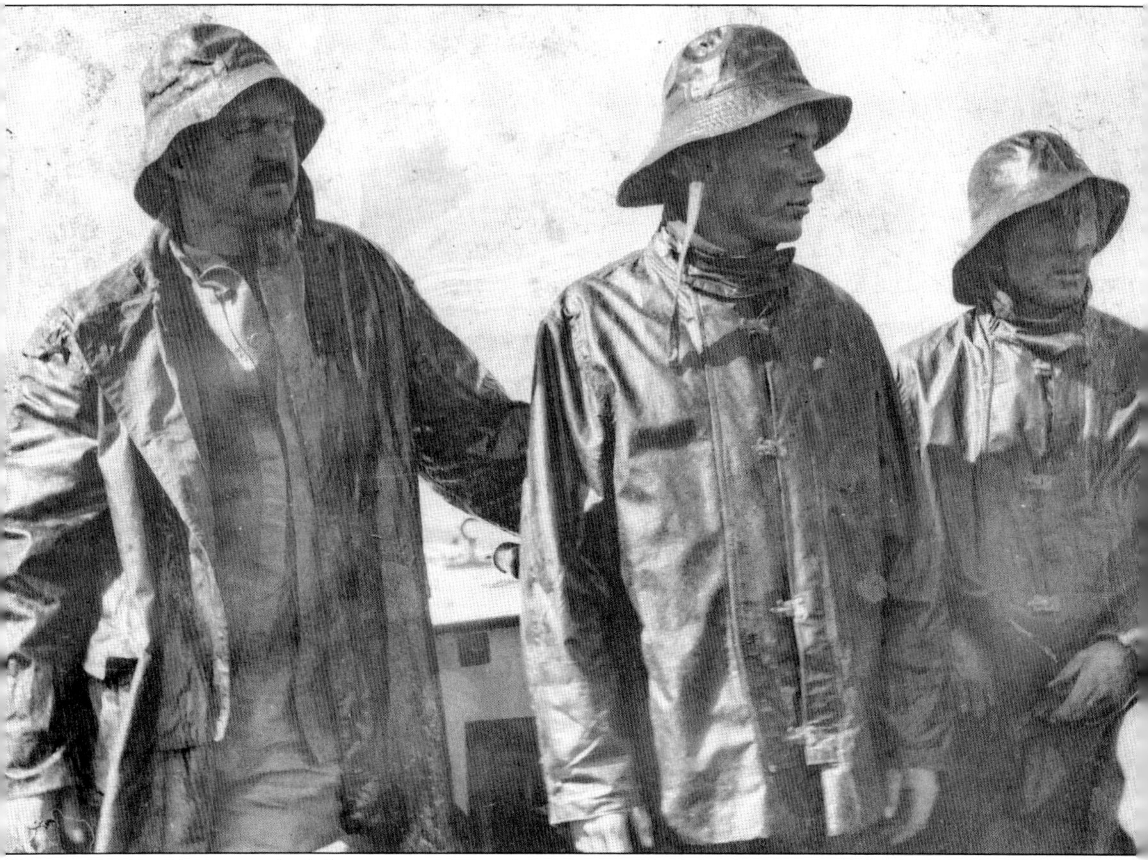

Over the years, the lifesaving station and Coast Guard crews at Barnegat Light have been a constant bulwark against the unique dangers of Barnegat Inlet and its outer shoals. One such crew is pictured here around 1930 performing their duty aboard the station's type-T lifeboat. Over decades of service, scores of lifesavers gave their lives in the line of duty around the inlet. In one such incident in 1886, John Soper, Solomon Soper, and Samuel Perrine were all killed in an attempted lifeboat rescue of a massive bark that sank on the Barnegat shoals one mile east of the inlet. Others who went into the frigid February waters that day included William Inman, who was forced to retire from service due to his injuries. The outcome of every rescue had the potential to reverberate up and down Barnegat Bay and change lives, families, and history. Names of those who served are the same that define the history of Barnegat Light and other communities in the area: Soper, Applegate, Thompson, Inman, Perrine, Falkinburg, Brown, Birdsall, and Ridgway, to name a few.

Four

Brownsville Becomes Barnegat City

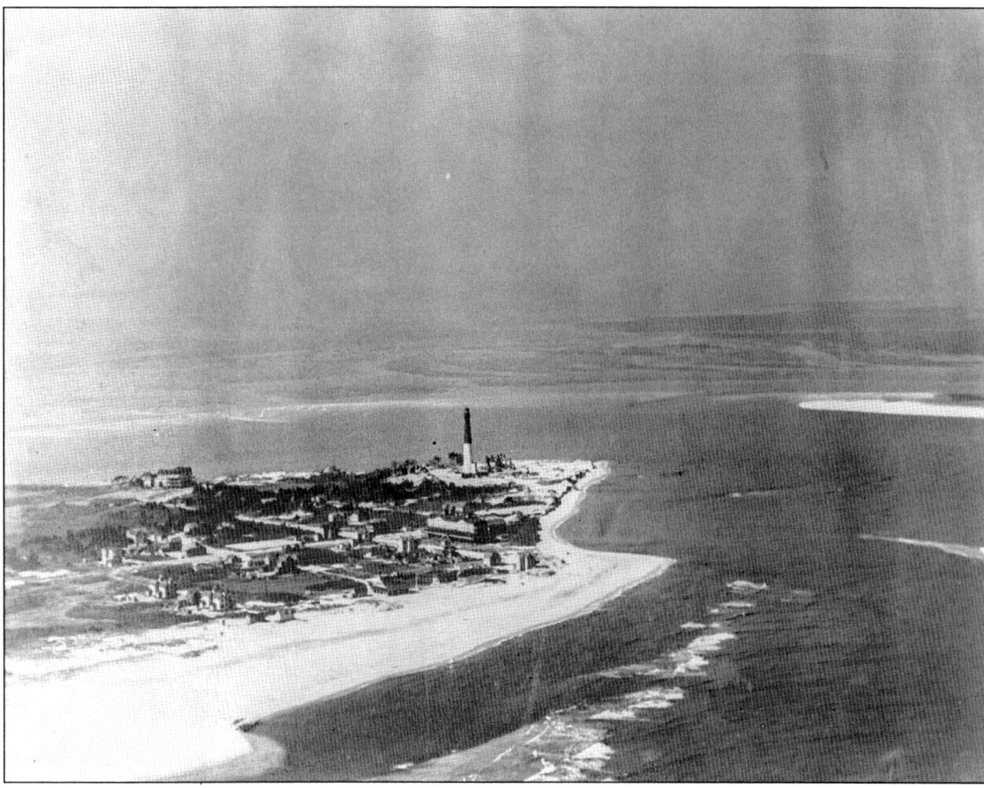

By the late 19th century, Barnegat Beach remained a sparse outpost of fishermen and lifesavers. With the Brown family owning so much land, locals took to calling the area "Brownsville." This c. 1910 aerial view of Barnegat Inlet shows the developed town of Barnegat City that quickly sprouted out of the sands before the century was out. (Courtesy of the National Archives and Records Administration.)

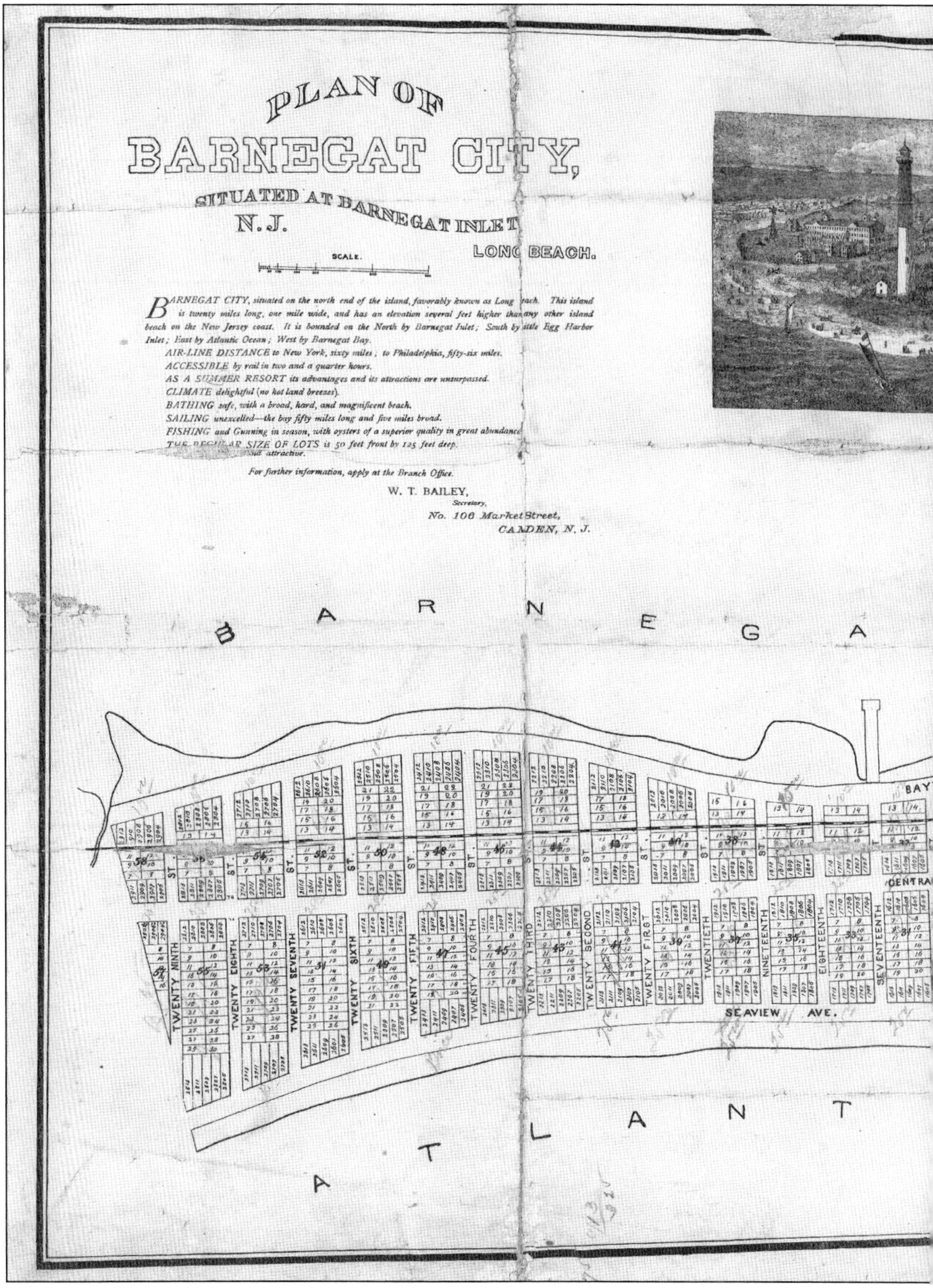

This 1880s development plan by Camden financiers William Bailey and Benjamin Archer changed the course of town history. Aiming to create the next Atlantic City, the developers had plans for wide boulevards, railroad connections with Philadelphia and New York, and cavernous hotels. Other sleepy Jersey shore towns and deserted acres of beachfront up and down the coast were

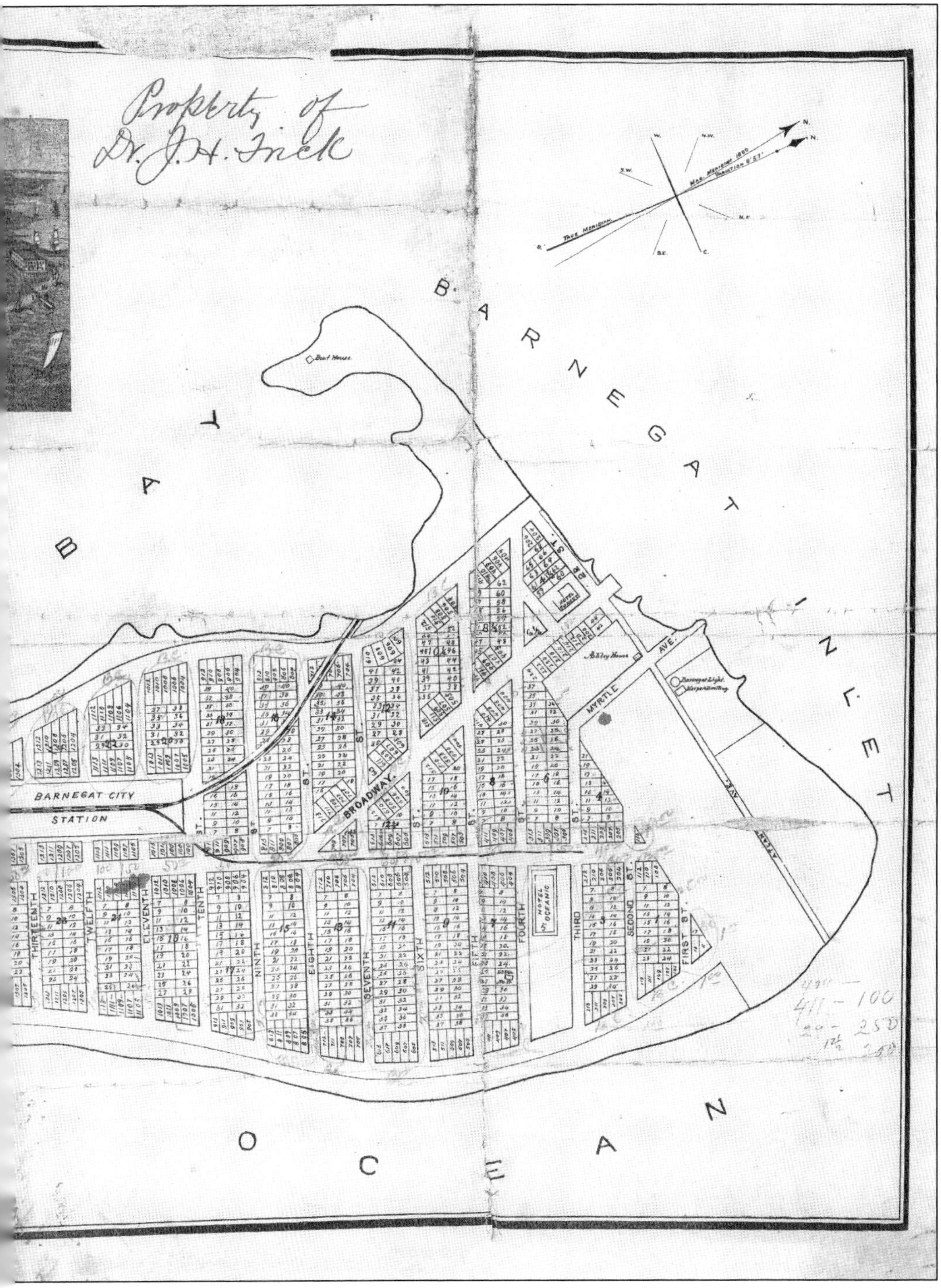

similarly bought up by bankers in the big cities. The great game for providing entertainment-rich retreats for coal-choked masses in eastern cities was afoot in the late 19th century. The streets and lots Bailey and Archer laid out here were not fully realized for nearly a century, but the plan did, literally, chart the future of Barnegat Light.

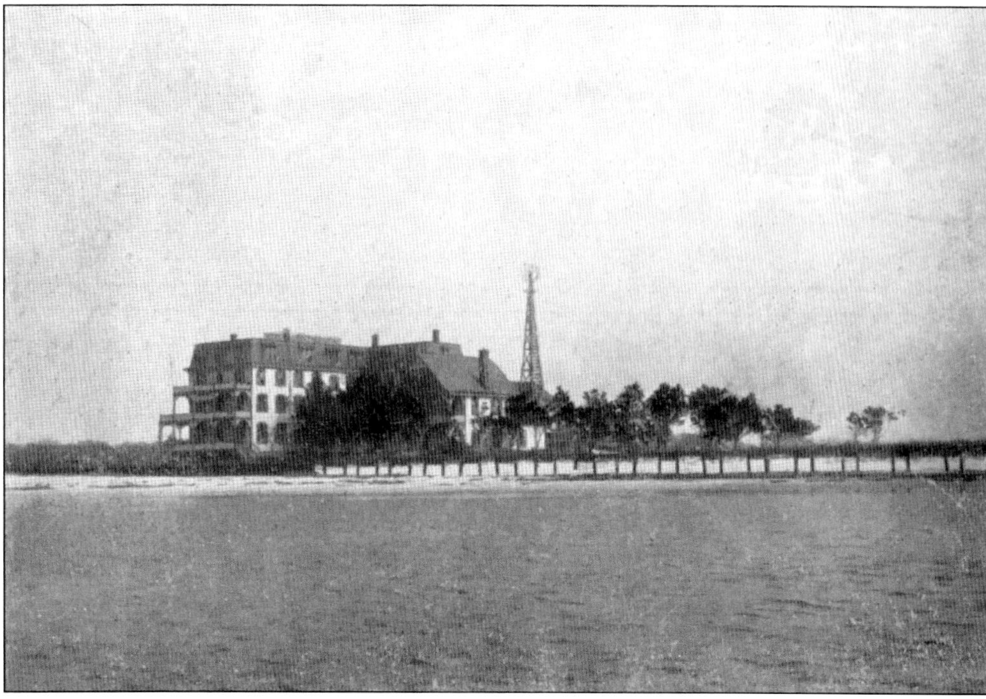

One of the first additions as part of the 1880s development plan was a bayside hotel at the end of Broadway, pictured in this undated postcard. Opened in 1883, the hotel was initially called the San Souci but renamed just a few years later the Sunset. Its current location would be in the bay, but at the time, the bay shore was about 100 yards northwest.

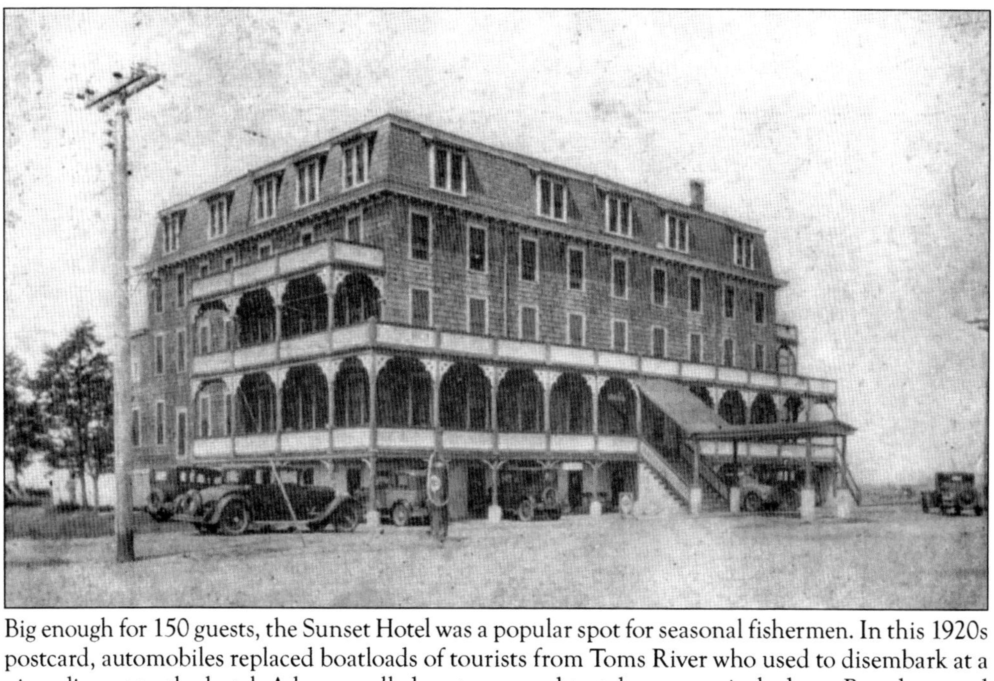

Big enough for 150 guests, the Sunset Hotel was a popular spot for seasonal fishermen. In this 1920s postcard, automobiles replaced boatloads of tourists from Toms River who used to disembark at a pier adjacent to the hotel. A horse-pulled cart was used to take new arrivals down Broadway and along Fourth Street to other new lodgings.

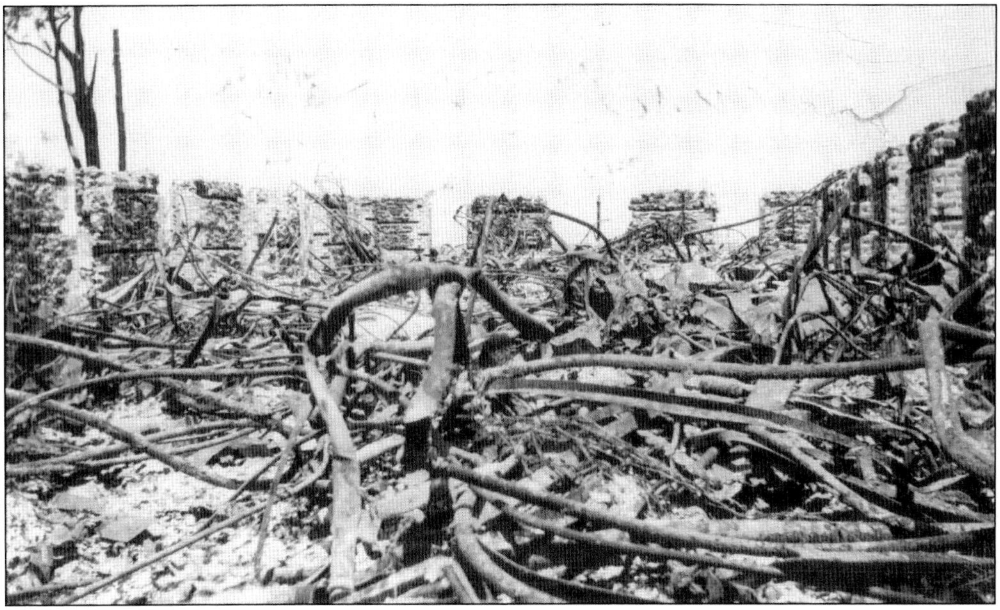

On June 26, 1932, a fire engulfed the old Sunset Hotel, which had been struggling to stay open. Flames fanned by a strong southwest wind sent smoke, fire, and embers into the sky toward the lighthouse. Witnesses were worried the embers might set fire to the landmark too. The flames could be seen for miles around. After it was extinguished, little was left, as seen here.

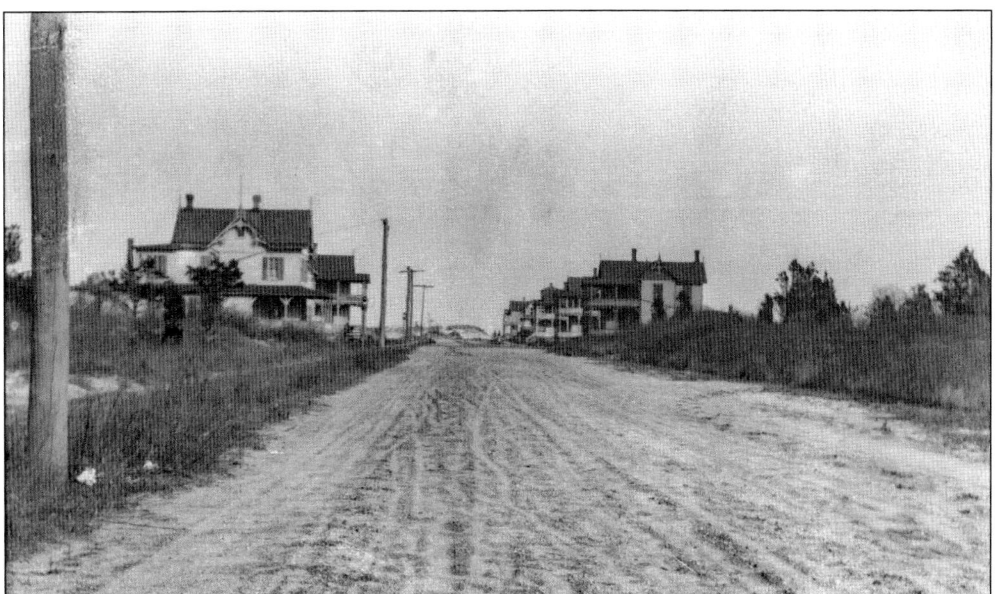

This c. 1910 view of West and East Fourth Streets shows some of the most visible improvements made during the 1880s. The wide and clear road was designed with comfort and ease in mind. A horse cart brought guests from the Sunset pier down to these cottages, six of which were built in nearly identical fashion, while several more were added throughout the 1890s.

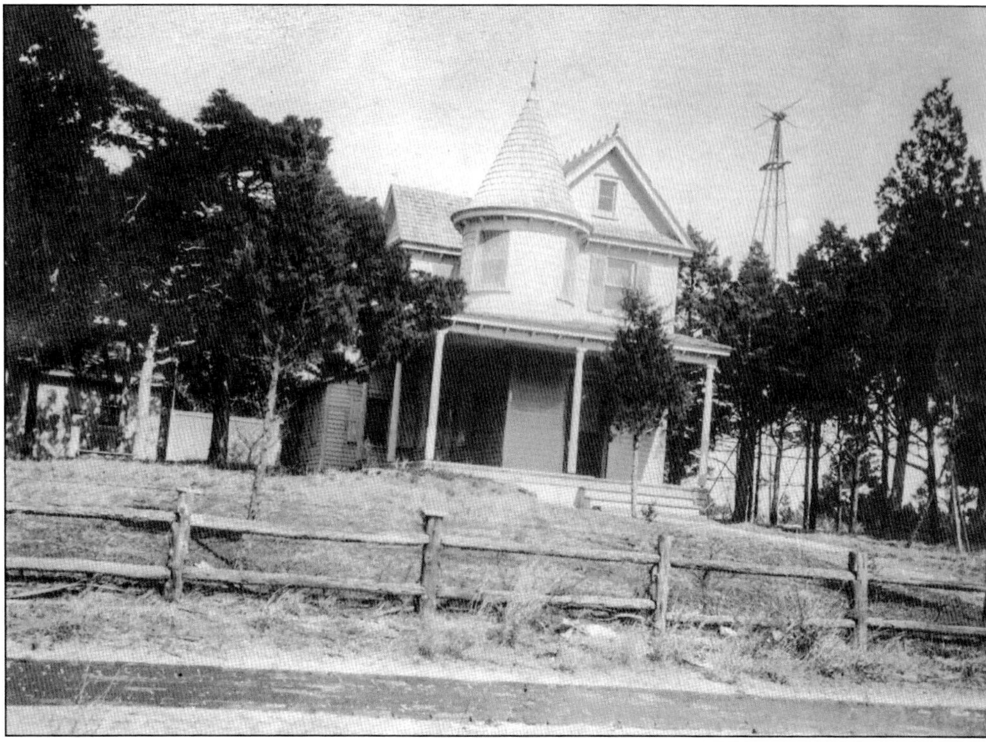

In the middle of West Fourth Street, this grand homestead was built for William Bailey atop a high dune. Later, William Frick would live here while serving as mayor of Barnegat City. The cottage has survived to the present day, appearing virtually the same as it did when it was new, right down to the fence posts.

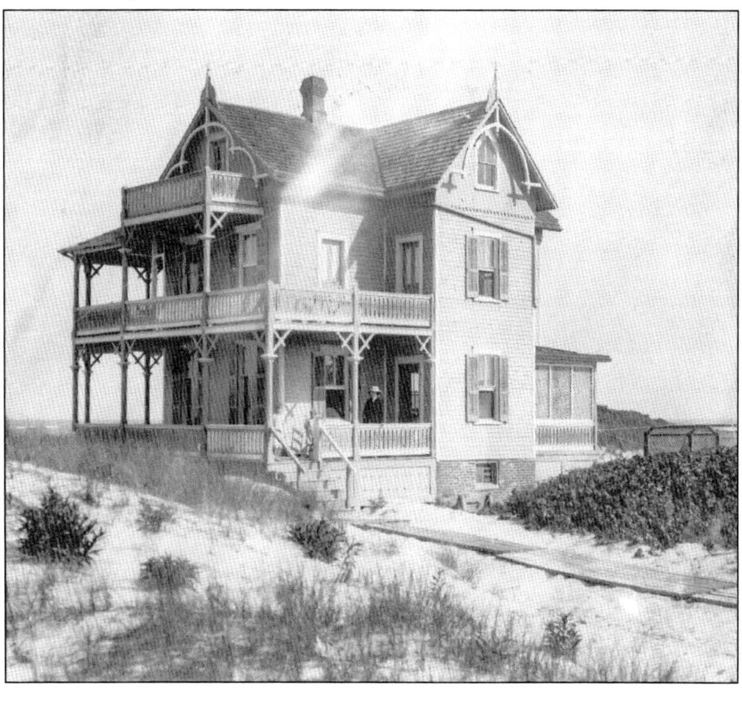

Seen here at the end of East Fourth Street on the south side is one of the six nearly identical cottages planned by William Bailey and Benjamin Archer's Barnegat City Beach Association. Many of the original investors were the first to buy property. At the time the street was laid out, the water's edge was a healthy distance from the end of Fourth Street.

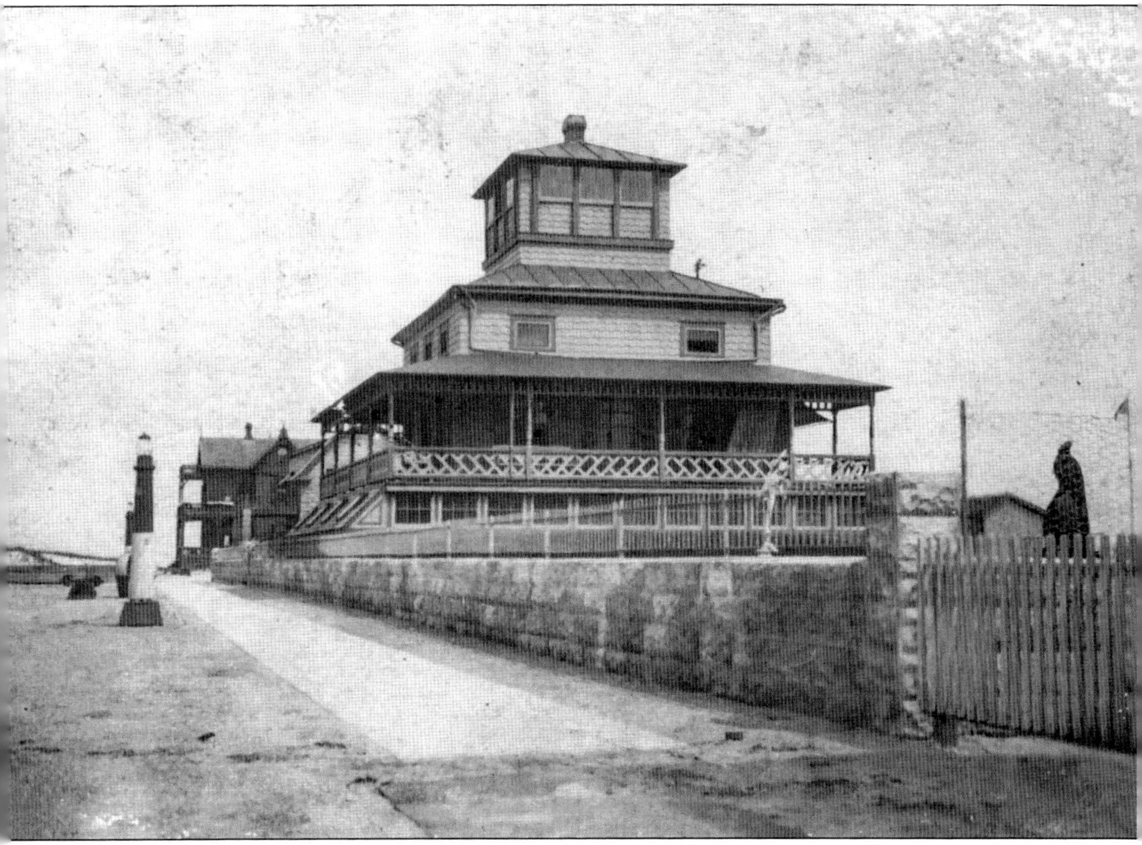

In the mid-1890s, two houses on the south side of East Fourth Street were added. The square house in the foreground was bought in 1897 by a New Yorker named John Haddock, who added his own style to the grounds with walls and lighthouse streetlights. The distinctive widow's peak was added in 1899. Haddock began a habit of beachcombing the flotsam that washed up from wrecks. His collection of mastheads, ship's wheels, and other paraphernalia soon became legendary. After Haddock's death, Sunset owner Dick Myers bought it in 1920 and held onto it for many years. An artesian well, of which there were several under Barnegat City, provided fresh water on the property and was shared with anyone who wanted it. Sandwiched between this and the dark beachfront cottage in the background was another small but unique house built entirely out of stone that helped break up Fourth Street's architectural conformity.

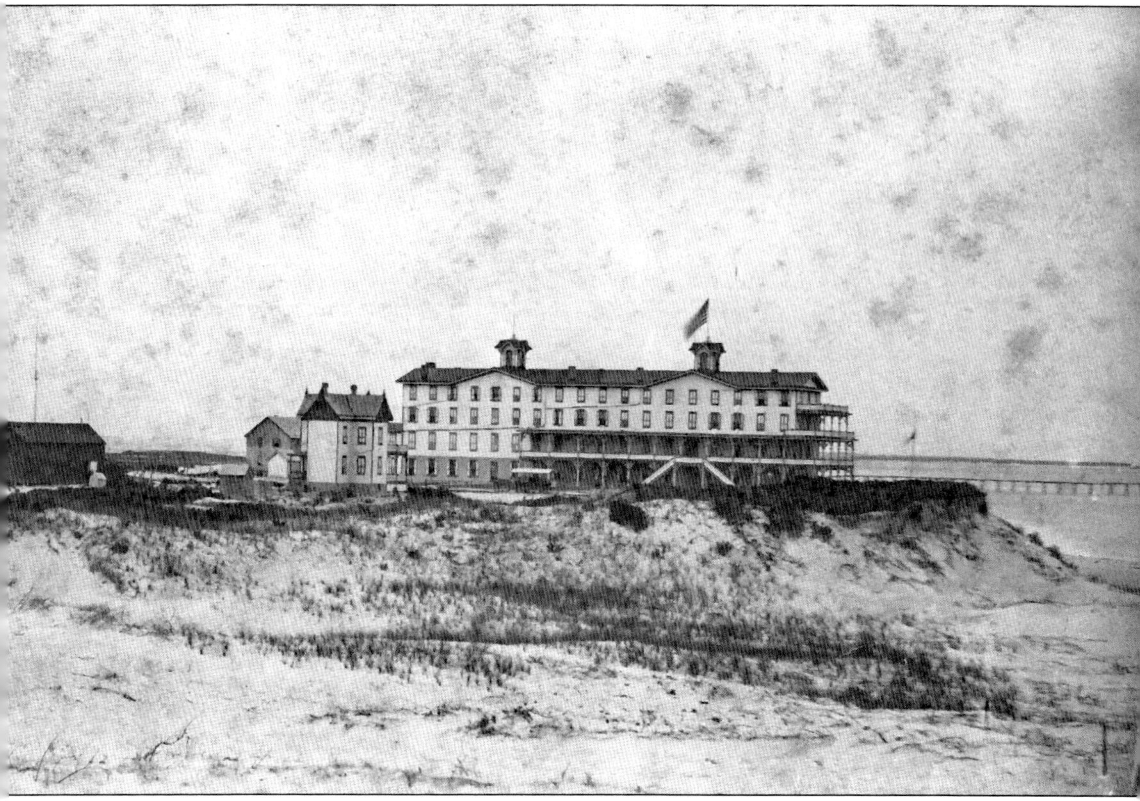

The anchor of Fourth Street, and the reason why all the cottages were built there, was the Oceanic Hotel. With four floors and accommodations for 200, the hotel was initially built on the very edge of the dunes, as seen in this c. 1883 photograph, leveling them in the process and tempting fate. An attempted ocean-side pier, soon lost to heavy seas and never rebuilt, can be seen extending into the Atlantic from nearby Third Street behind the Oceanic. The hotel was heavily promoted in Philadelphia and Camden as the centerpiece of the new Barnegat City resort, which existed in marketing materials only. The town still bore no official name but was commonly referred to as Barnegat Beach at that time to differentiate it from the mainland town of Barnegat. Whereas Atlantic City was promoting the idea of day trips via a direct rail link to Philadelphia, Barnegat City's marketers had overnight and weeklong stays in mind, appealing to a different class of tourists.

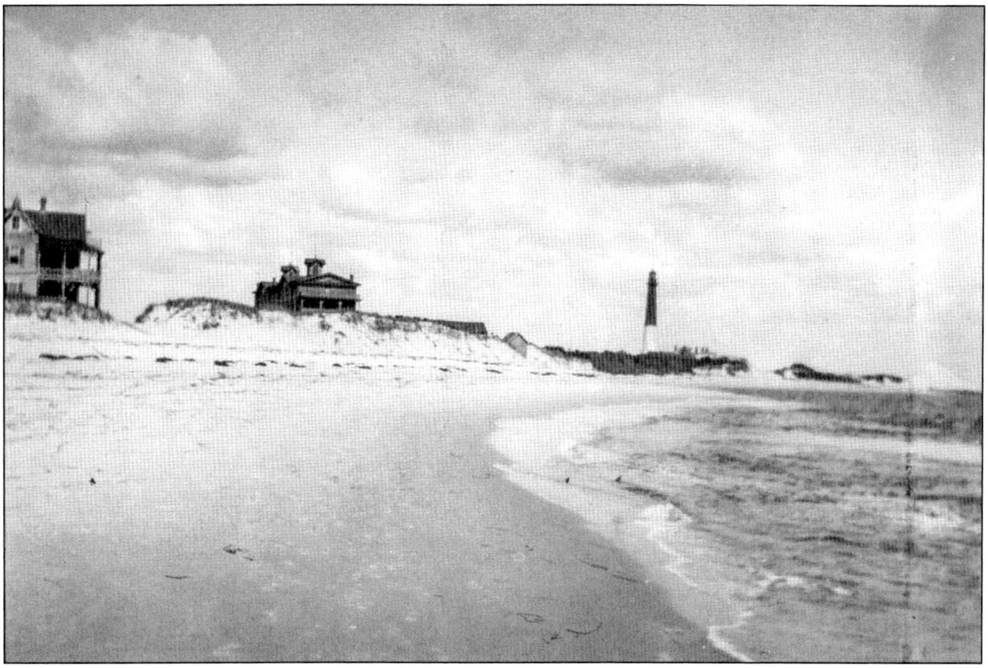

The southward march of Barnegat Inlet also affected the ocean-side shoreline. The ocean slowly advanced on East Fourth Street, beginning soon after the Oceanic Hotel was built dangerously close to it. Less than three years later, in about 1885, the hotel had to be moved back to the eastern end of the block, as pictured here. Also seen is the hotel's former site, now touching the water's edge.

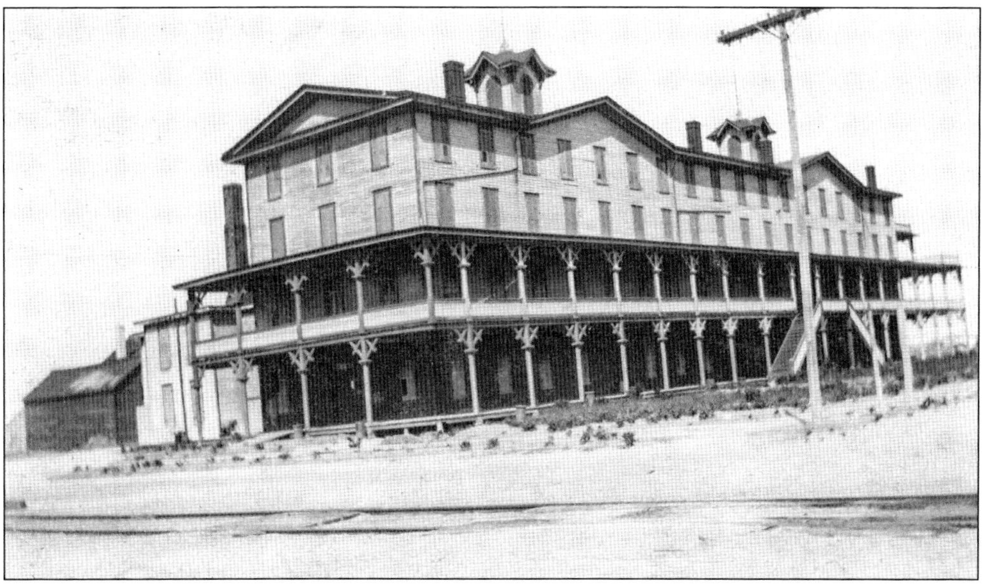

In its new location at the corner of East Fourth Street and what was planned to be the north-to-south island road known as Central Avenue, or "the Boulevard," the Oceanic Hotel was upgraded with a wraparound two-story porch, while the newly arrived railroad built a platform for guests in front of the hotel.

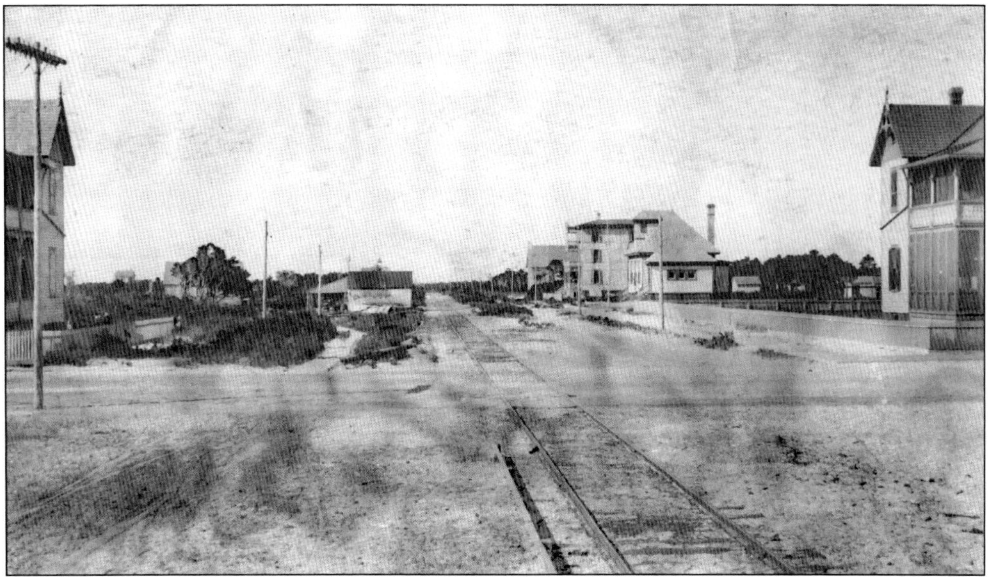

The formerly sandy path used by some on horse-drawn carriages to move goods to and from nearby High Point and other towns was by the early 1900s a well-traveled rail line bringing as many or more visitors as the steamboats that operated between Barnegat City and Barnegat or Toms River. Electrification also arrived around this time, although the town still used oil street lamps for many years.

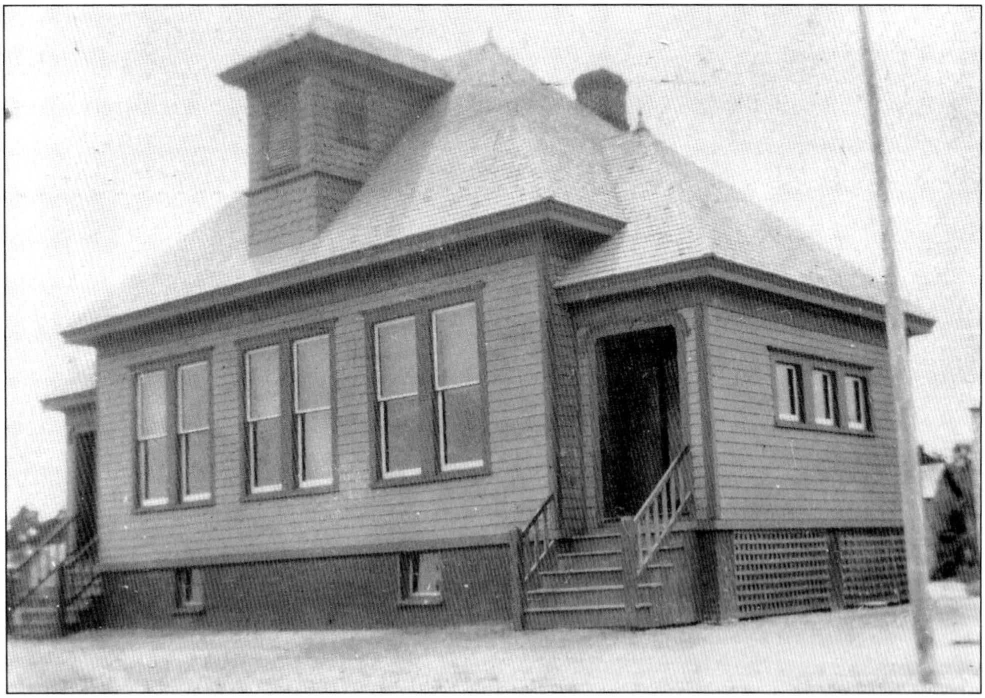

A growing town meant more children. A local teacher taught them in a small cottage on Third Street, but by the late 1890s, it was too small. A new, larger one-room school, seen here, opened in 1903 on the corner of West Fifth Street and Central Avenue. (Courtesy of the Ocean County Historical Society.)

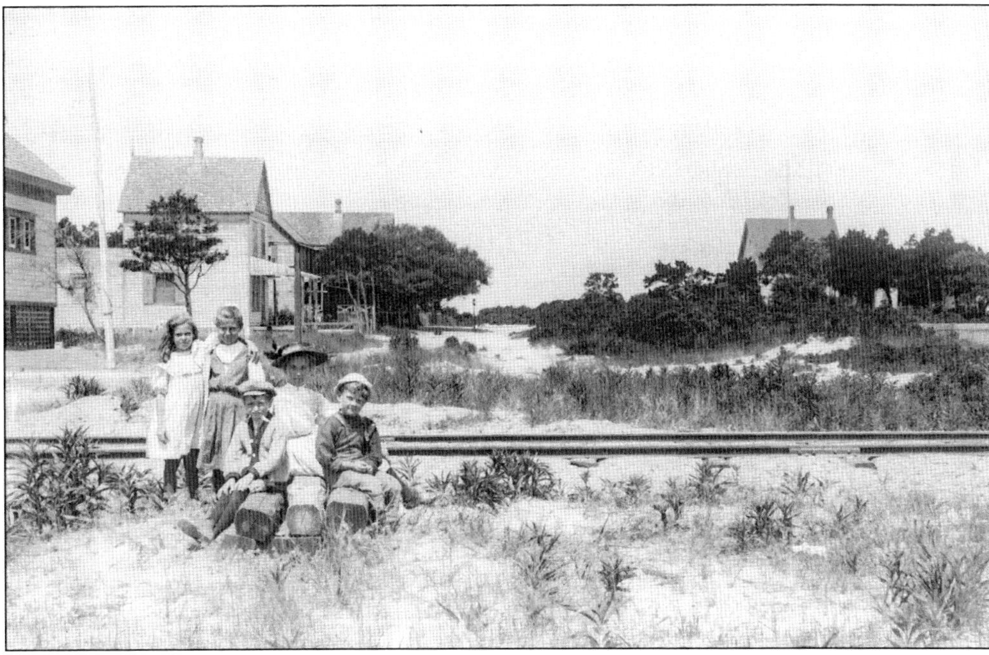

This c. 1910 view of West Fifth Street exemplifies the duality of turn-of-the-century Barnegat City; the developed was side-by-side with the wild. From left to right, a new modern school, Joe Peckworth's two-story cottage with the town ice house in the rear, and the Social Hotel were still only accessible by meandering sandy paths amidst thick brush.

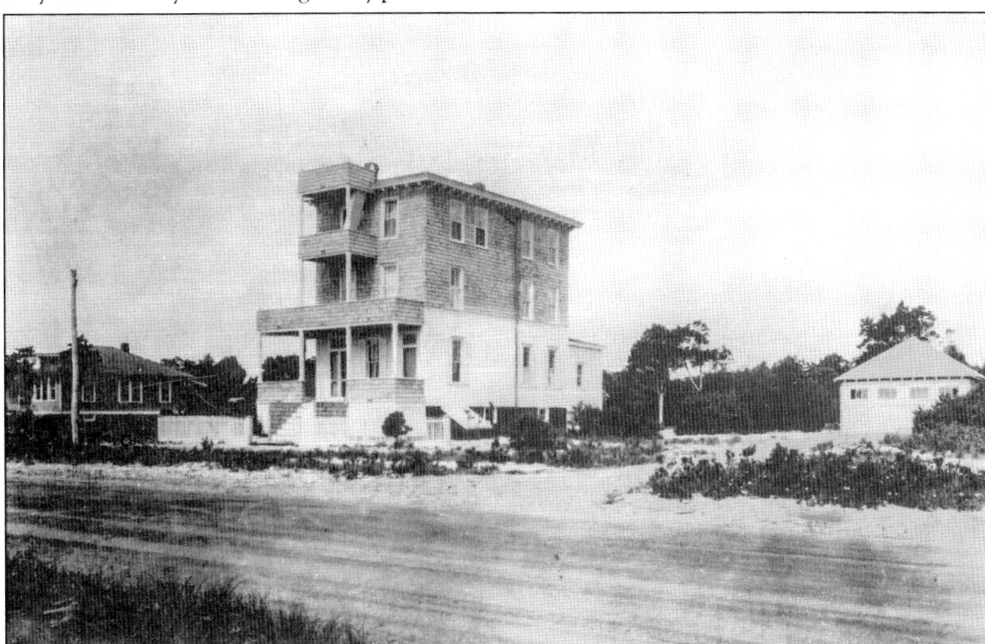

Using the signal flag system, houses such as this one at West Sixth Street and Central Avenue were built every 50 miles up and down the East Coast during the Spanish-American War of 1898 to warn of naval attack. A special Coast Guard crew manned the station at all times, but nothing came of the fears, and the war ended later in 1898, leaving behind this relic.

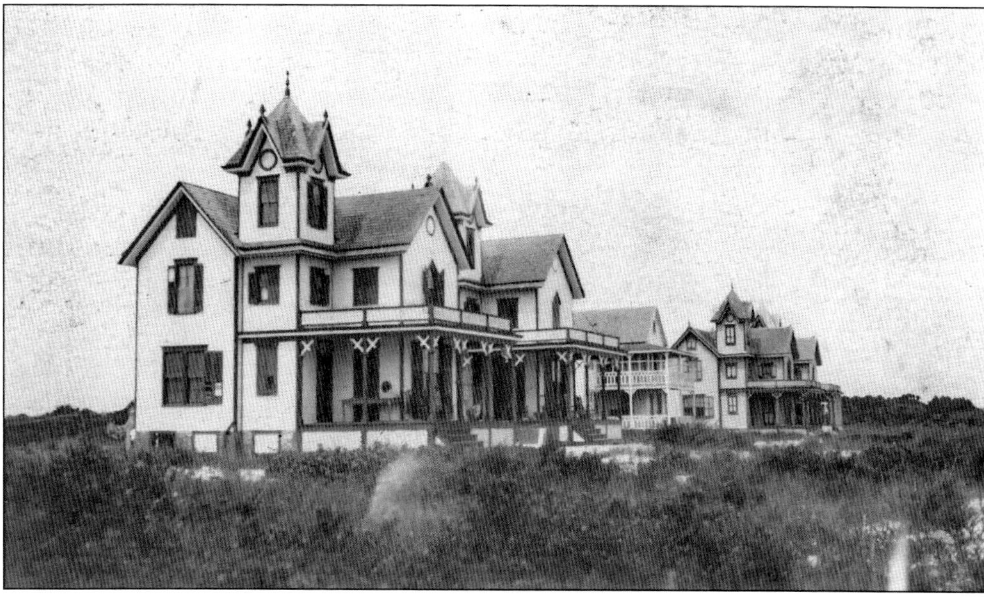

East Sixth Street is pictured here with another row of large cottages of nearly identical style. Along with the cluster on Fourth Street, the Barnegat City Land Company, the building arm of William Bailey and Benjamin Archer's venture, was seeking to advertise the kind of attractive town they could build with additional investors.

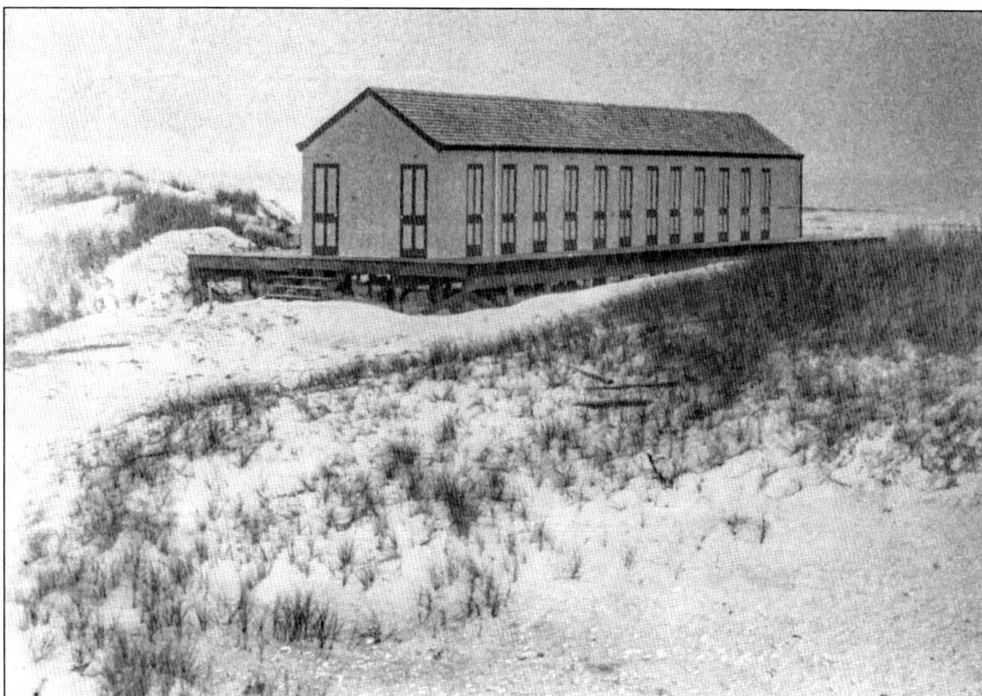

At the very end of the sands that would become East Eighth Street stood this bathhouse for guests of the Oceanic Hotel on East Fourth Street. A small boardwalk was built along the beachfront connecting the two. As with the ocean-side pier, it did not last long against the mighty Atlantic. The bathhouse, though, stood for nearly 40 years before it was torn down in the 1920s.

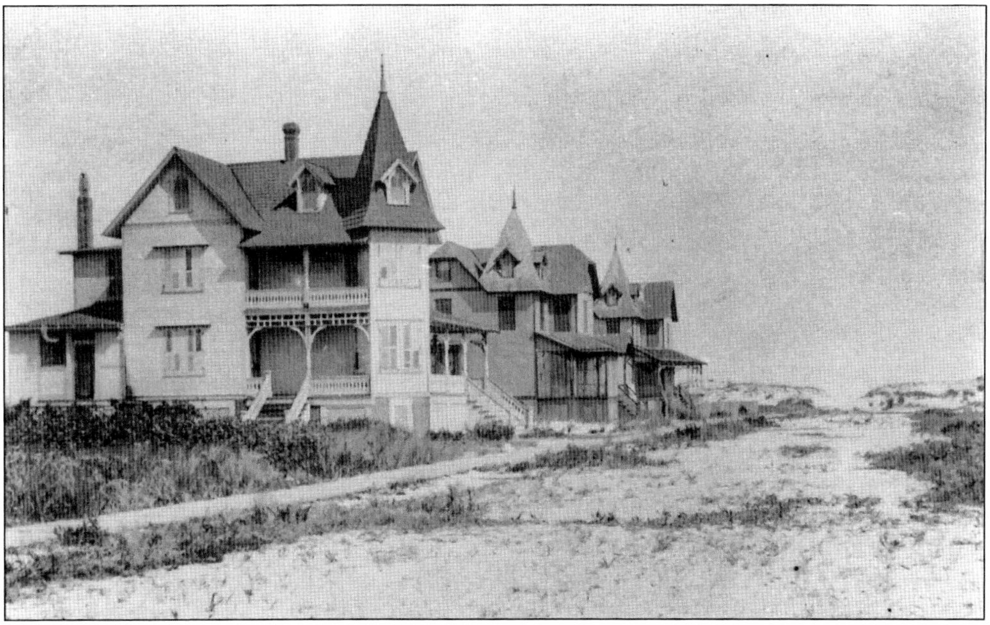

This row of houses on East Twelfth Street followed the advertising vein of construction, showcasing what could be. Another large and unique house was also built on the corner with Central Avenue, which Benjamin Archer took for his own. The house at left was recently owned for many years by renowned local artist Ed Heitman.

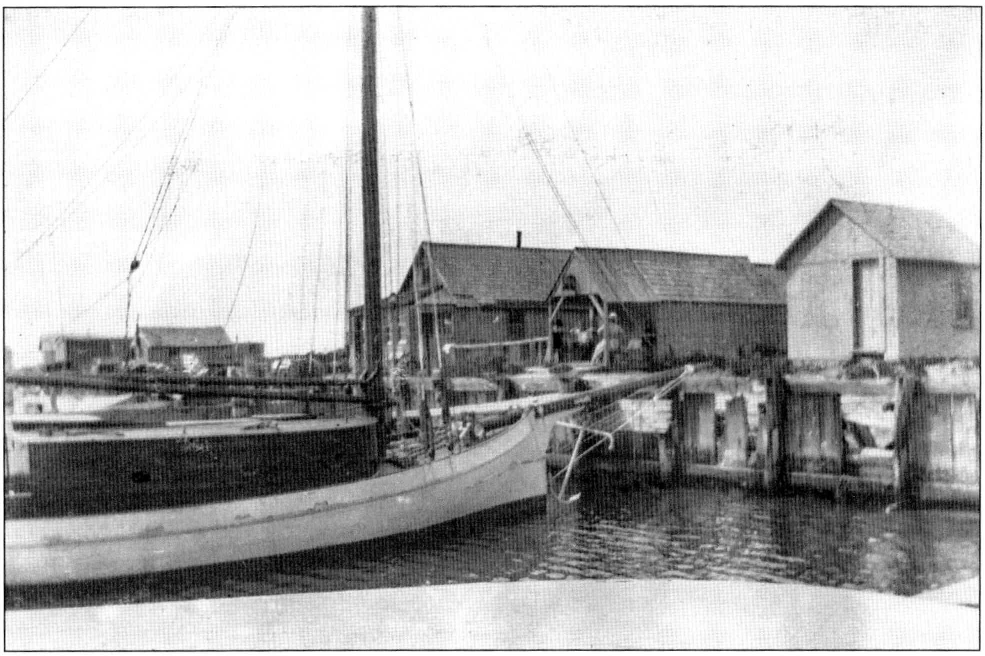

The long spit of land at the end of West Sixth Street was the site of the Barnegat City harbor, pictured here. Rows of fishing cottages lined a wooden bulkhead, while fishing boats filled the port. As Camden and Philadelphia bankers lived in their grand cottages on the ocean side, longtime local families and blue-collar newcomers continued to make their lives as baymen and fishermen along the bayside of Barnegat City.

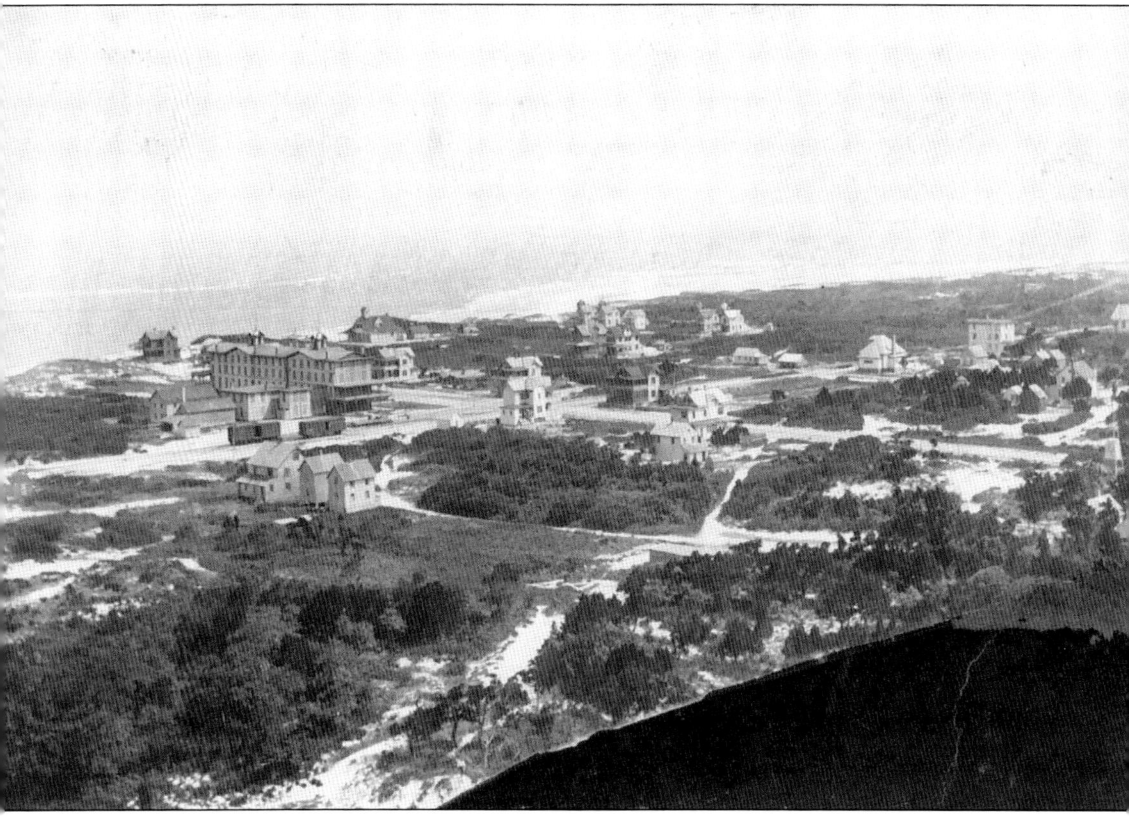

With the exception of East Twelfth Street and the West Sixth Street harbor, this bird's-eye view taken from the lighthouse shows the full extent of Barnegat City at its most developed around 1910. Nearly 20 years of promotion and investment in Camden and Philadelphia failed to realize any more of William Bailey and Benjamin Archer's dream of a new bustling shore resort. After Archer's death in 1903 and Bailey's in 1908, the pace and urgency of development waned. The grand hotels on either side of Barnegat City struggled to remain in business, changing hands several times. A typhoid scare in the late 1910s effectively killed the Oceanic Hotel's future. The Sunset Hotel carried on until it was destroyed by fire in 1932. The bayside pier and horse cart were abandoned in favor of the railroad and, ultimately, the arrival of the automobile in 1914.

Five

Planes, Trains, and Automobiles

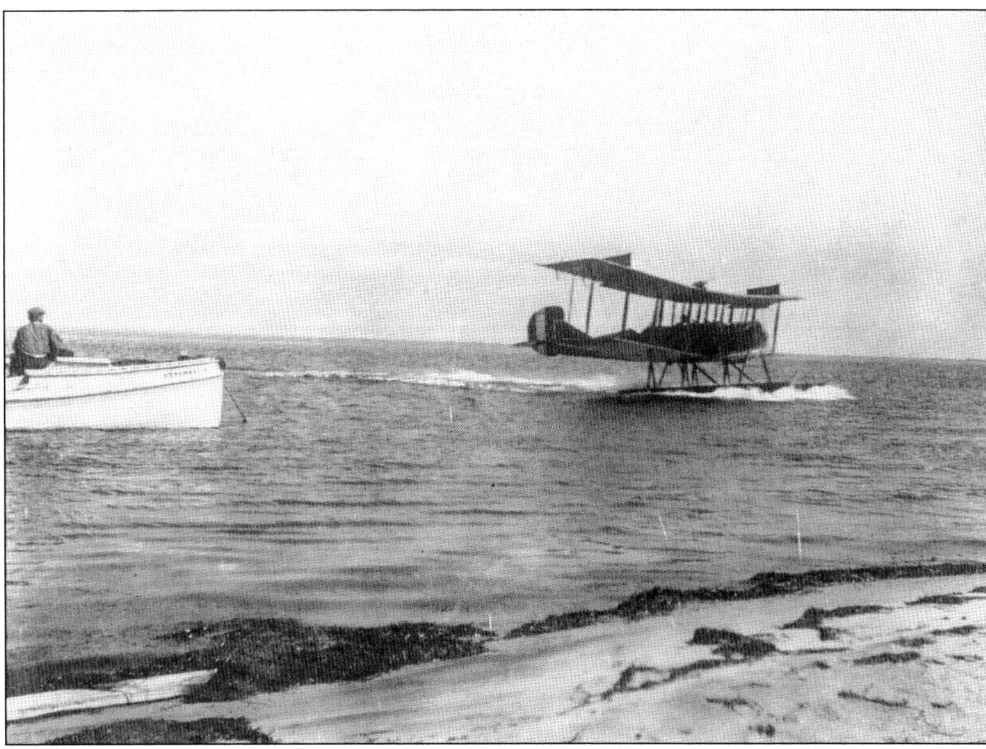

The 20th century saw even more signs of modernity creep into Barnegat City. This large seaplane would arrive on the bay and park near the Sunset Hotel, seen here c. 1915. The US Mail sometimes came by boat from Barnegat or by train. In later years seen here, it was delivered by air to Barnegat City and High Point on the north end of the island.

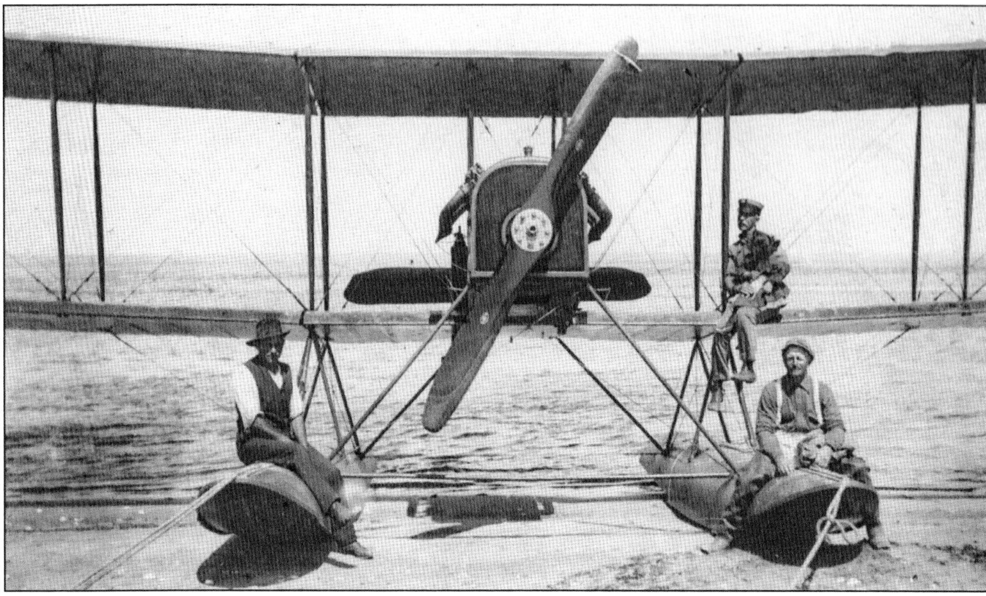
With a population of barely 150, by 1920, the sight of a plane, or anything out of the ordinary, would bring the town out. Here, from left to right, Edward Bennett, an unidentified person holding one of the men's daughters, and Joshua Shreve pose on the massive airplane. In the coming years, manned flying objects would become a regular part of life at Barnegat City.

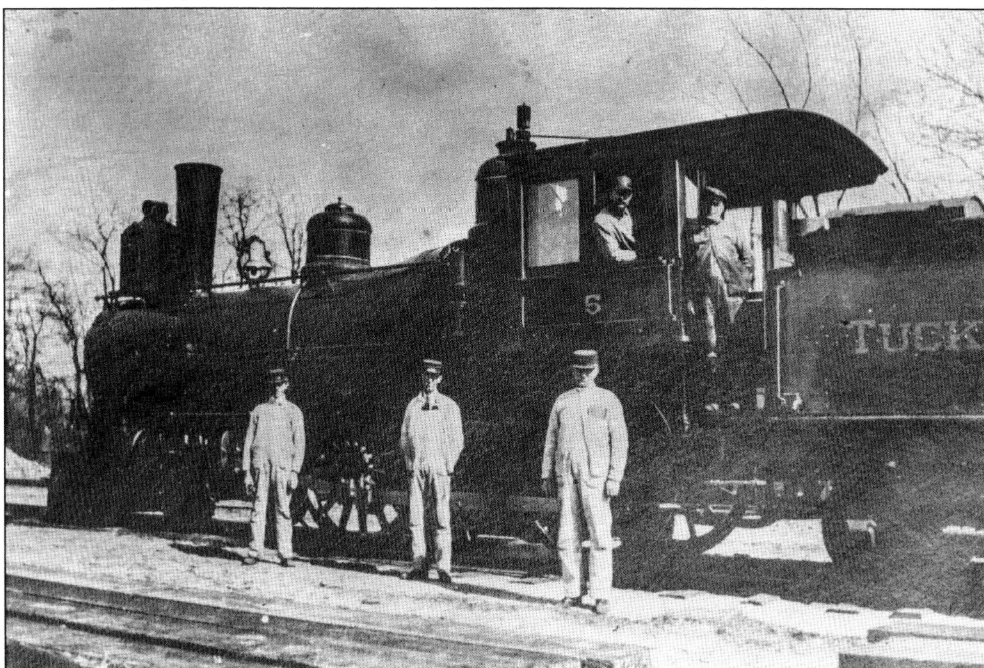

The railroad was the most significant arrival on Long Beach Island since the European settlers. A bridge from the mainland to the middle of the island was constructed in 1886, along with a north and south road. Operated by the Tuckerton Railroad, locomotive No. 5, the last in service, is pictured here with, from left to right, brakeman Thomas Chattin, brakeman Howard Shinn, (unidentified), conductor George Wills, and fireman Edward Ireland.

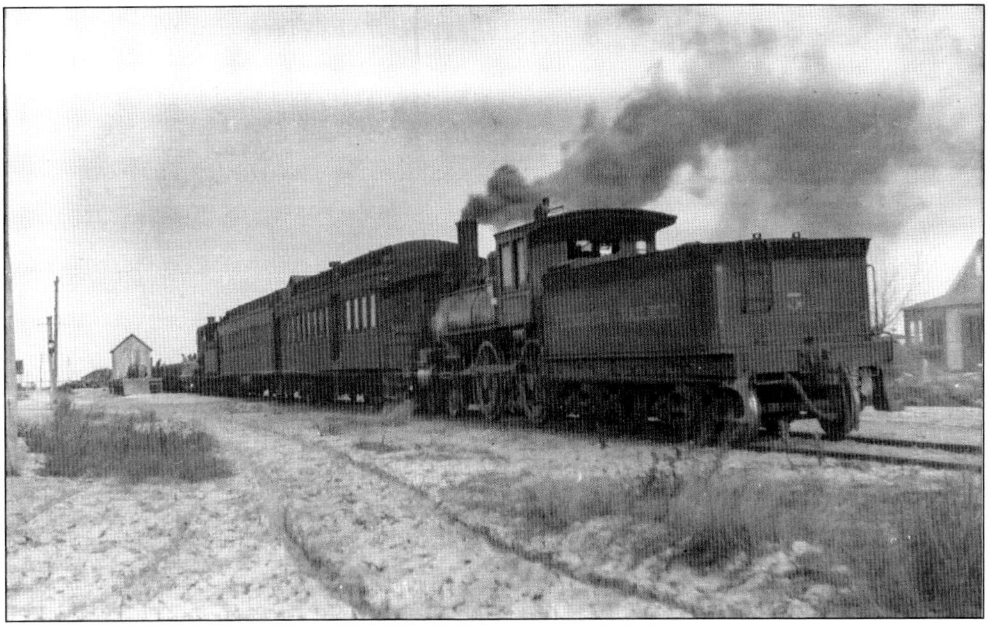

This undated photograph shows a typical Tuckerton Railroad train arriving in Barnegat City near Fifth Street. Cargo and a fresh catch often outnumbered passengers. At the terminus of the north road at Barnegat City Junction in Ship Bottom, passengers would transfer to a southbound train toward Beach Haven or continue west over the bridge on the roads to regional towns or to Philadelphia or New York City.

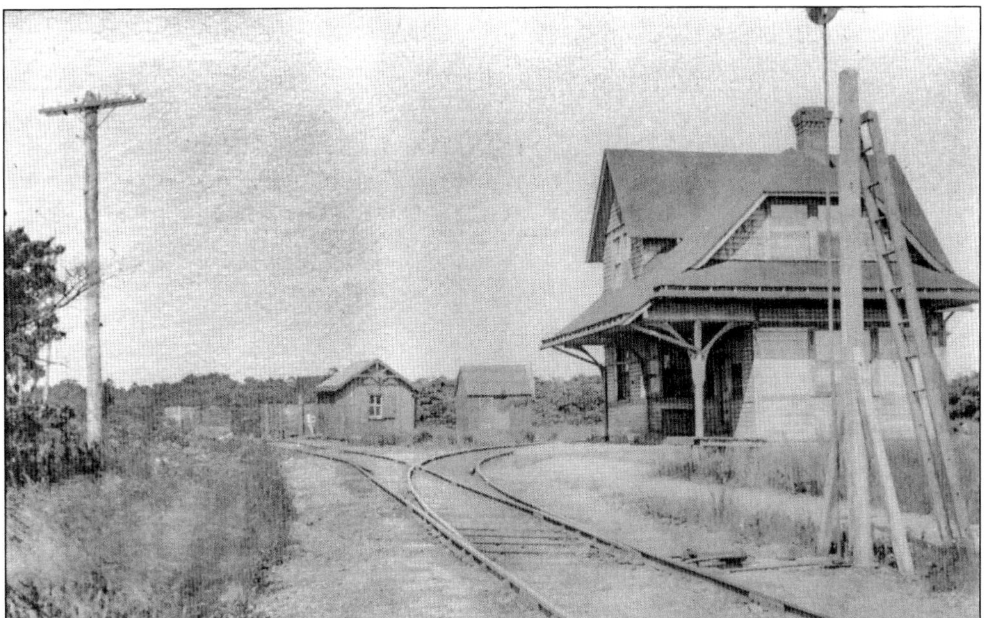

Barnegat City Station, as shown in this undated postcard, was built on West Eleventh Street in 1885. Based on the Barnegat City Beach Association plans, the spur to the left was for a grand future port at the West Sixth Street harbor that was never built. Unlike the rest of Long Beach Island, the tracks through Barnegat City from Ninth to Third Streets actually overlapped Central Avenue.

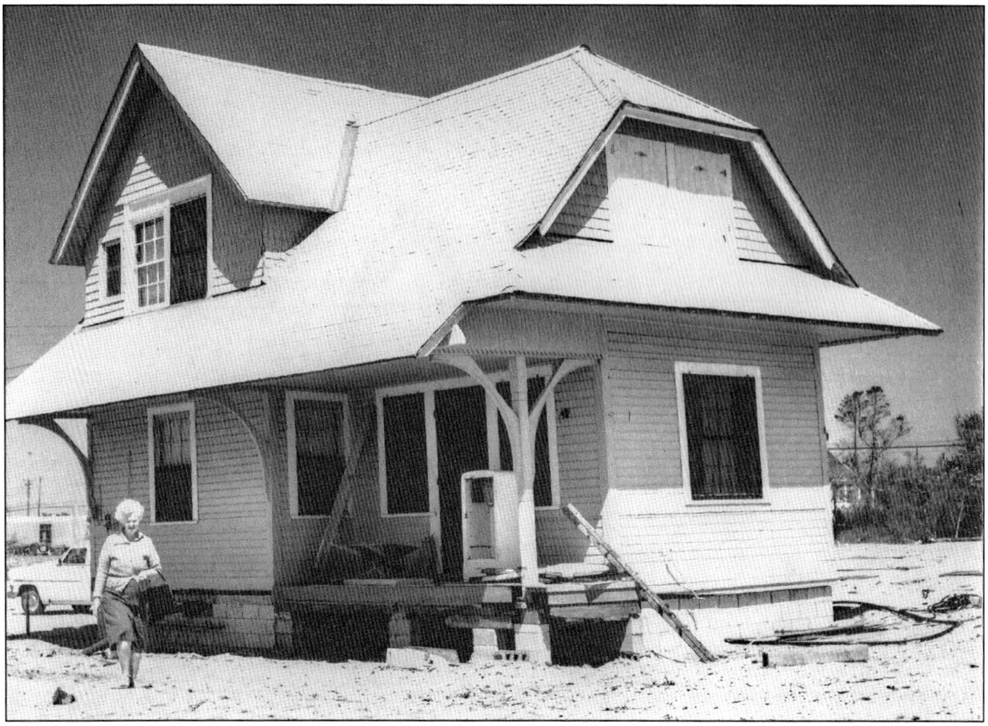

Of 12 stations that served the line on Long Beach Island, Barnegat City's was the only one to survive to the present day. The station underwent several renovations, as seen in this photograph from the 1950s. It was converted into a private residence in the 1930s after the railroad was shuttered.

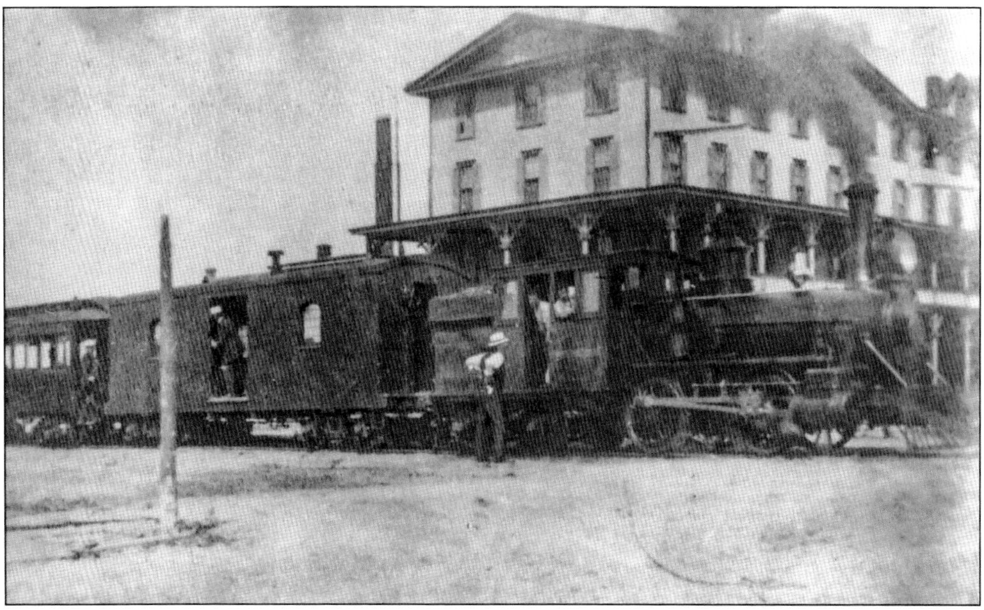

The famous *Yellow Jacket* train, so named for the dark green Baldwin 0-4-4t Forney locomotive called the *Harvey Cedars* and the bright yellow passenger cars it pulled, is seen here at the Oceanic Hotel around 1900. Between 1894 and 1908, the *Yellow Jacket* was a familiar and beloved sight on the north end of the island for the short-lived Manahawkin & Long Beach Transportation Co.

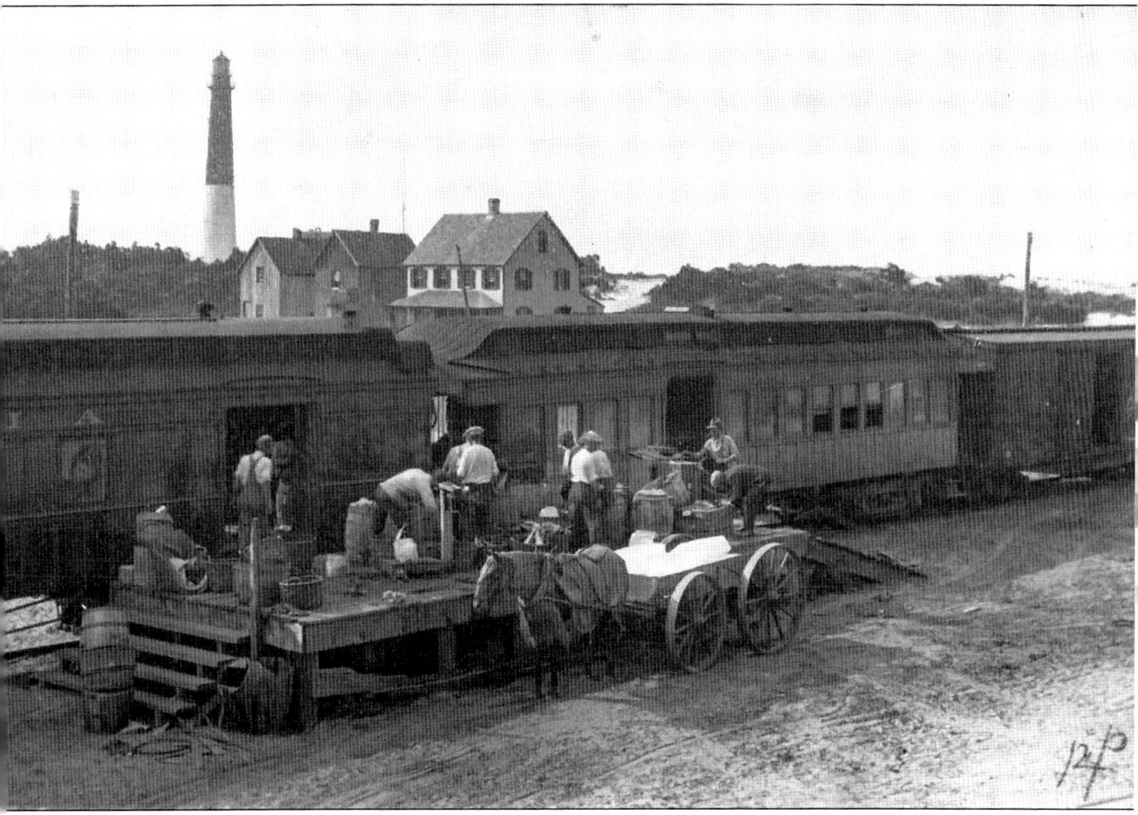

The Tuckerton Railroad (TRR)'s Long Beach Island spur suffered through fits and starts between 1886 and the early 1910s. The Pennsylvania Railroad owned several of the area lines. Various sections were spun off into their own companies, such as the Long Beach Railroad, the Philadelphia & Beach Haven Railroad, Barnegat Railroad, and the Manahawkin & Long Beach Transportation Company. John Ashley Brown was a director of several mainland lines that led to the island roads. During occasional stock market panics, companies like these went under. Most winters, the lines petitioned for service to be discontinued until spring. The *Yellow Jacket* was reasonably profitable for much of this time. Movement of freight became as significant a source of business for the TRR as passenger travel. This scene of the Oceanic Hotel station was typical of many stops. The hotels and railroads were intimately linked; hotel developers often sat on the boards of the railroads. This helped to bring the railroad and hotel guests to town at the start. But when the lines and hotels struggled, this intermingled ownership often compounded financial troubles.

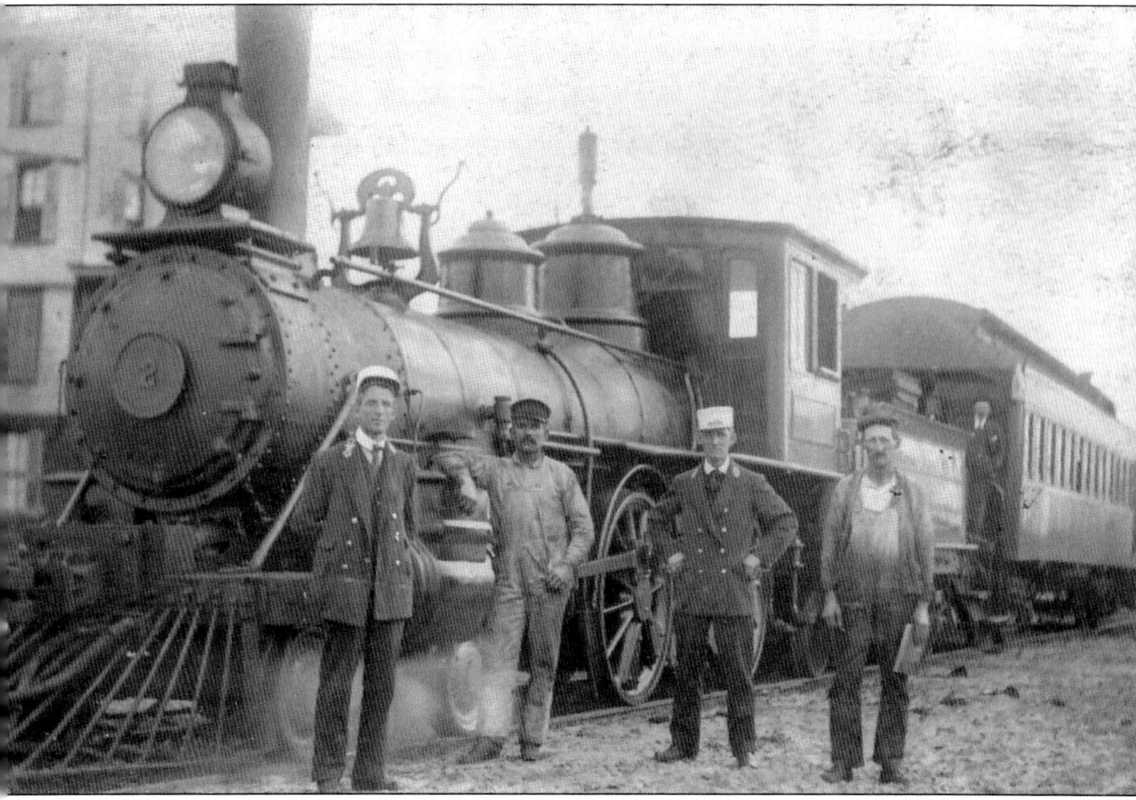

Standing with engine No. 2 are, from left to right, Al Brown, Al Sprague, Alex Inman, and Clarence Bennett in front of the Oceanic Hotel around 1908. Like the crews of the lifesaving stations in Barnegat City and elsewhere on Long Beach Island, the trains were run by family and friends whom everyone knew. When it shut down for the winter or due to growing operational losses in the 1900s and 1910s, fishermen who came to rely upon the trains to get their catch to market, along with property owners who thought building near the tracks would lead to higher values, complained and got mayors and congressmen involved. Most often the corporate machinations were efforts to force the growing debts each company was incurring on the parent companies. The construction of the automobile bridge in 1914 was the first mortal blow. The construction of a road to Barnegat City in 1920 was another. In 1923, the Barnegat line was discontinued. When the railroad bridge was washed out in 1935, the end had arrived.

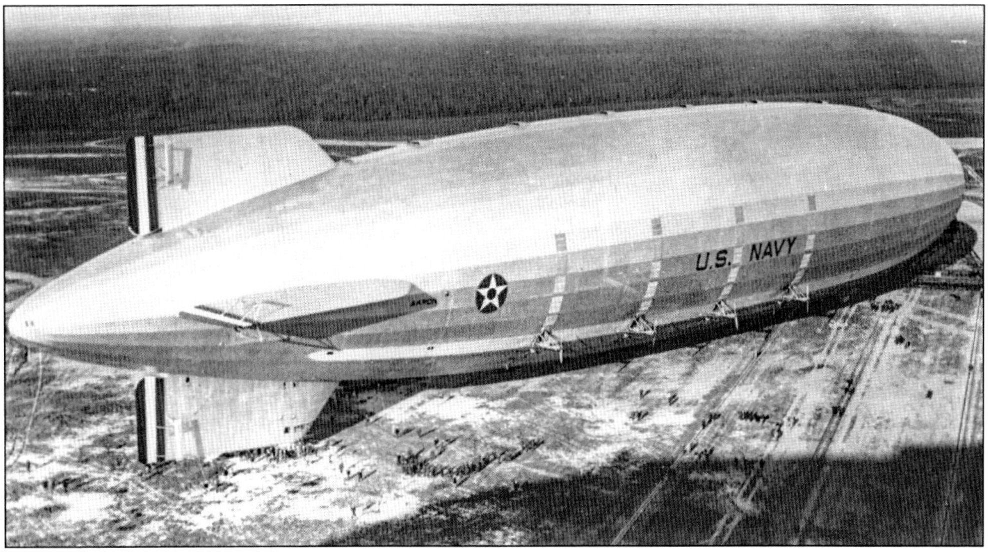

Air travel continued to be a fact of life at Barnegat City, but never more so than the 1930s, when leviathans of the sky began passing overhead. The Lakehurst Naval Air Station became the East Coast port for all dirigible travel, a rapidly growing military and commercial industry. The USS *Akron* is seen here on the field in the shadow of the massive 966-foot hangar No. 1.

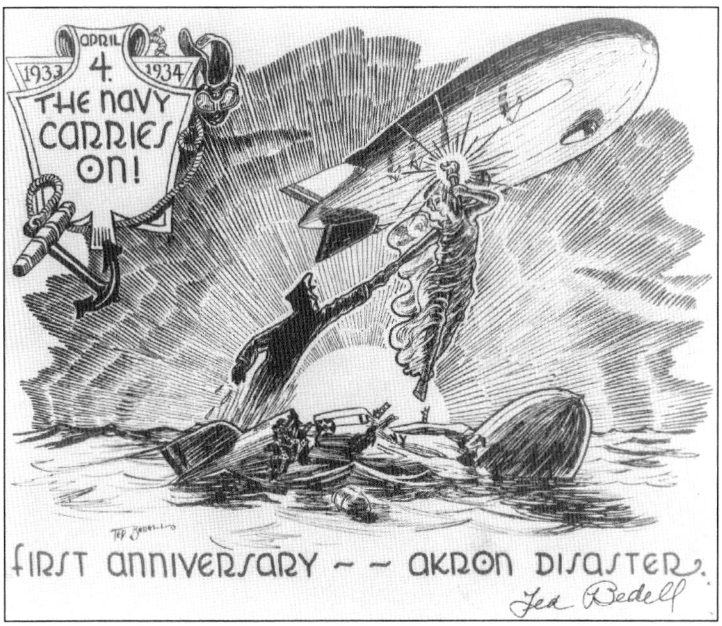

Built by the Goodyear Corporation in cooperation with the German Zeppelin Corporation, the ZRS-4 USS *Akron*, 785 feet in length, was the largest airship ever built at the time. Designed for long-distance naval reconnaissance, its crash on April 4, 1933, off Barnegat City, commemorated in this print, was international news largely forgotten today.

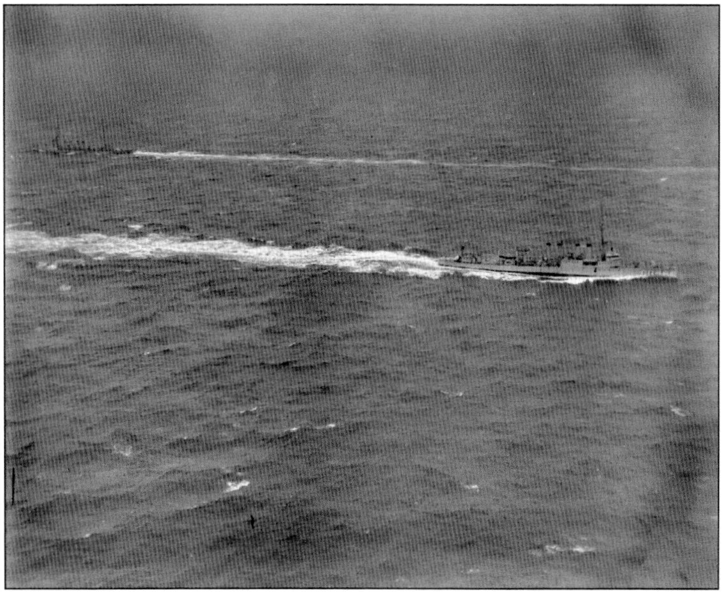

Search and rescue efforts, seen here, began early on the morning of April 4, 1933. The Barnegat City Coast Guard Station sent out its boats, while efforts were coordinated through the station on East Seventh Street. Doctors were flown in by seaplane. Elsewhere, every port from New York to Philadelphia offered assistance. Crowds of family and friends waited anxiously for any word.

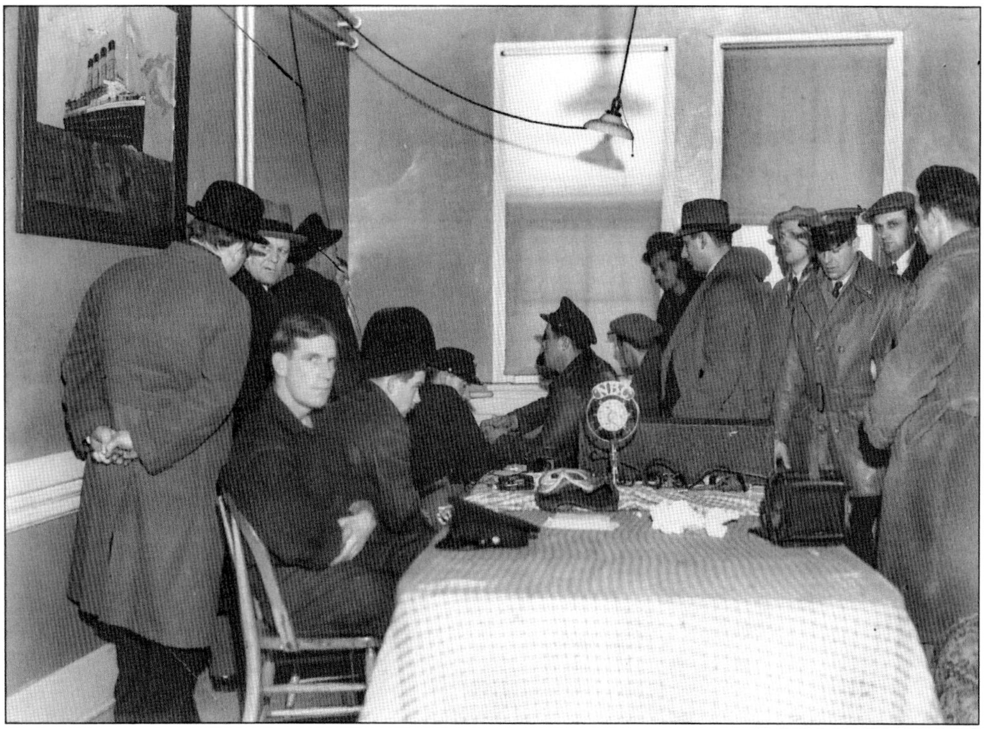

International news crews descended on Barnegat City, congregating in this room at the Coast Guard station and broadcasting radio reports to the waiting world. The *Akron* had flown for three years and was flying the day of the crash with a packed complement of 76 men, including the head of the Navy's Bureau of Aeronautics, Rear Adm. William Moffett.

By the afternoon of the crash, search vessels located some floating debris, pictured here, confirming their worst fears. A German tanker, *Phoebus*, passing by the area reported it had recovered four men, one of whom died before being brought aboard. Of the crew of 76, only three survived the catastrophe. Few victims were recovered, and most of the debris drifted and sank over a wide area to the south.

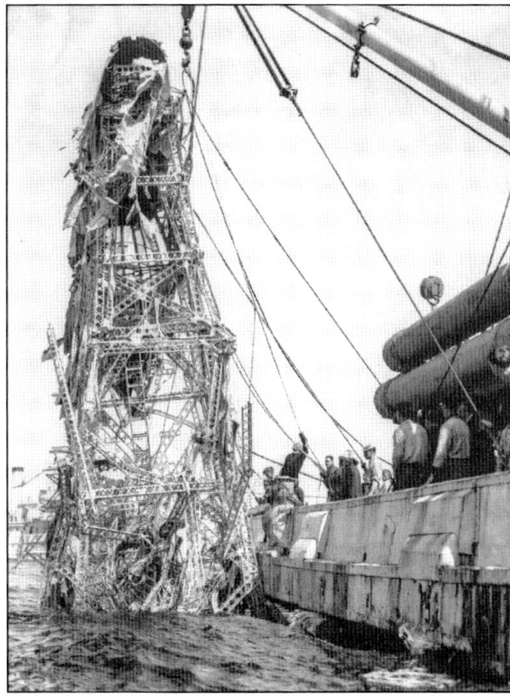

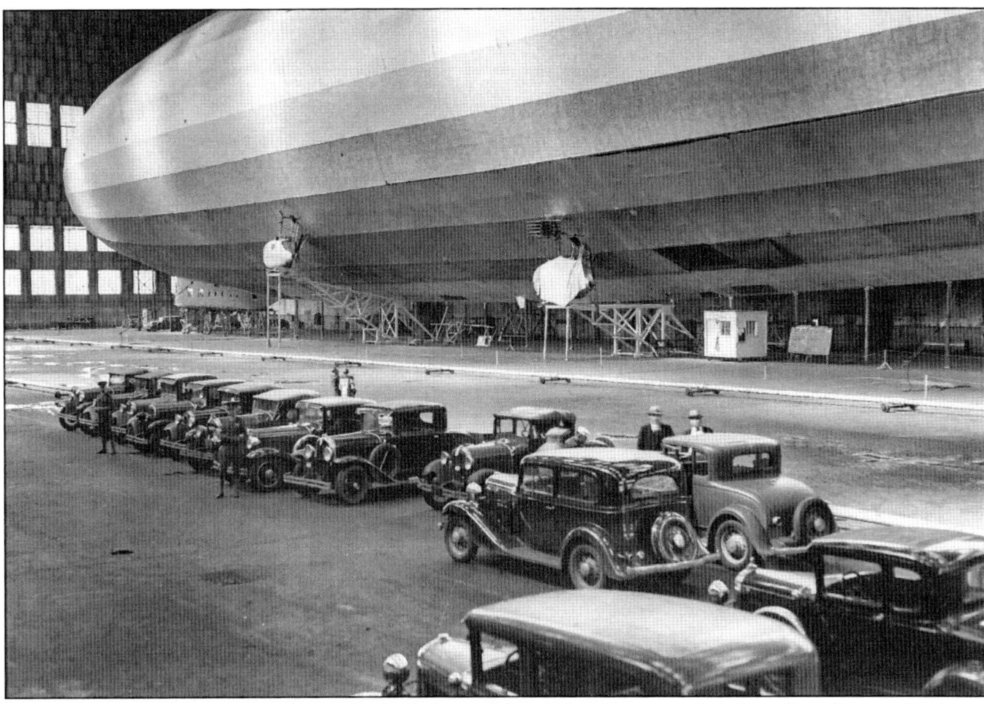

This haunting photograph from the Lakehurst Naval Air Station, the day after the crash, shows cars belonging to members of the USS *Akron* crew. An investigation revealed that thunderstorms pushed the mighty ship down while a combination of conditions and human error led to the helmsman dipping the tail into the ocean, leading to the loss of the *Akron*. A lack of life rings contributed to the mass casualties.

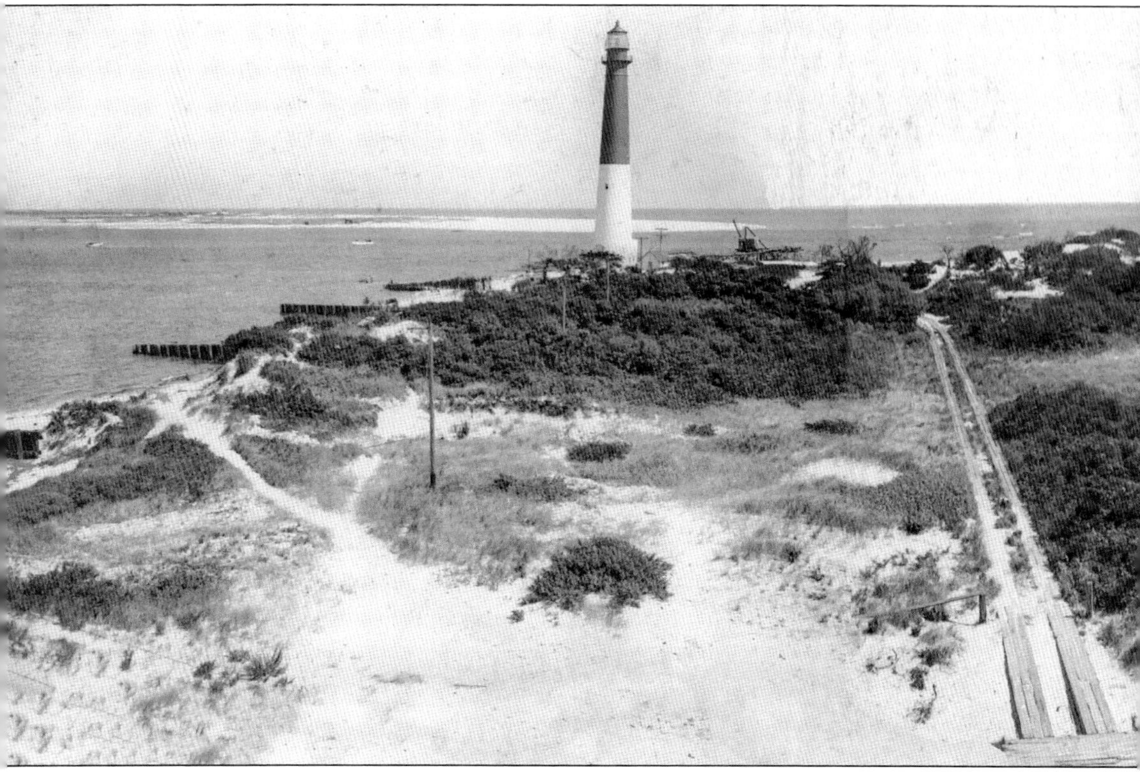

Taken from the roof of the Sunset Hotel around 1925, this panoramic view of Barnegat City features the automobiles that had begun to transform the town in ways that William Bailey and Benjamin Archer would have welcomed. The ability of Americans to transport themselves from place to place at ease and without using public transportation revolutionized the way developers marketed projects and to whom. The concept of a day trip by car was fast becoming an option for

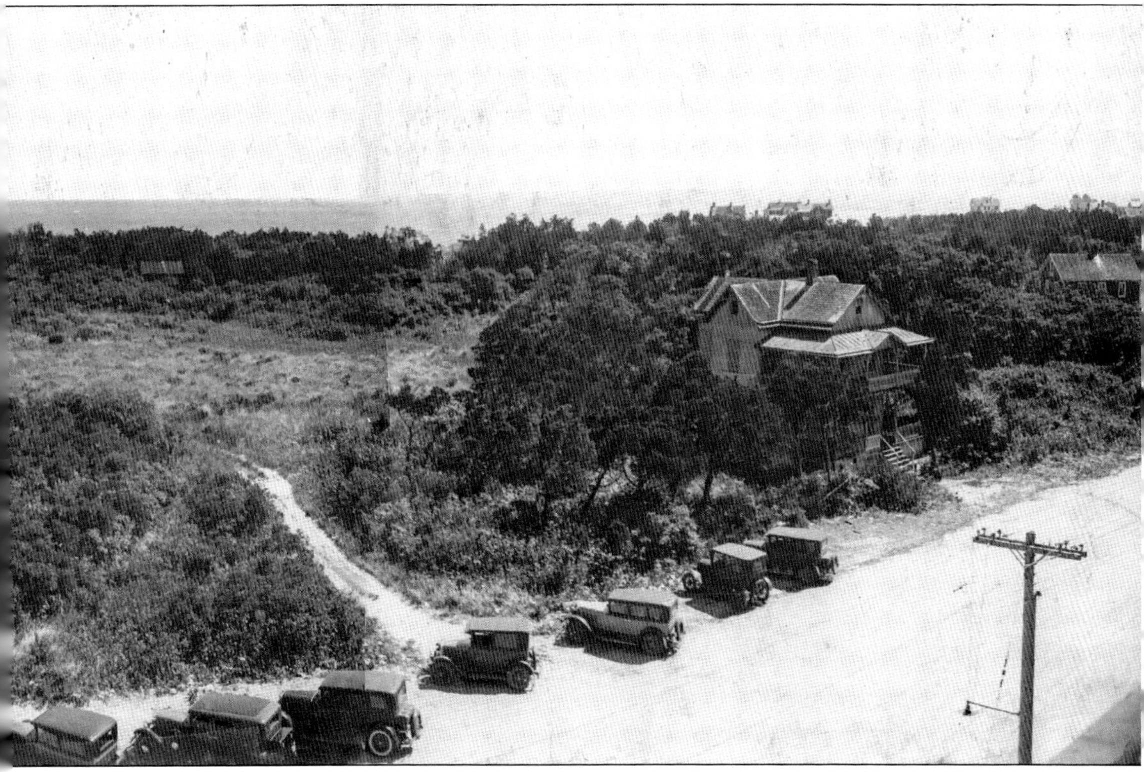

the average American. Meanwhile, trains had a limited attraction for the shore tourist due to the uncomfortable, long, and dirty conditions a ride entailed in those days of open rail cars. The grassy meadow in the shadow of Barnegat Lighthouse seen here would soon become a massive parking lot that encouraged automobile tourists to visit Barnegat City and see the landmark.

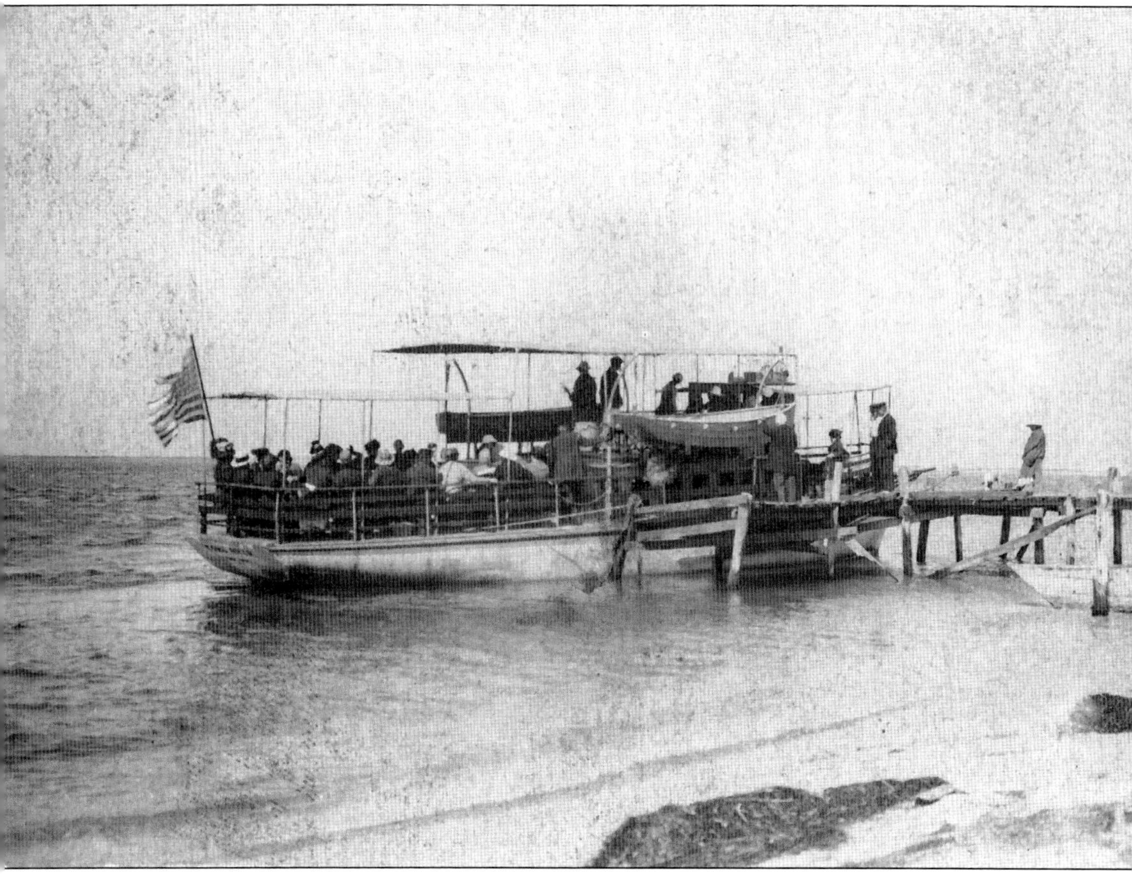

The days of boating to Barnegat Beach from the mainland or taking a ferry from Toms River were long gone, as echoed by this 1914 postcard. Pleasure boating and excursion boats, though, would be making a strong return to Barnegat City beginning in the 1930s, when recreational boating became a tourist business thanks to the automobile's ability to make vacation destinations and road trips an unintimidating idea for the average tourist. Boat rentals became a big business for local fishermen, who discovered charters as a new source of income and justification for buying a second vessel. Cruises that ran up and down the length of Barnegat Bay from Atlantic City to Manasquan began shortly after World War II. Some who moved into Barnegat City could afford their own pleasure boats, inviting family and friends to go out fishing for the day. Tourism, like so much of what happened in Barnegat City over the years, became a family affair.

Six

The Summers of Terror

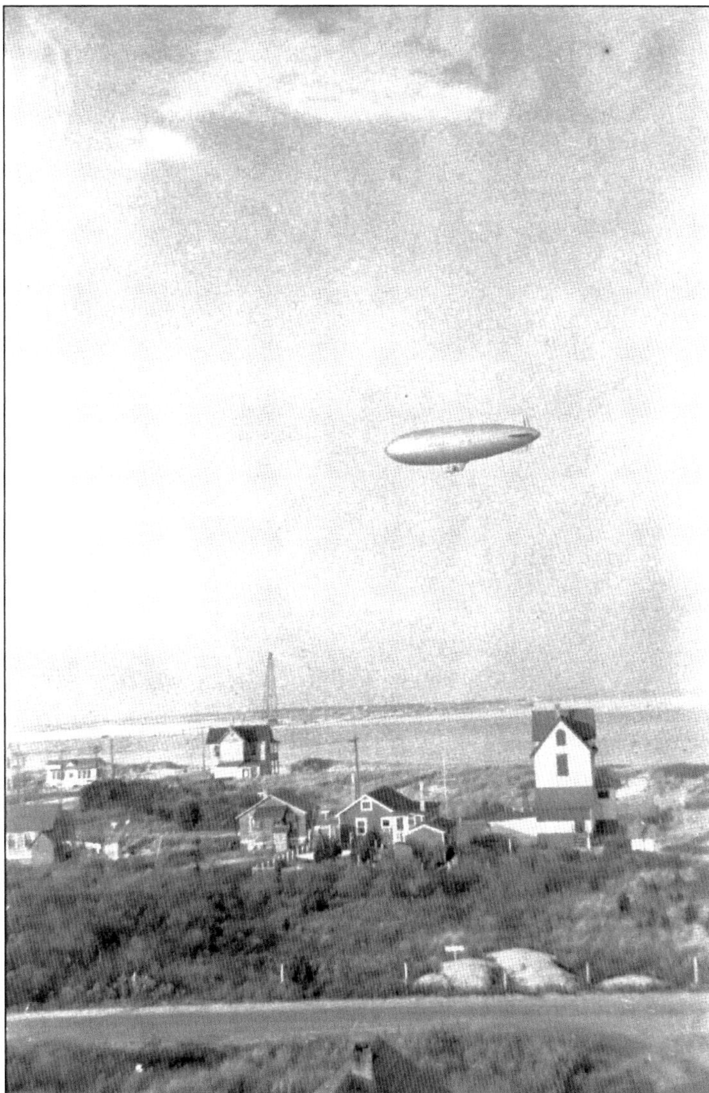

Development of lighter-than-air craft, such as the USS *Akron*, was part of efforts to be ready for the next great war. In December 1941, that preparation was justified when the United States entered World War II. Smaller blimps now patrolled the skies over Barnegat City, pictured here, which was also used as a navigational point from which they would watch for enemy fleets, especially submarines.

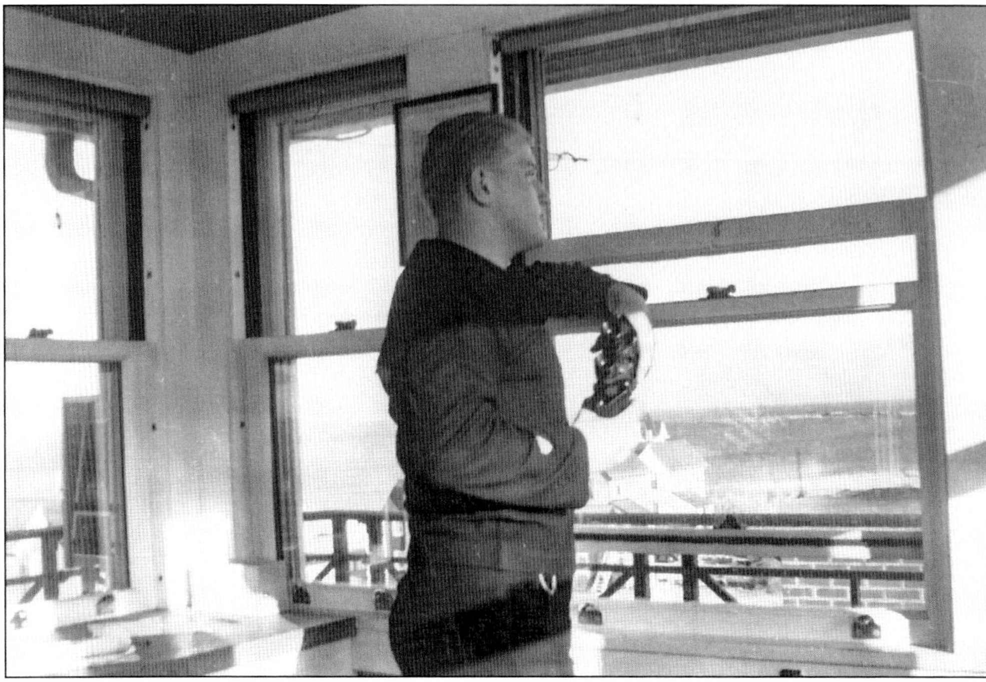

On the ground at Barnegat City, Coast Guardsmen were put on observation duty, too, as Coast Guardsman Klinewski is demonstrating here. Units from the Army were stationed on Long Beach Island and ordered to patrol the beaches in anticipation of possible amphibious landings. The prospect of German bombing raids and invasion were taken seriously in the first months of the war, although they were highly improbable.

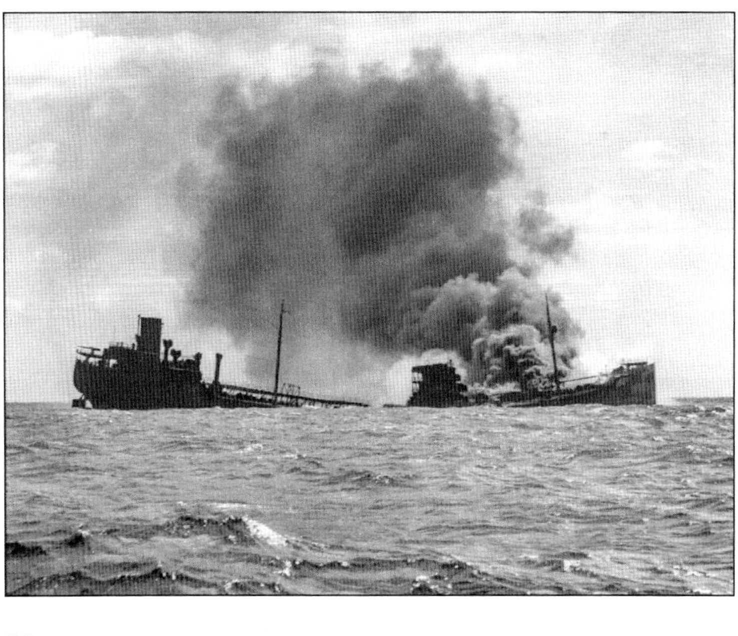

One of the first signs that the war had truly arrived on the home front came in February 1942. The Standard Oil Company tanker *R.P. Resor*, pictured here, was broken in half by torpedoes from the *U578* north of Barnegat Inlet, killing nearly 40. Oil spread from the hold and polluted the waters. The *Resor* was the 24th ship sunk along the East Coast since December.

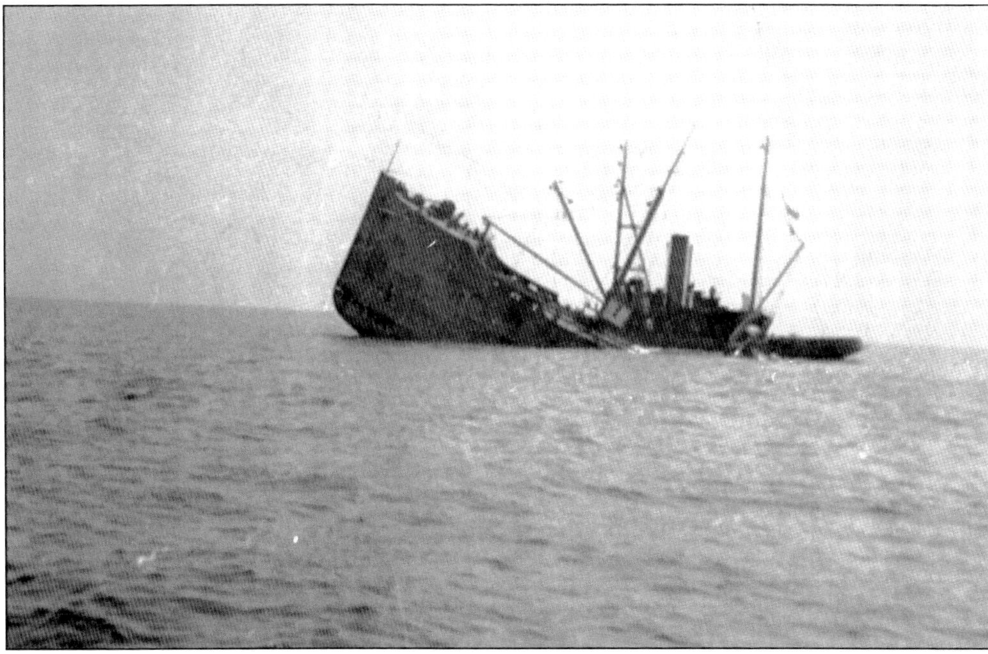

On March 10, 1942, the tanker *Gulf Trade* was attacked by the *U588* within a few miles of the Barnegat City beach, killing 18. In the coming weeks, the broken hulk of the ship, seen here shortly after the attack, still remained above water after spilling her cargo. The oil that washed up gave Barnegat Light its distinctive black-streaked sand. Navy pilots strafed the wreck for target practice.

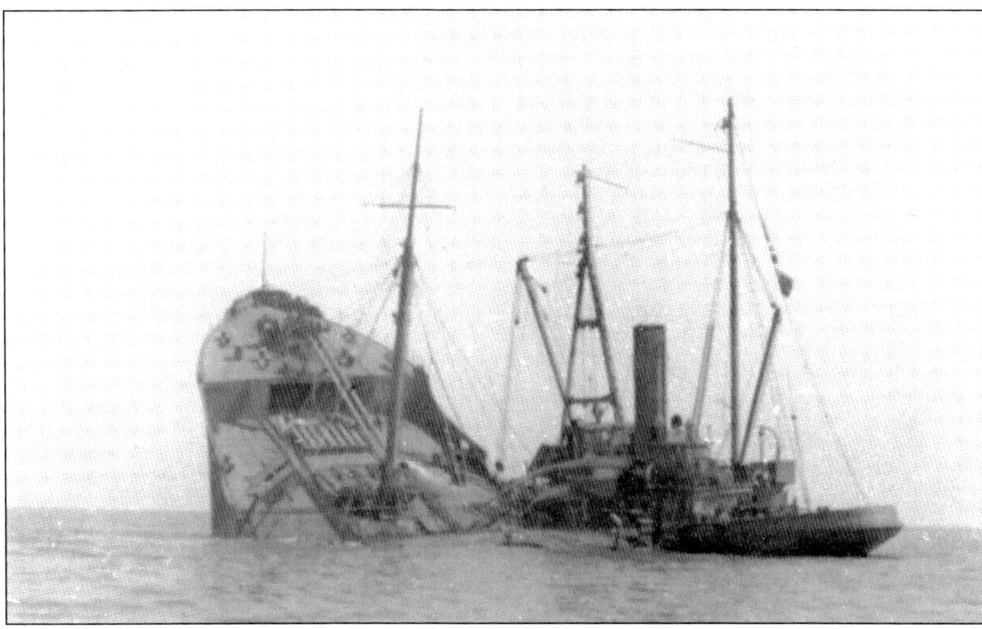

During the rescue of the survivors of the *Gulf Trade*, the *U588* attempted to fire on the Coast Guard cutters that arrived on scene. The bow, seen here, sank within a few days. The stern remained afloat and was ultimately towed away to deeper water where it could not affect marine traffic using the well-traveled and now targeted shipping lanes just beyond Barnegat Inlet.

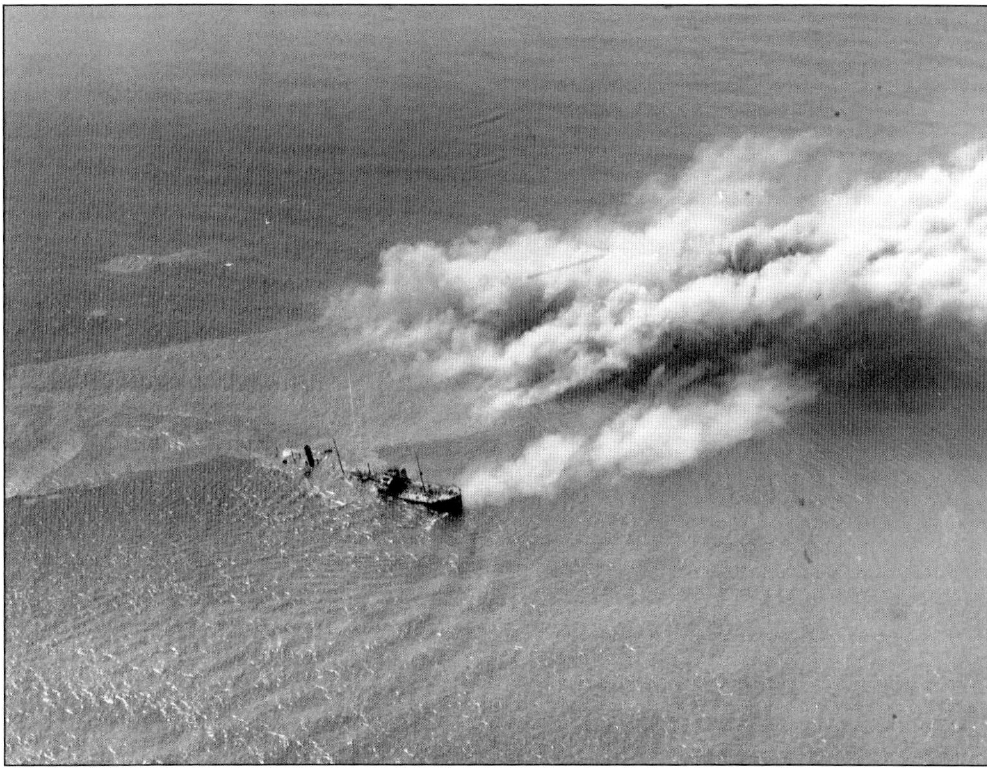

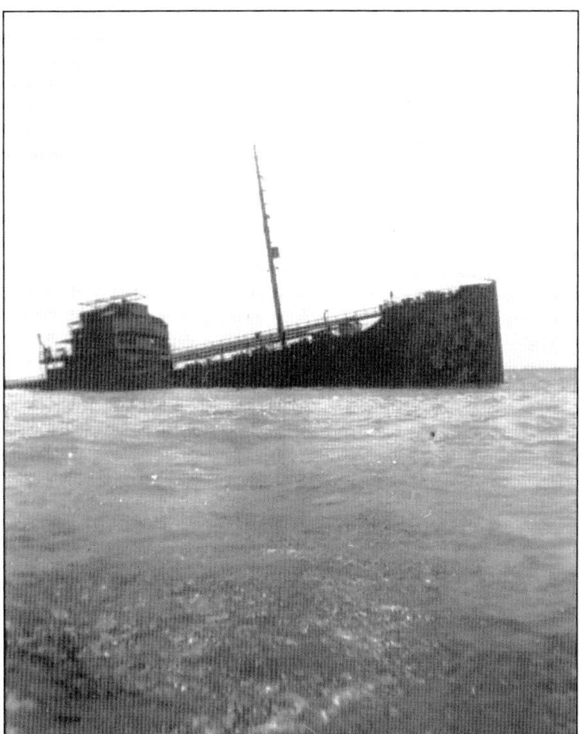

Just before Memorial Day, the tanker *Persephone* was passing Long Beach Island in an armed convoy, which now practiced maneuvers to counter submarine targeting. Nonetheless, the *U593* chased the group and focused on the last tanker in the line. After several attempts, torpedoes found the *Persephone*. The aftermath is pictured here from one of the blimp escorts.

Like the other tankers, the hits amidship broke the *Persephone* in half, sending the stern straight to the bottom. Oil on the water's surface caught fire and burned the bow section, seen derelict in this photograph. Luckily, calm conditions during daylight allowed for 28 of the crew to quickly escape. Nine died in the attack.

The *Persephone's* stern section was sitting in relatively shallow water, causing several vessels to hit the underwater obstacle. The Coast Guard used explosives to collapse the wreck further. The bow section pictured here never sank and was towed to New York, where it was scrapped. A portion of its oil was also salvaged.

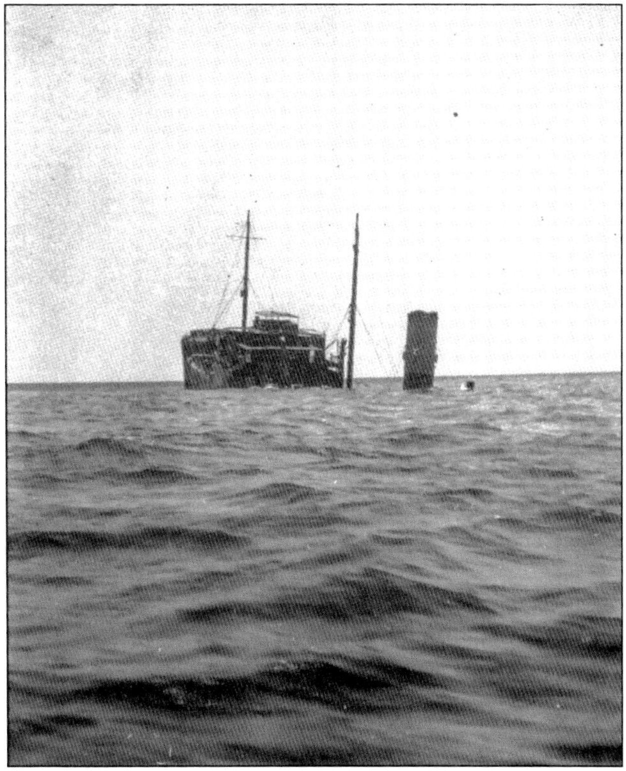

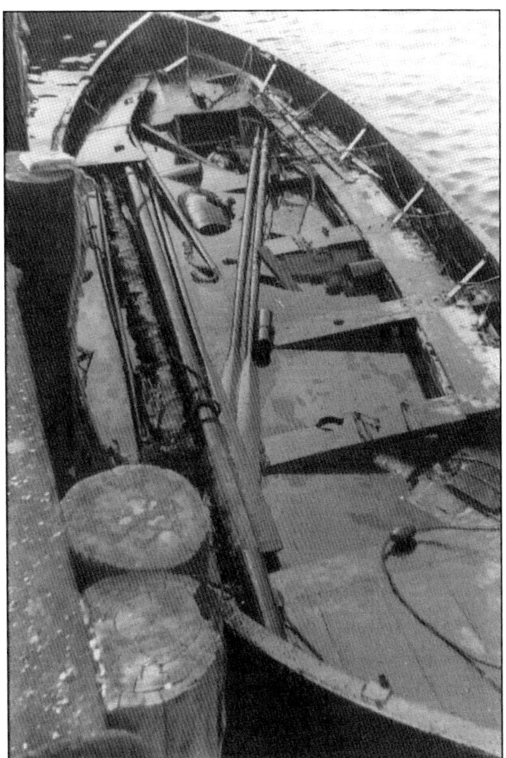

When the *Persephone* was hit, the explosion was seen and heard all across Barnegat City. The Coast Guard, along with local fishermen, sped out through the inlet in their boats as part of a rescue effort. All returned safely with the 28 survivors. One of the *Persephone* lifeboats is pictured filled with oil.

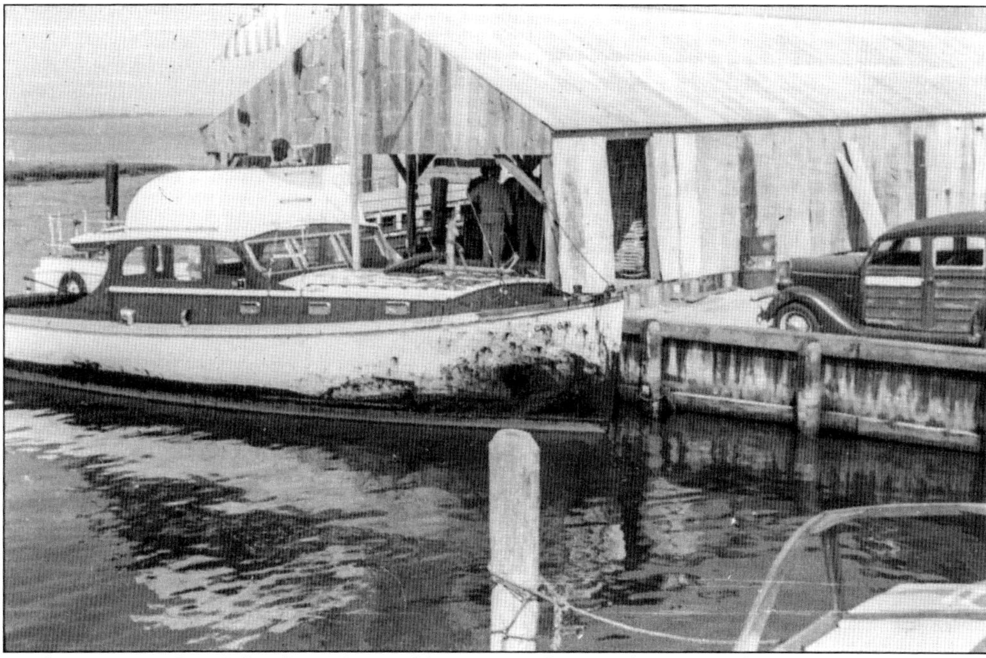

At the Barnegat City School on West Fifth Street and Central Avenue, the teacher saw the scene out the window, stopped class, and took the children up to the beach to witness history firsthand. After the fishermen returned, their boats were stained with oil, like the *Princess Pat* seen here back at the West Sixth Street docks.

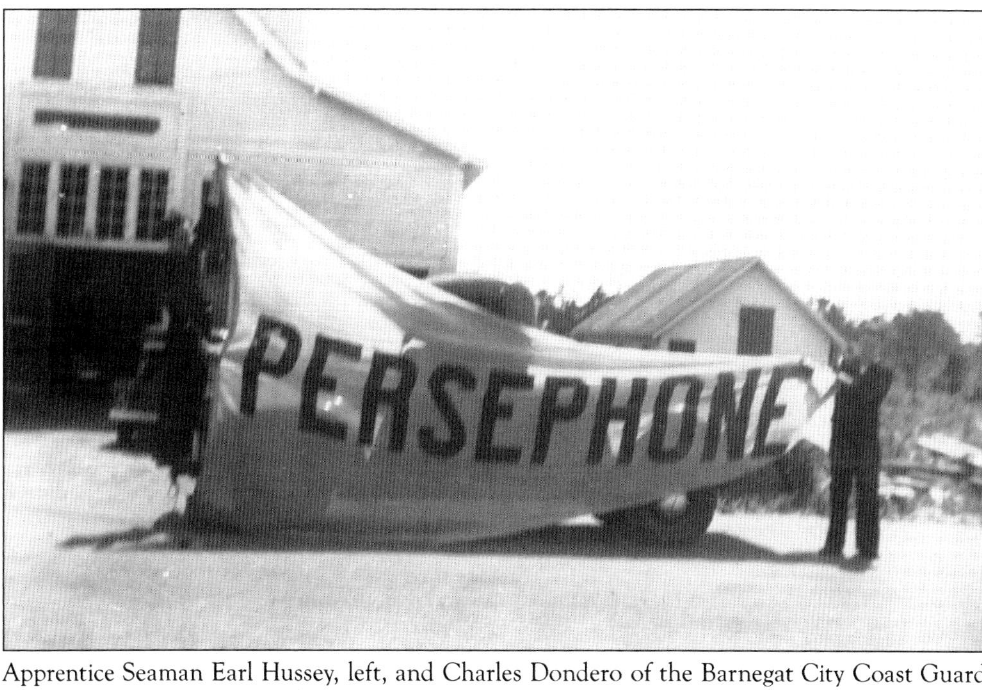

Apprentice Seaman Earl Hussey, left, and Charles Dondero of the Barnegat City Coast Guard Station stand between the old and new station on East Seventh Street with a trophy from the wreck. It was said that someone later made off with the flag, although the men were given several items by the grateful survivors.

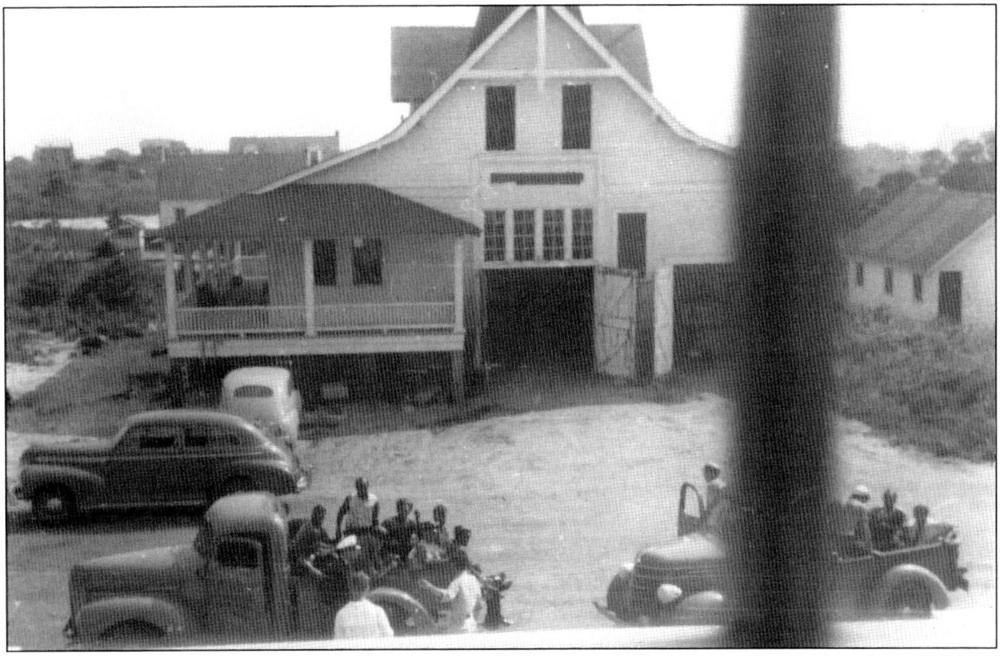

As seen here, the crew of the *Persephone* was coated in oil when they were rescued. When children got small amounts on their feet from the beaches, either from washed up oil or tar added by the Army to discourage amphibious landings, the sticky stuff could be harmlessly burned off with a little kerosene. For the sailors, knives would be needed to cut clothing loose, followed by lengthy bathing.

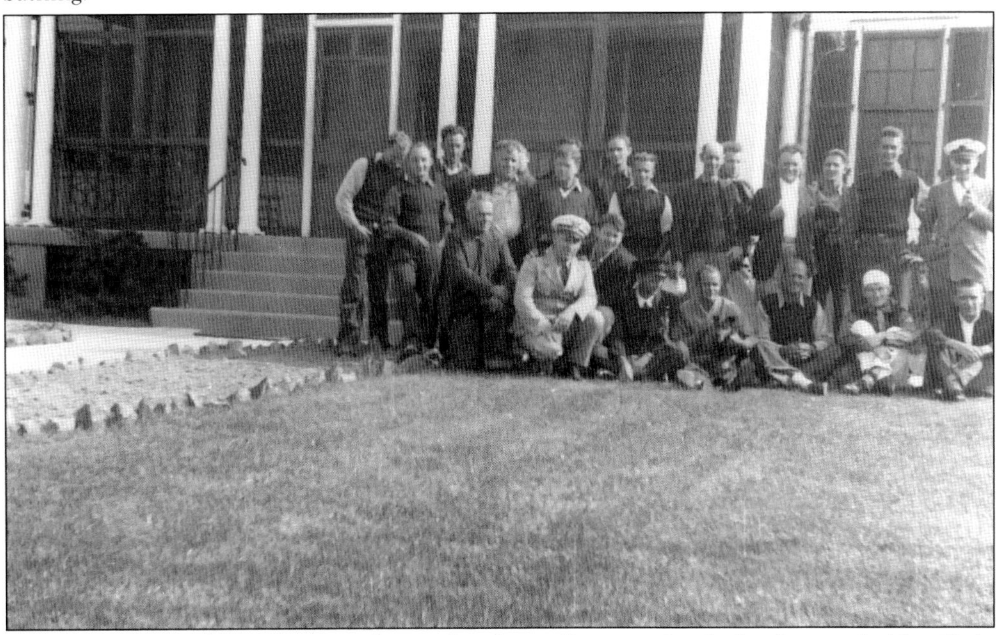

After their rescue, the 28 men stayed several nights in Barnegat City before leaving for New York. Here the mostly Panamanian crew pose with the station bosun, Leroy Howell, before a bus arrived for them. One returned to Barnegat City every weekend until he was due to be shipped out in July. On his last visit, he drowned in the surf.

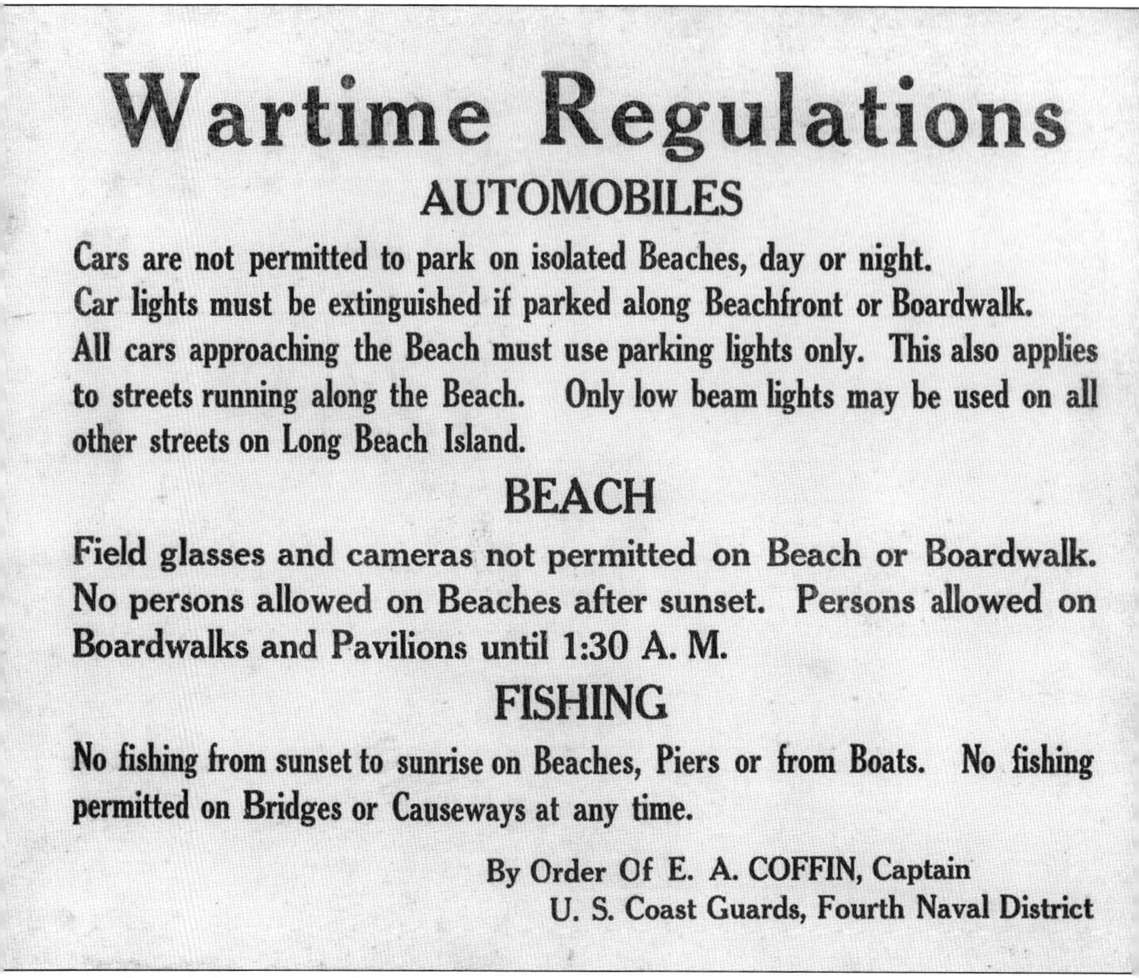

Wartime Regulations

AUTOMOBILES

Cars are not permitted to park on isolated Beaches, day or night.
Car lights must be extinguished if parked along Beachfront or Boardwalk.
All cars approaching the Beach must use parking lights only. This also applies to streets running along the Beach. Only low beam lights may be used on all other streets on Long Beach Island.

BEACH

Field glasses and cameras not permitted on Beach or Boardwalk.
No persons allowed on Beaches after sunset. Persons allowed on Boardwalks and Pavilions until 1:30 A. M.

FISHING

No fishing from sunset to sunrise on Beaches, Piers or from Boats. No fishing permitted on Bridges or Causeways at any time.

By Order Of E. A. COFFIN, Captain
U. S. Coast Guards, Fourth Naval District

Through the summer of 1942, German U-boats managed to attack and sink 609 merchant and Naval vessels from the Gulf of Mexico to the coast of Maine. The speed and relentlessness of the campaign gave the Germans the element of surprise. American efforts to counter submarine warfare were slow to be realized, although the British could provide plentiful tips. Traveling in convoys, having anti-submarine naval support on the sea and in the air, following a zigzag course, and, most importantly, utilizing coastal blackouts, were all soon implemented. The blackout rules on this poster made it clear that no lights of any significance could be on at night. Against a dark backdrop, a blacked out ship was indistinguishable through the periscope of a U-boat. Without these measures, the massacre of American supply lines off the East Coast in early 1942 may have continued; this tactic was known as a tonnage war, and had been used to terrifying effect upon the British Isles for three years at that point.

Seven

Life by the Sea

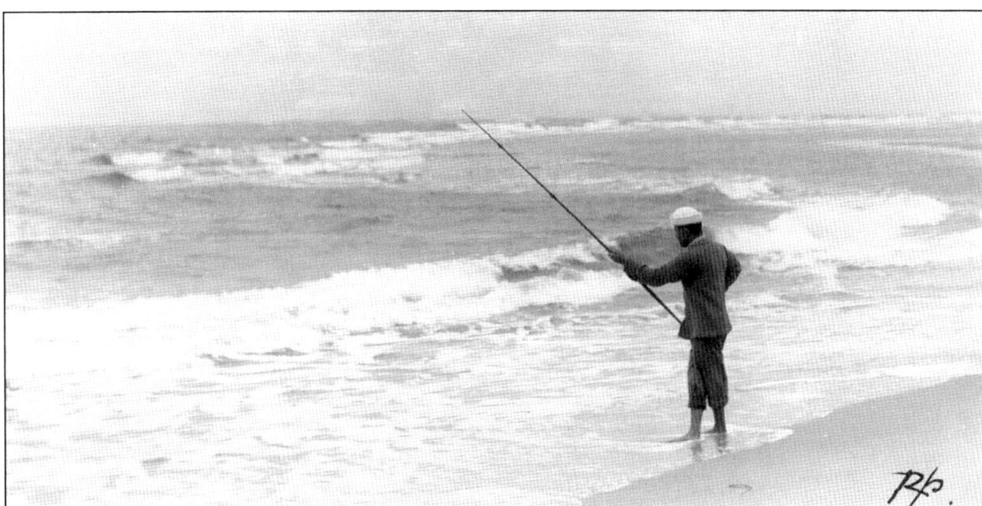

The first and foremost historic reason for coming to Barnegat Inlet was the fishing. It was and still is renowned for the variety and quantity of fish accessible by boat or by shore. More species were plentiful in days gone by, but quotas have attempted to correct for overfishing. Surfcasting was a favorite of many, as demonstrated in this postcard.

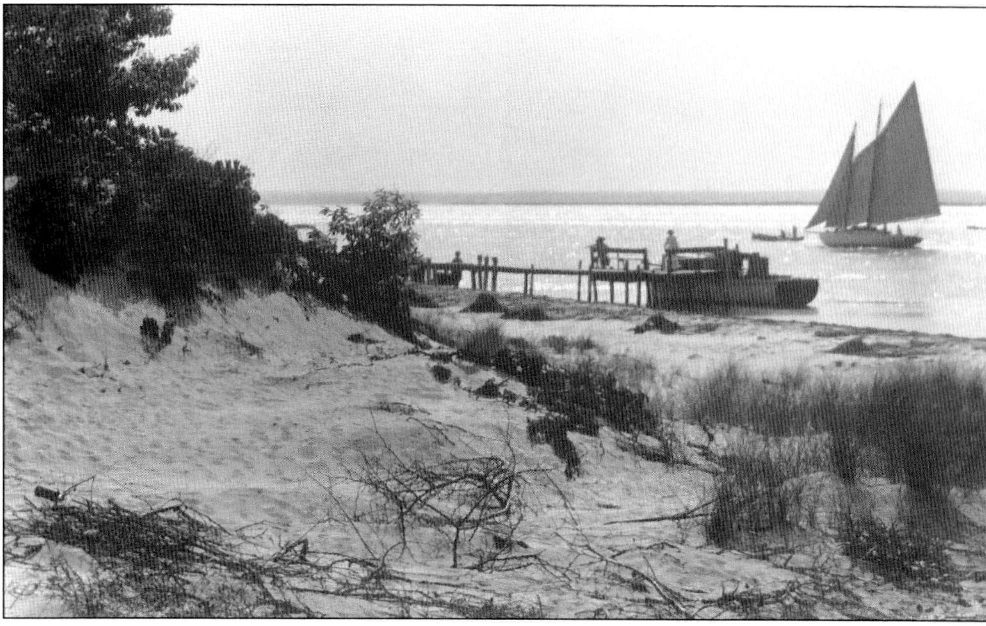

Sailing attracted countless vacationers and locals. The Sunset Hotel pier and nearby West Sixth Street harbor were popular spots for mooring up for the night. Often, sailboats would drop anchor in the calm bay, coming ashore to resupply. At times, hundreds of sails could be seen around Barnegat City, whose tides meant calm days were a rarity while the inlet gave ready, though always challenging, access to the bay.

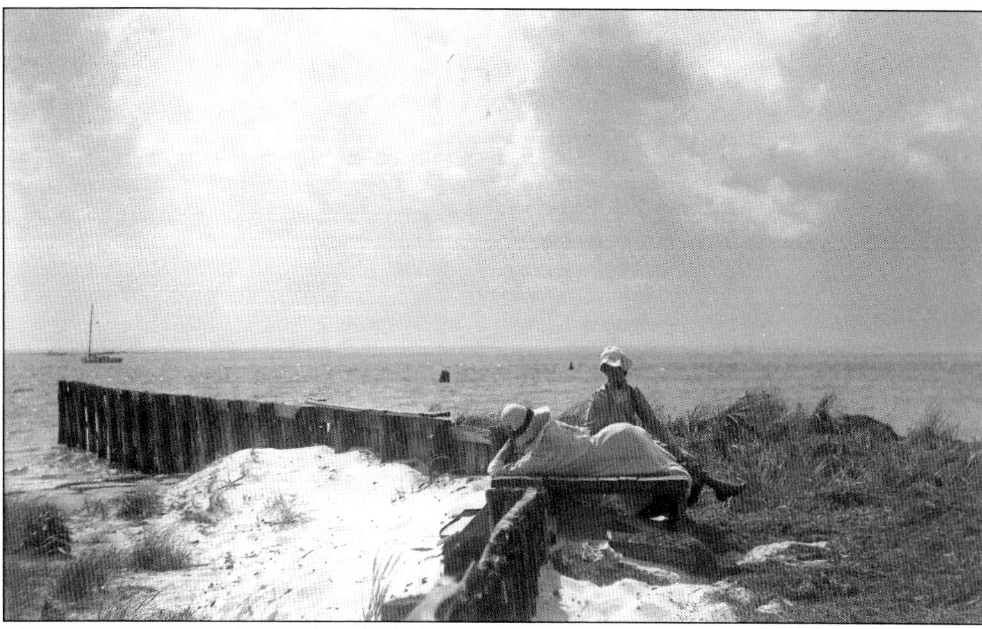

The idea of sitting on a beach, though clothed, became a fashionable American practice starting in the late 1800s. Many lived in Camden, Philadelphia, or New York and came to places like Barnegat City for the supposedly restorative properties of sea air, but also because the skies were clear and not choked by smog from the factory-filled cities. These c. 1900 bathers are enjoying the bay shore near the lighthouse.

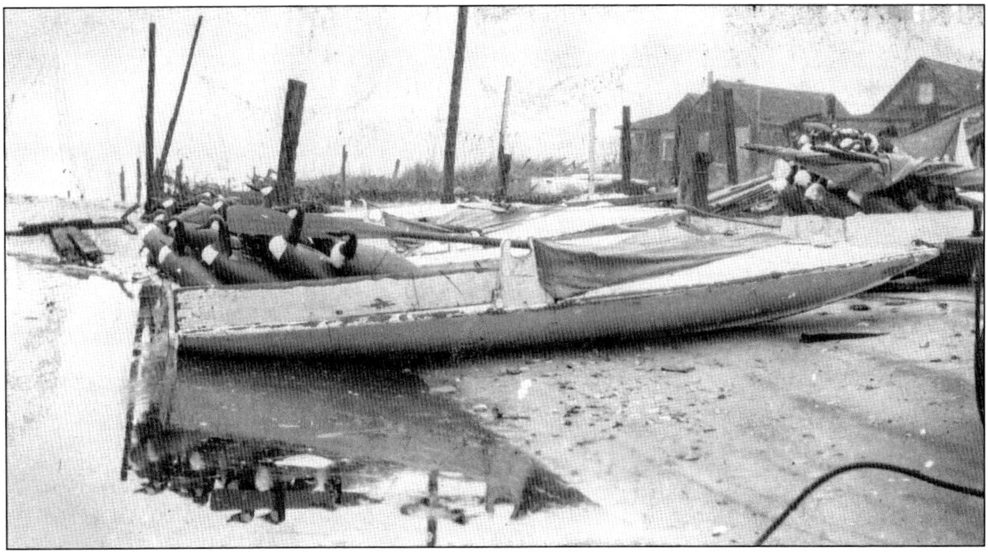

J.H. Perrine's boat shop in the mainland town of Barnegat patented these sneakbox boats used for hunting waterfowl. The fall hunting tradition in Barnegat Bay attracted men from across the country in droves. Decoys like those seen piled at the rear of this sneakbox at the West Sixth Street harbor around 1920 were used to lure flocks in, while camouflaged hunters lay in wait.

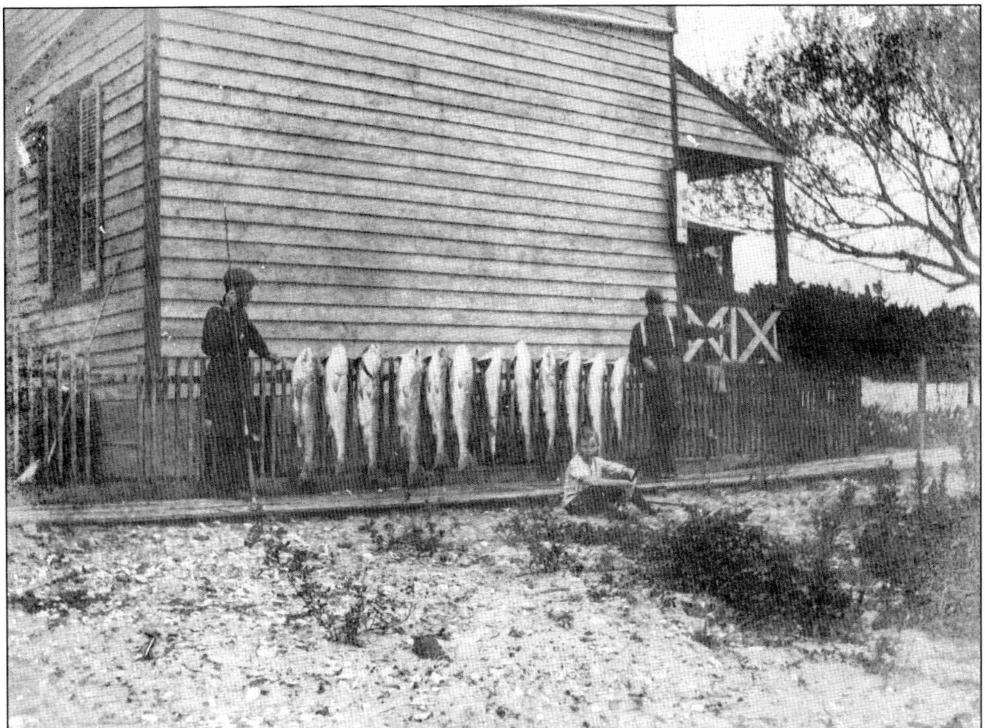

Fishing grew to become a competitive sport. Tournaments began to see who could catch the most, the biggest, or the rarest. Sometimes, the person who claimed a new record would not even be trying, but simply cast a line from the beach any old day and come back with a whopper. Other times, anglers such as those pictured here would get right down to business.

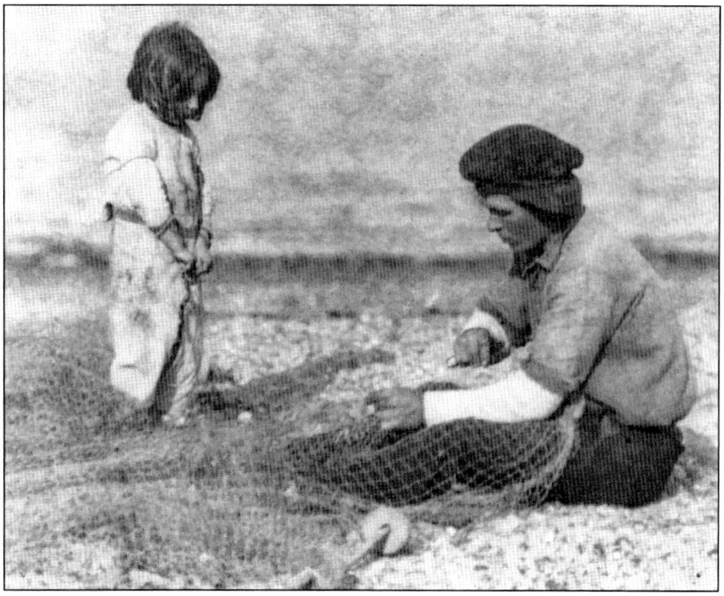

In whatever form it took, the skill of bringing home a catch involved the whole family. Like lifesaving and the trains, a father would teach a child the trade, as this pair are doing. In this way, some Barnegat Light families are third-, fourth-, fifth-, and even sixth-generation fishermen.

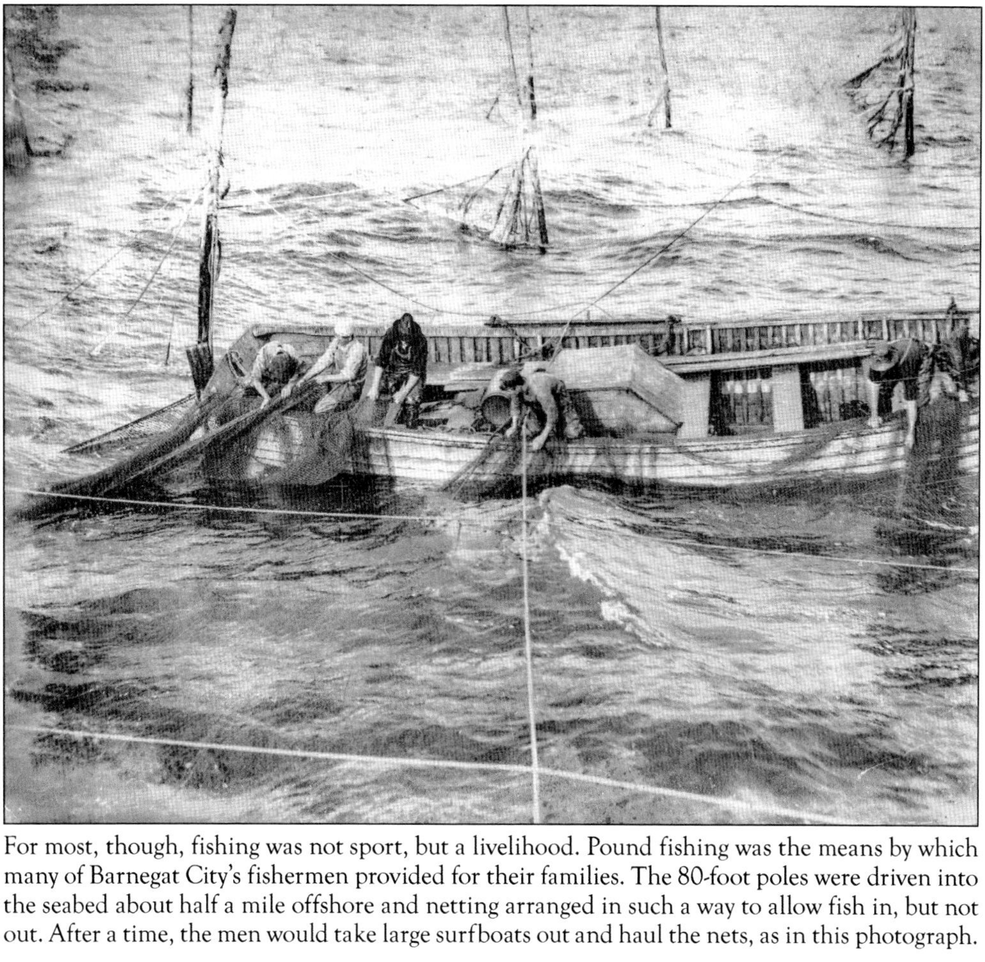

For most, though, fishing was not sport, but a livelihood. Pound fishing was the means by which many of Barnegat City's fishermen provided for their families. The 80-foot poles were driven into the seabed about half a mile offshore and netting arranged in such a way to allow fish in, but not out. After a time, the men would take large surfboats out and haul the nets, as in this photograph.

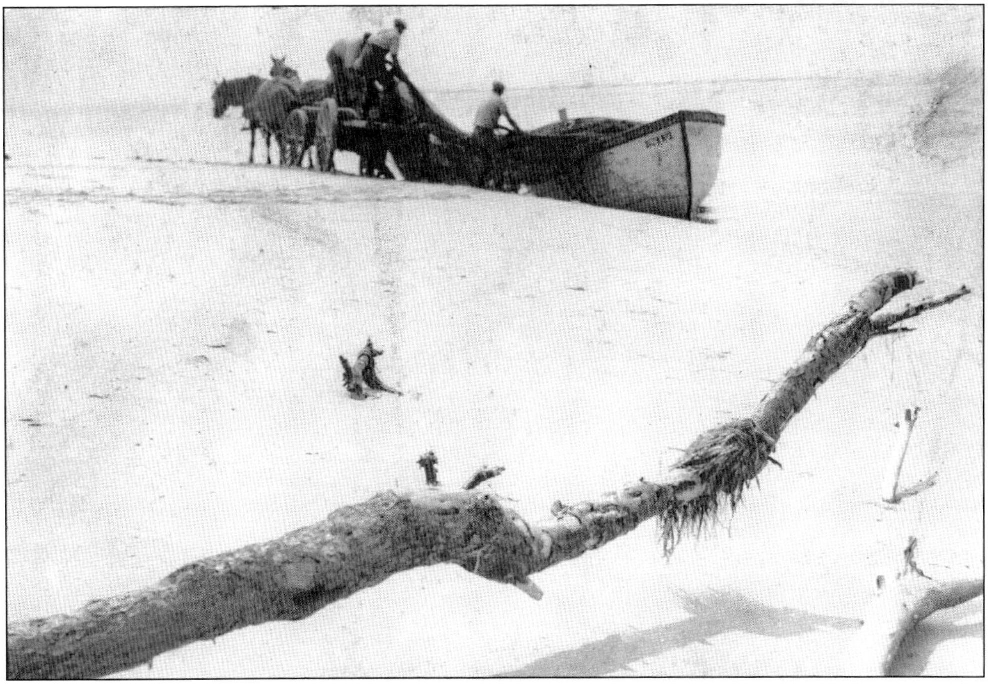

Getting the nets loaded with fish into the pound boats was only the first hurdle to bringing the catch to market. Getting the boats up on the beach came next. This effort involved the horses pictured here, of which Barnegat City had several for such purposes. In later years, the boats docked at the West Sixth Street and West Eighteenth Street docks.

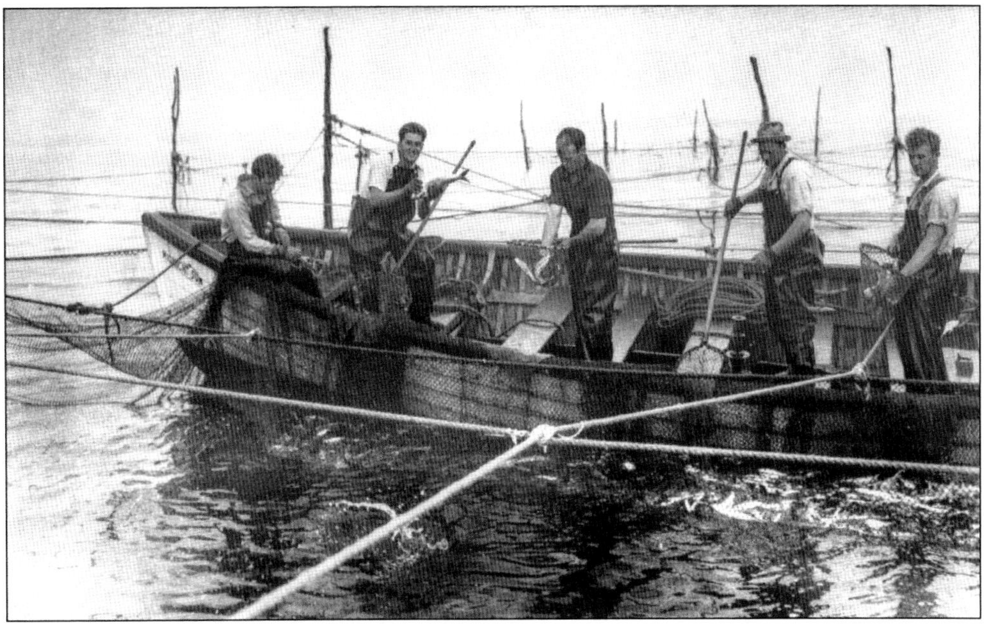

Seen here in the industry's later years, pound fishing lasted as a Jersey shore tradition until the early 1950s when long-lining took over. However they were caught, men continued to catch bounties from the Atlantic. Old Dutch, British, and German settlers gave way to Scandinavian settlers in the early 1900s as Barnegat Inlet continued to attract those looking for new opportunities by the sea.

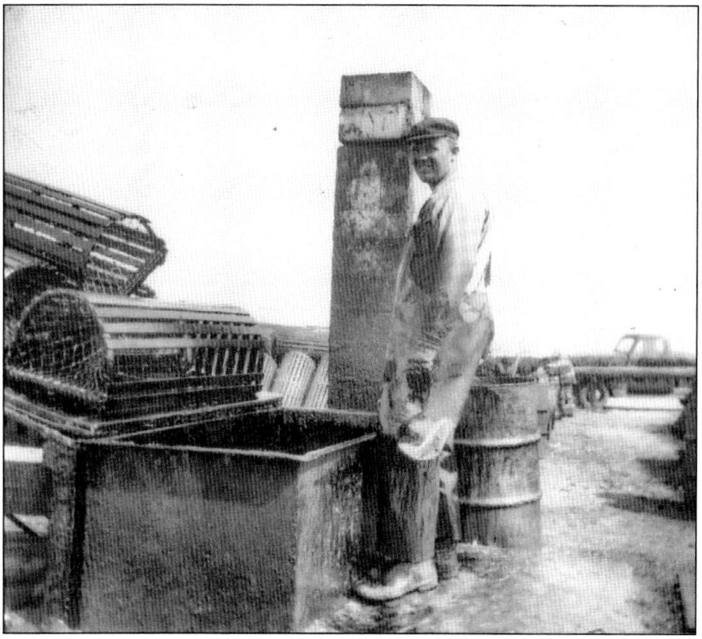

Another local industry was pot fishing. Lobster pots were tarred in large containers at the docks by the hundreds, as Axel Jacobsen demonstrates here. Lobsters used to be so plentiful that lobster salad sandwiches could be had at Applegate's General Store on West Fourth Street for pennies. Over the years, they were overfished and are now harder to find in deeper waters.

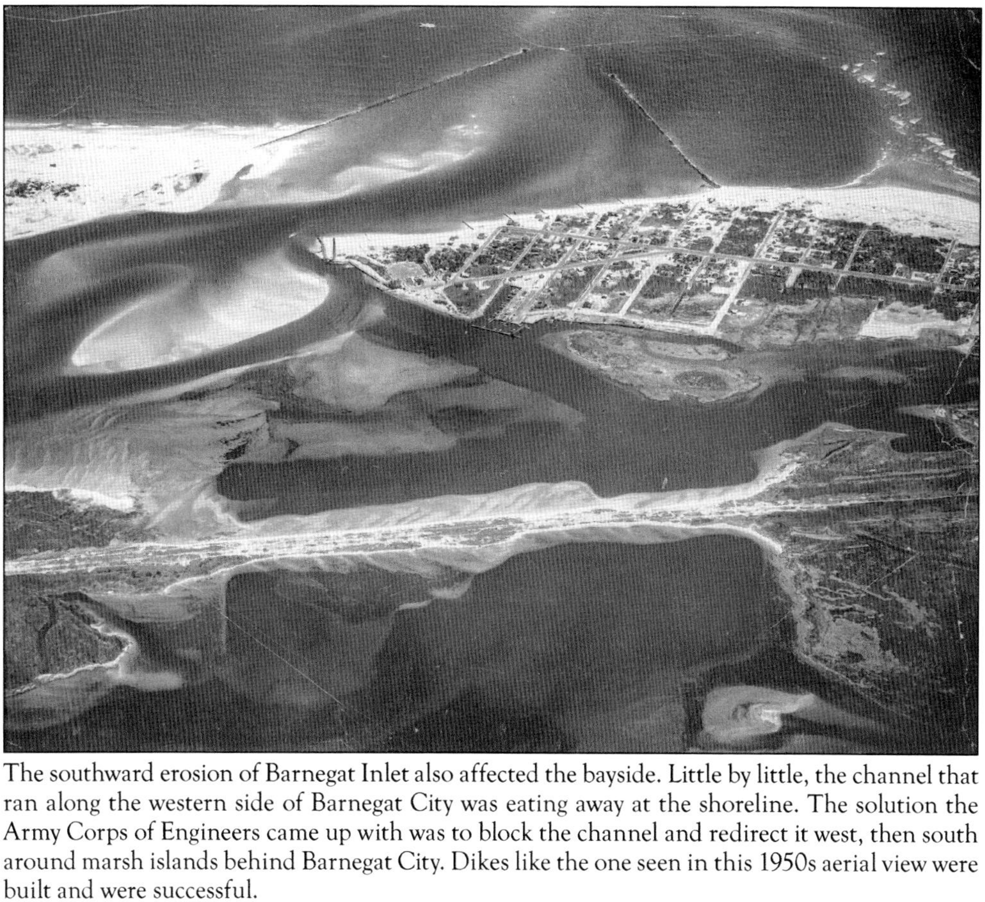

The southward erosion of Barnegat Inlet also affected the bayside. Little by little, the channel that ran along the western side of Barnegat City was eating away at the shoreline. The solution the Army Corps of Engineers came up with was to block the channel and redirect it west, then south around marsh islands behind Barnegat City. Dikes like the one seen in this 1950s aerial view were built and were successful.

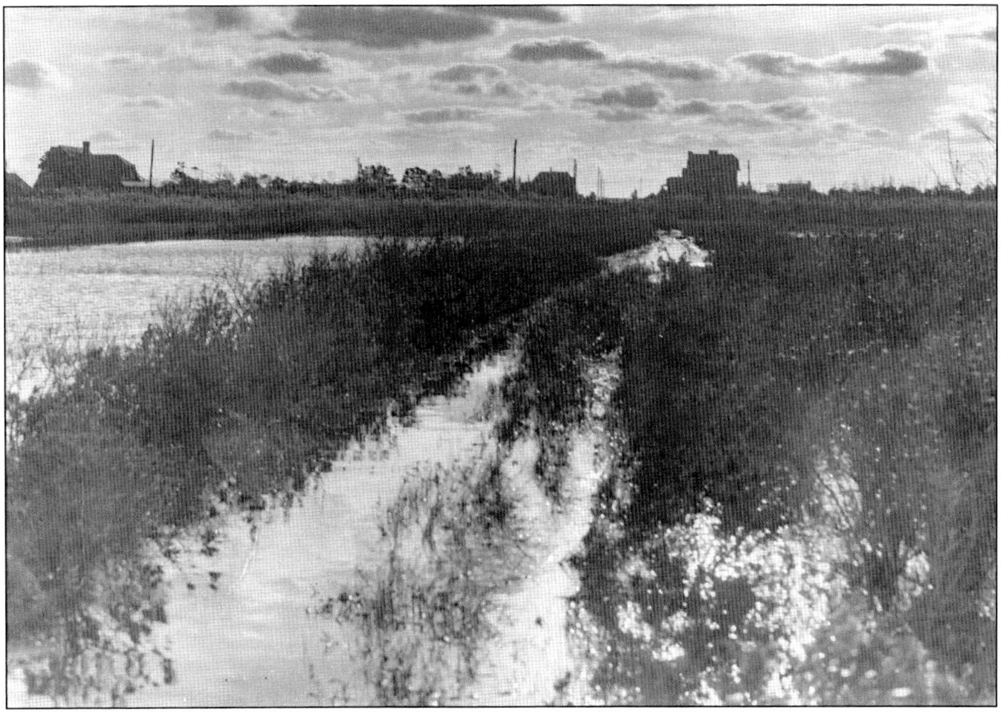

Even with engineering efforts to stem the tides, flooding is a normal part of life on Long Beach Island, especially the bayside. Meadows flooded and drained regularly, acting like natural sponges to regulate the water levels. In the mid-20th century, massive development, primarily by filling in these meadows, resulted in more frequent town flooding. This scene from West Twelfth Street in Barnegat City became one of those filled-in meadows.

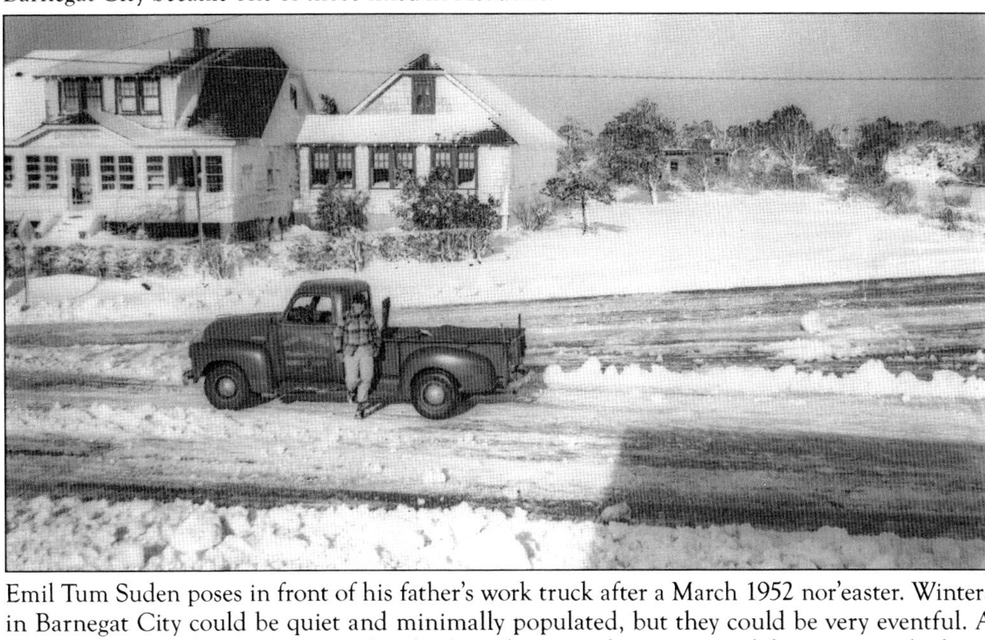

Emil Tum Suden poses in front of his father's work truck after a March 1952 nor'easter. Winters in Barnegat City could be quiet and minimally populated, but they could be very eventful. A snowy beach was always a jarring sight after brutal summer heat waves and days spent sunbathing. However, cold-weather nor'easters were the culprits of some of the worst damage the town ever saw.

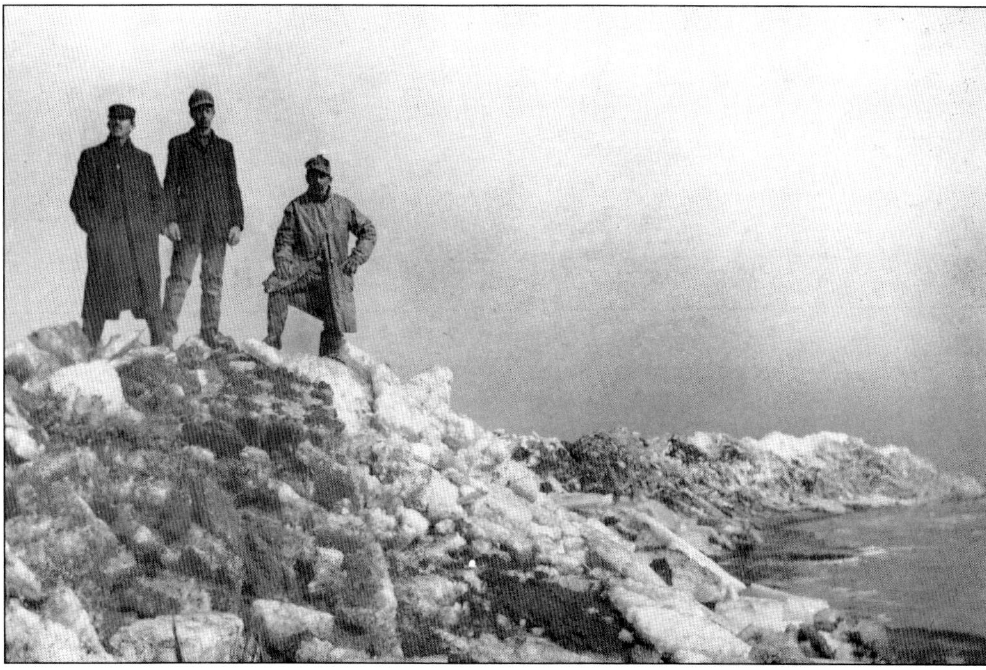

One of the primary concerns about cold snaps was whether or not Barnegat Bay would freeze. If it did, the eventual, and usually sudden, thaw would result in ice flows that could choke the bay and Barnegat Inlet, preventing any fishing. When it surged ashore and piled up during a storm, the damage could be devastating. These men are standing atop one such pileup.

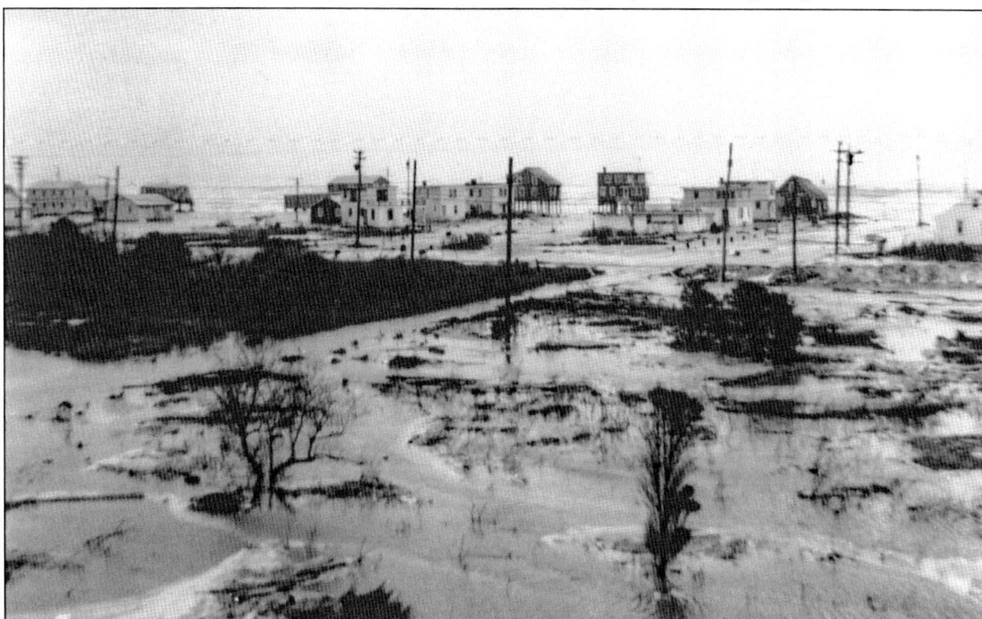

The Ash Wednesday Storm of March 1962 was the most damaging storm ever to strike Barnegat Light. This view, looking east along Twenty-Eighth Street, shows how it was one of many places on Long Beach Island where the Atlantic Ocean and Barnegat Bay met. Five record high tides due to a stalled storm caused unprecedented devastation that many recall in hushed tones.

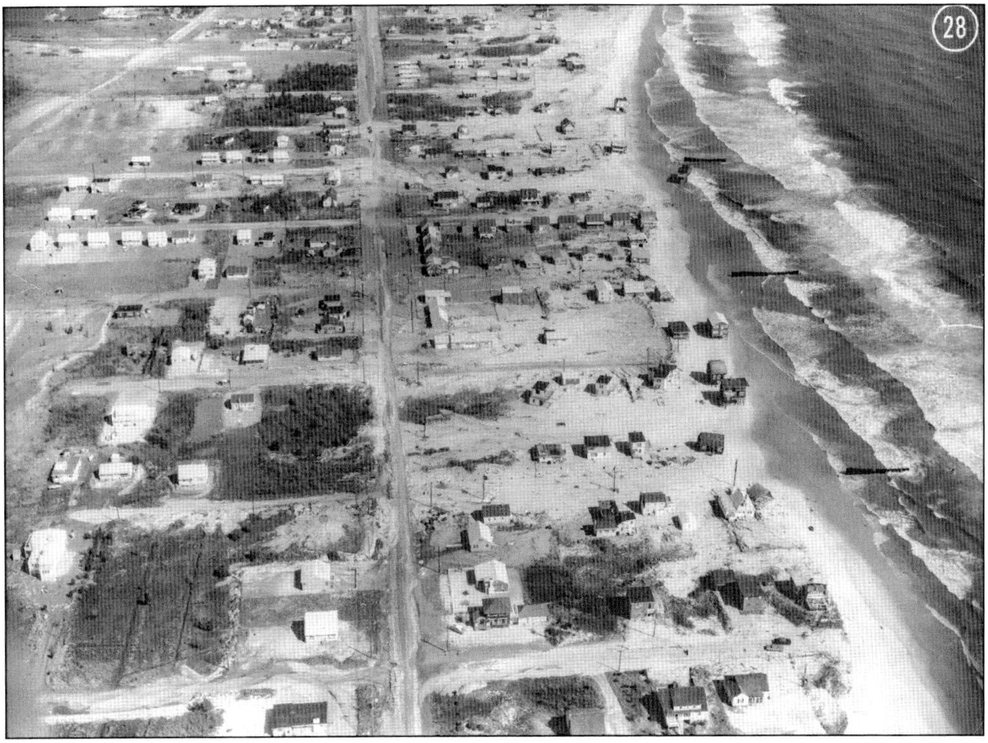

This aerial view from Nineteenth Street (top) to Twenty-Ninth Street shows the casualties from the March 1962 storm. The beach and dunes were washed down the eastern blocks and streets. Beachfront houses were now oceanfront. One such house in the water on the Twenty-Fifth Street beach was ordered moved, even though the lot had not. The owner gave it up, and authorities dynamited it to clear the new beach.

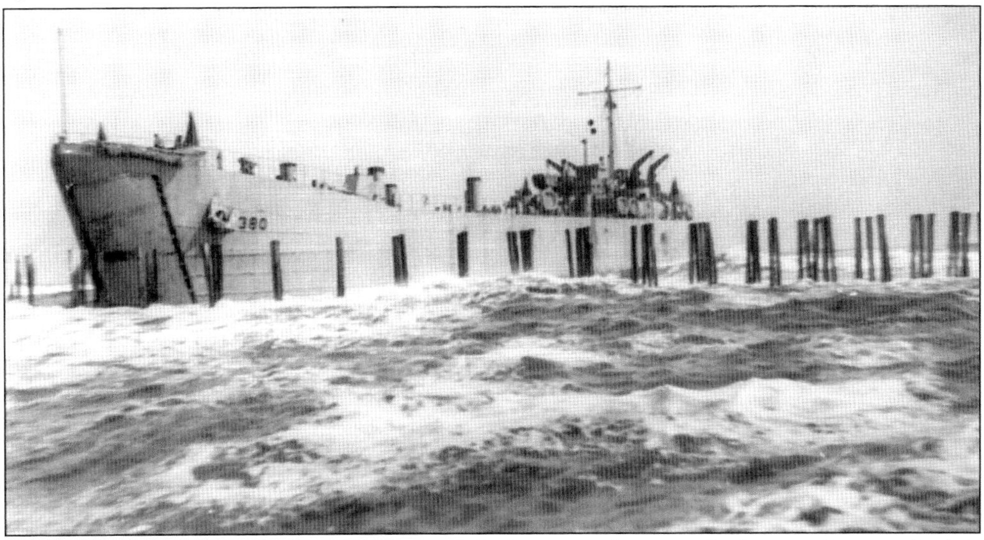

After storms passed, residents could expect to find strange things washed up on Barnegat Light's beaches. In the 19th century, it was often a stranded ship. In the 20th century, Navy vessels were not an uncommon sight. This tank landing ship was driven into the new diagonal Eighth Street Inlet jetty, which extended far out into the water in 1943.

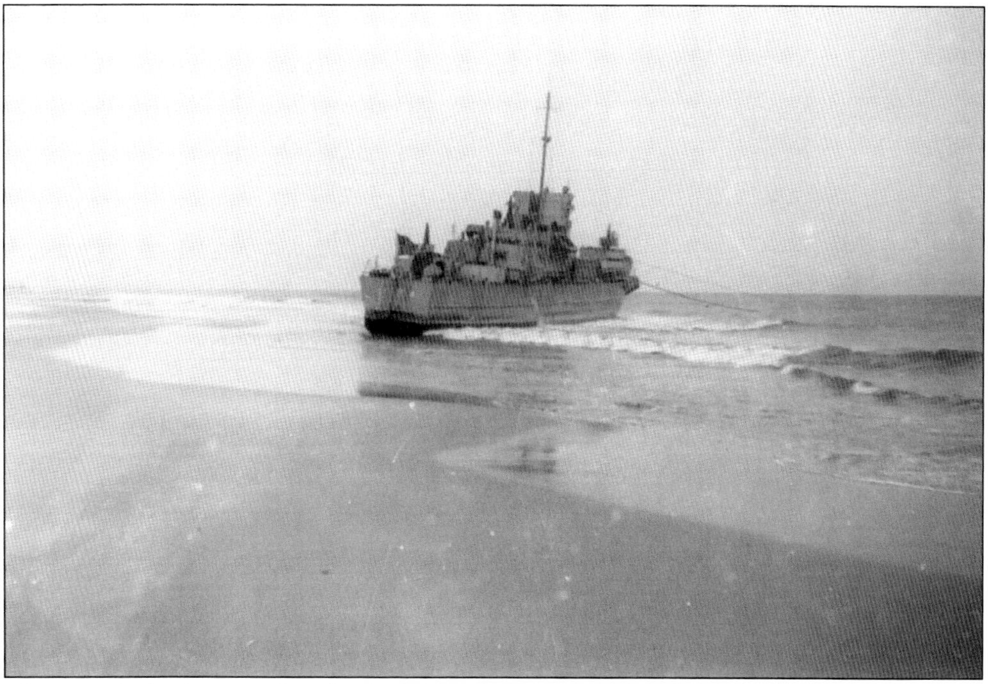

Also in 1943, this Navy medium landing ship was driven up on the beach. Beachings became more common in the late 20th century. Like their wrongly accused ancestors, the Barnegat Pirates, local fishermen became adept at dragging boats off the beach using whatever equipment was available. This time, their efforts were not met with unverifiable rumors of plunder due to the isolated nature of the island.

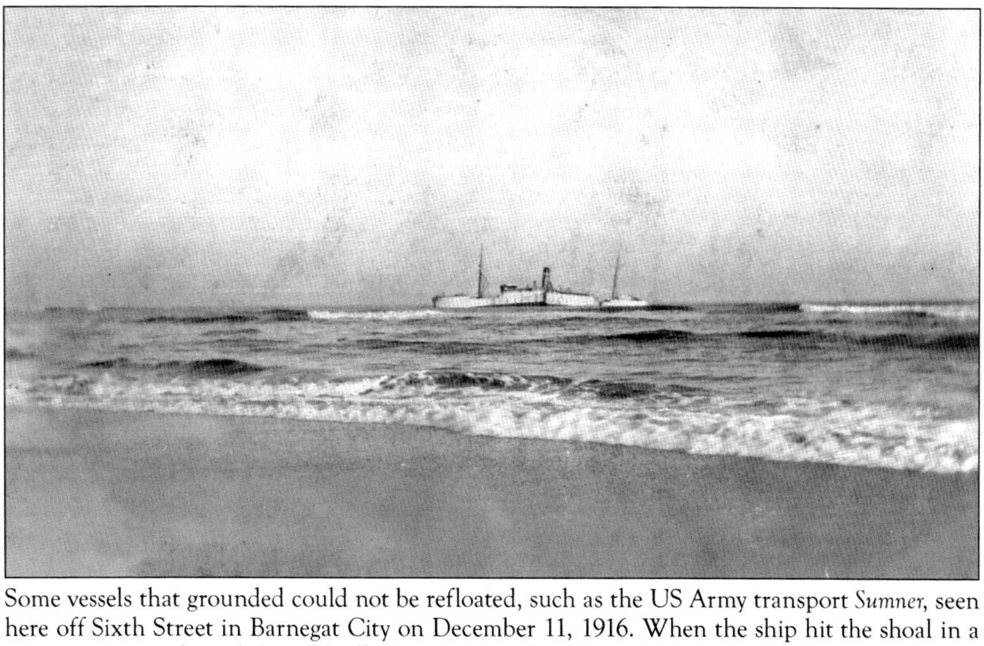

Some vessels that grounded could not be refloated, such as the US Army transport *Sumner*, seen here off Sixth Street in Barnegat City on December 11, 1916. When the ship hit the shoal in a storm, it was stuck, and the surf rolled it enough to break the ship's back. The *Sumner* was not in deep enough water to sink, so it simply settled and fell apart over months.

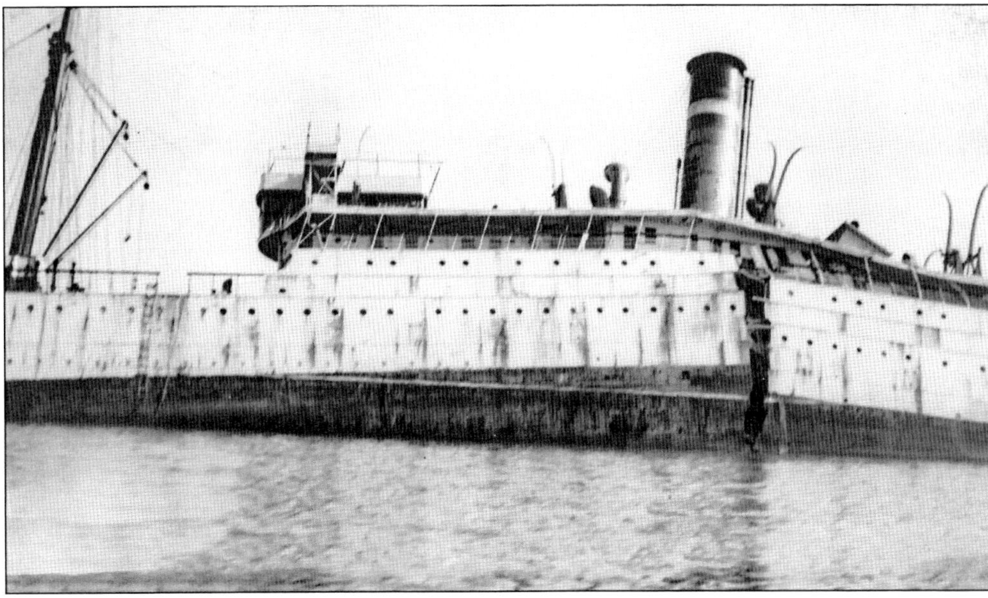

Over 230 soldiers were evacuated with help from the Barnegat City Coast Guard Station. In the initial hours after the grounding, the *Sumner's* 120-man crew remained aboard, attempting to get the ship off the bar. They eventually gave up after the keel was broken, as seen here, and salvage impossible, leaving the ship to its fate.

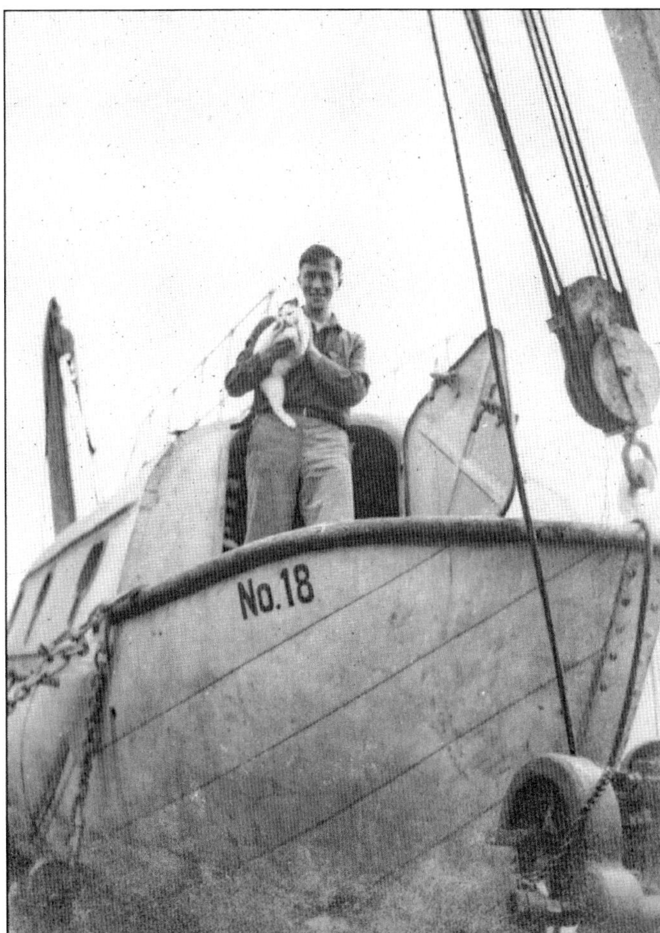

At 351 feet, the *Sumner*, a retrofitted German passenger liner known as the *Rhaetia*, was one of the largest ships to go down off Barnegat Light. Owing to the shallow shoals, its sinking was very public and drawn out. After all aboard were brought to the East Sixth Street harbor, including the feline passenger disembarking in this photograph, little could be done but watch the vessel break up.

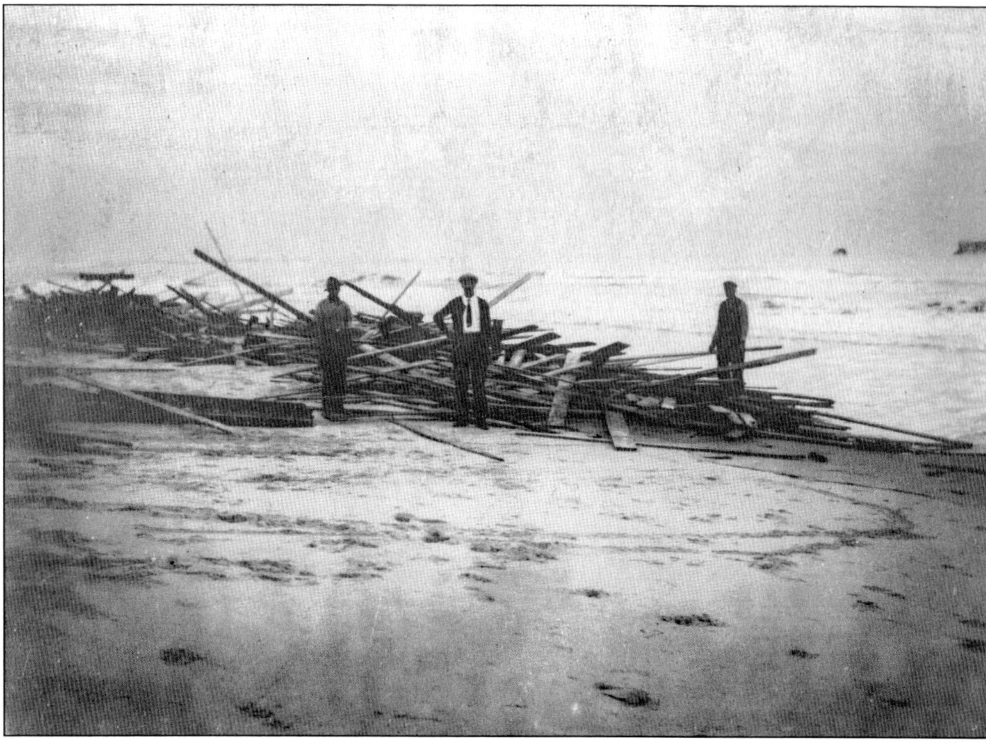

In an ironic twist, the deteriorating wreck of the *Sumner* claimed another ship a year later, the drifting schooner *J.A. Holmes* loaded with lumber from Maine. As the *Holmes* broke apart and spilled her cargo, locals began a tried-and-true practice of using what the sea provided. Wood from the *Holmes* and other ships, if in good shape, was recycled to make repairs or build new cottages.

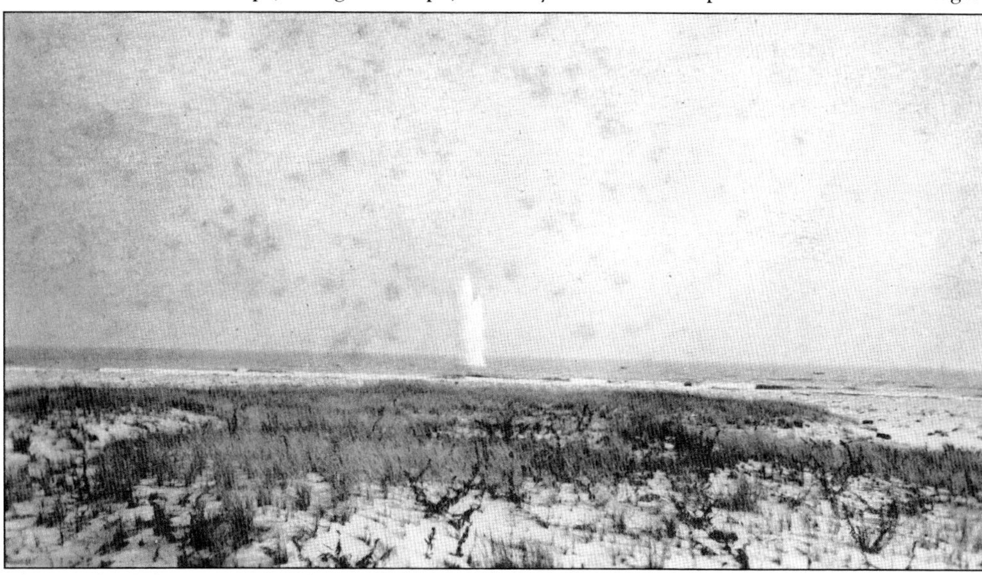

The wreck of the *Sumner* may have been out of sight by January 1919, but its influence could still be felt by passing ships. Like the 1942 wreck of the tanker *Gulf Trade*, merchant ships were hitting the submerged wreck. The Coast Guard, as later, decided explosives were the answer. The towering white column, well over 100 feet high in this photograph, suggests the effort was successful.

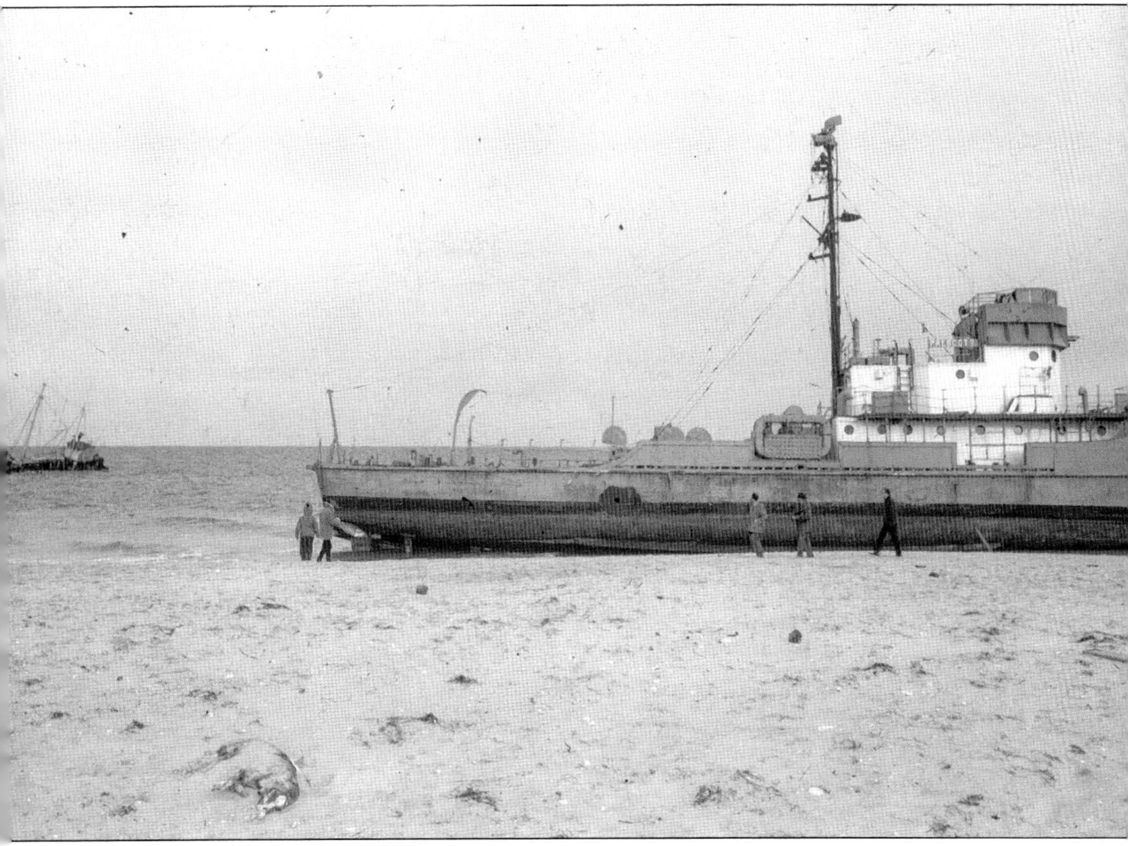

One of the few wrecks to leave a lasting visible remnant was that of the scalloper *Sea King*, pictured here on the left. Forced aground in a storm in February 1963, the ship was towing the decommissioned patrol craft sweeper *Prescott*, seen on the beach, from New York to Atlantic City for conversion into a scallop boat. In the days after the storm, locals used their experience to work the World War II minesweeper off the beach and on to a successful fishing career. The *Sea King*, sadly, had a hole, and attempts to raise it failed. The owner was asked to have it removed anyway, but after repeated attempts, he left it in the water off the Eleventh Street beach at Barnegat Light. The mast became a local landmark, eventually moving from 100 yards off the beach to 100 yards onto the beach, thanks to the eastward march of the shoreline in the 1990s.

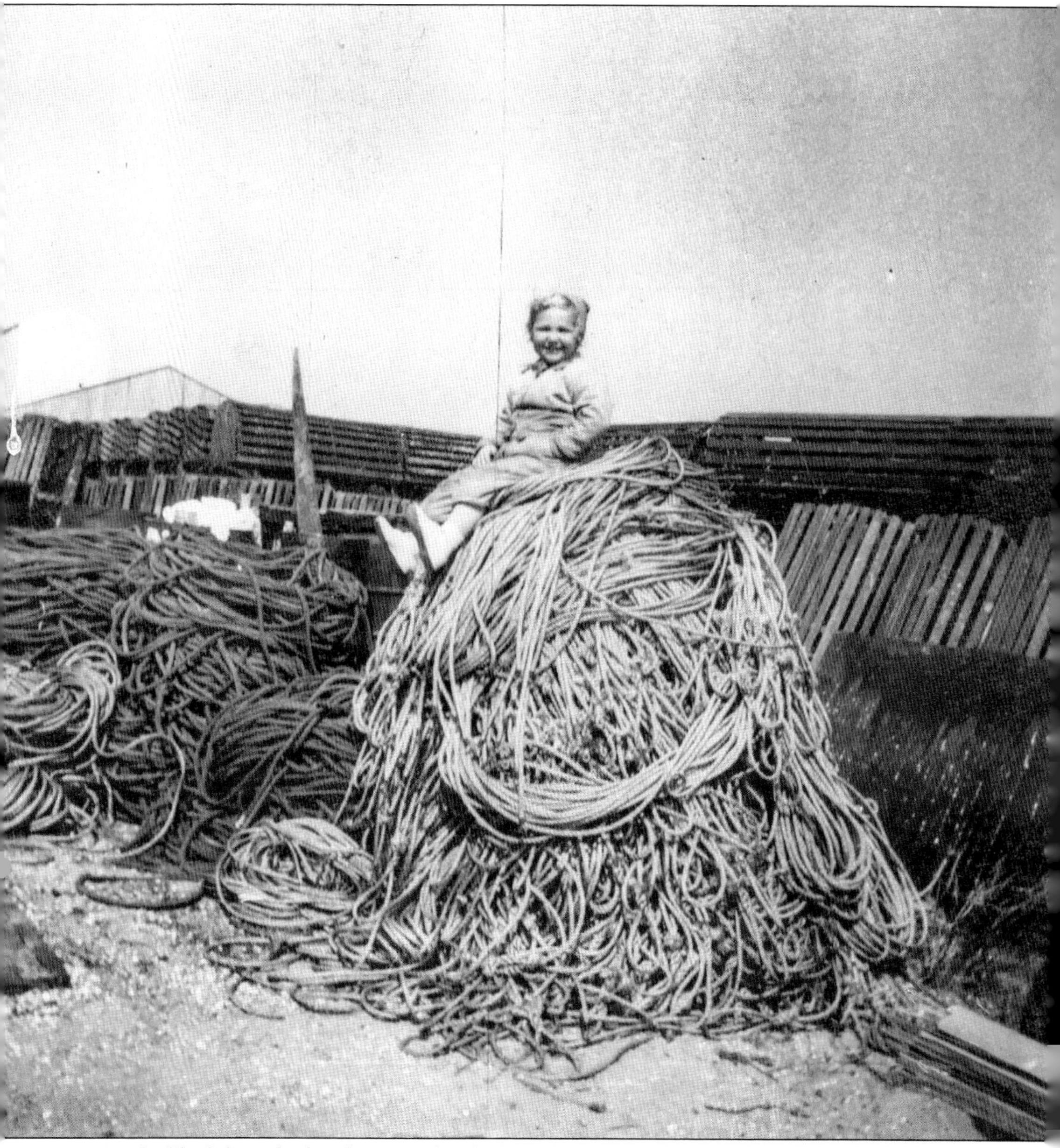

Profitable fishing had to be earned, often at great cost, whether it was an indebtedness or the ultimate sacrifice. Some would celebrate a good season in the local bars until the money ran out and it was time, and a necessity, to go out fishing again. For most, though, the life of a fisherman or bayman was about providing for his family. Children were raised around the trade. The young girl in this photograph sits atop a pile of shot lines among the fishing pots on West Eighteenth Street, one of the hubs of business in Barnegat Light. Sons often followed their fathers onto the boats they had once steered from the elder's lap. Lean years, even decades, could come and go before fisheries found success. Pound fishing gave way to longlining. Popular fisheries, such as blues and salmon, gave way to "junk" fisheries, like tilefish and dogfish, which were then made marketable and profitable. Where once lobster fishing was everywhere, now scalloping is one of the most plentiful. Adaptation has sustained the fleet at Barnegat Light for over a century.

Eight

Eroding the Past

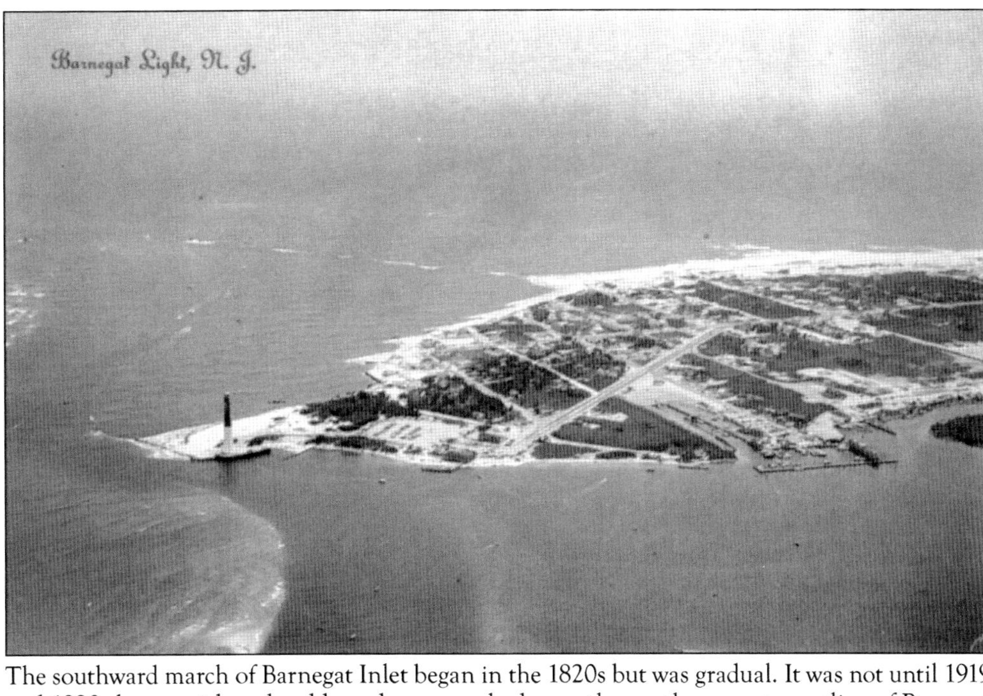

The southward march of Barnegat Inlet began in the 1820s but was gradual. It was not until 1919 and 1920 that a quick and sudden advance washed away the northernmost coastline of Barnegat City. This aerial view from the 1950s reveals the extent of the damage, most notably surrounding the Barnegat Lighthouse on three sides with very little buffer left for the next big storm.

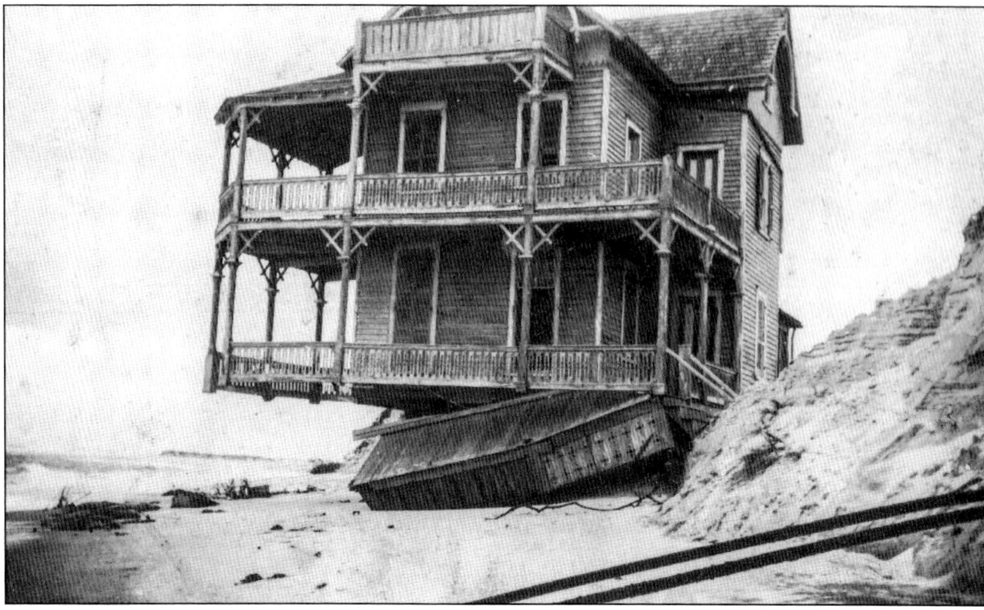

This beachfront cottage was the first to be undermined and abandoned on East Fourth Street in 1919. The exposed railroad tracks were part of the old Oceanic Hotel horse cart line from the days when the hotel was on the eastern end of the block. Sometimes, this kind of erosion could reverse itself just as quickly, a curious quirk of local tides that was as surprising as it was dependable.

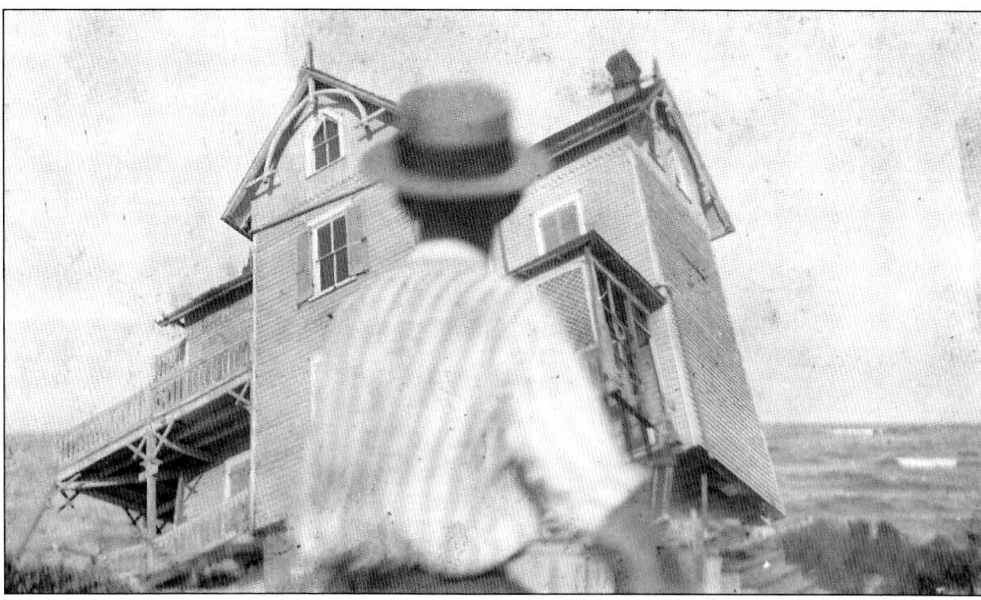

This man was among a crowd of local onlookers who gathered to watch the beachfront Melhorn family cottage fall into the surf. It was not one of the lucky ones to only flirt with disaster. Moving a house was, perhaps surprisingly for the times, neither uncommon nor extravagant. Several companies on Long Beach Island had equipment and horses for the job.

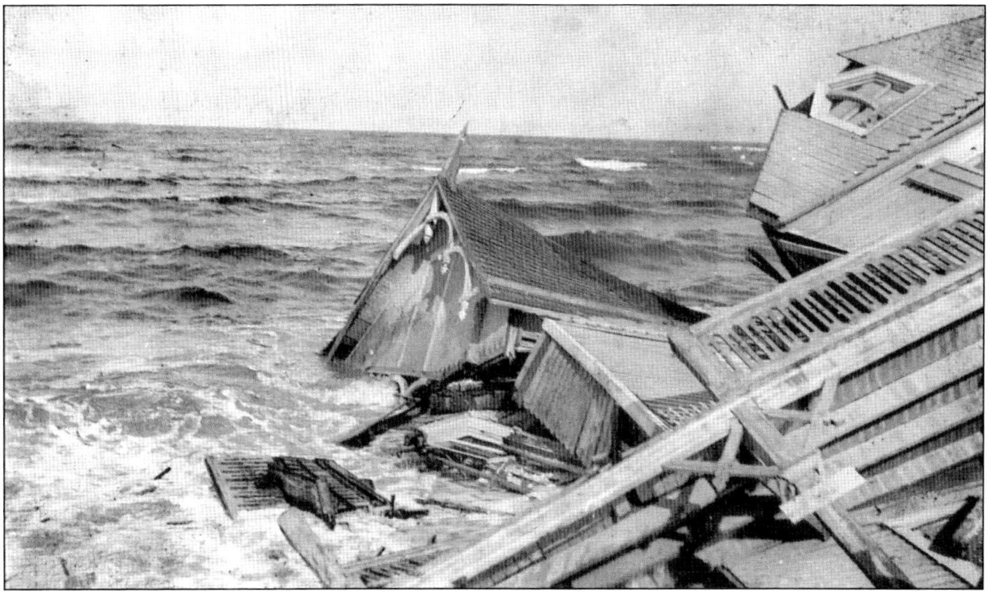

The sad remains of the 1880s cottage pictured here contributed to the diminishing hopes of development in the coming years. Frequent headlines appeared all across the region beginning in 1919, including Philadelphia and Camden, describing the plight of Barnegat City's eroding coastline, concentrated on the 1880s development from Third to Eighth Streets.

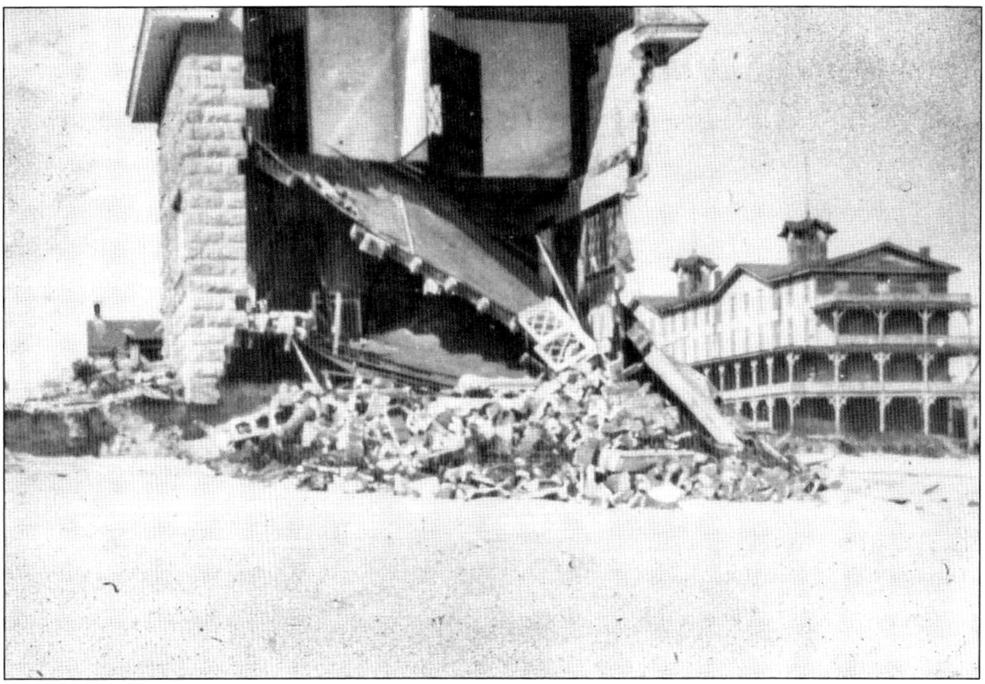

This unique all-stone house was the next to go on East Fourth Street, last owned by the Wolgamuth family. When it was undermined, locals salvaged what they could, as they had from the previous cottage. The recycling tradition of Barnegat City was strong and a necessity in a mostly isolated town where ready access to materials and foodstuffs was usually weeks off, and came in bulk for that reason.

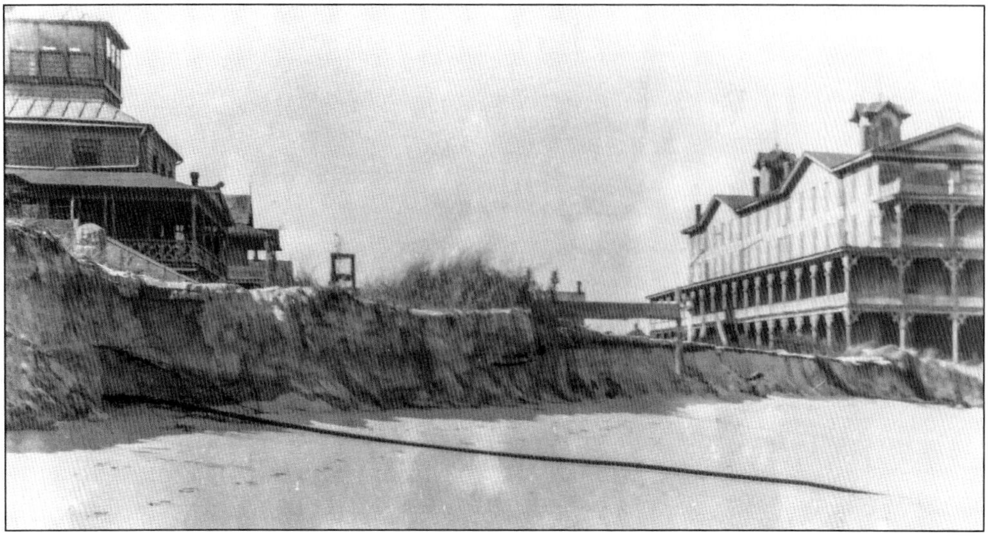

The march of the tide along the beach from the lighthouse to East Fifth Street kept on into 1920. The Haddock house and Oceanic Hotel were under a growing threat to join their neighbors lost to the surf, as seen in this 1920 photograph. Who would go next and when became a waiting game that attracted residents and tourists alike.

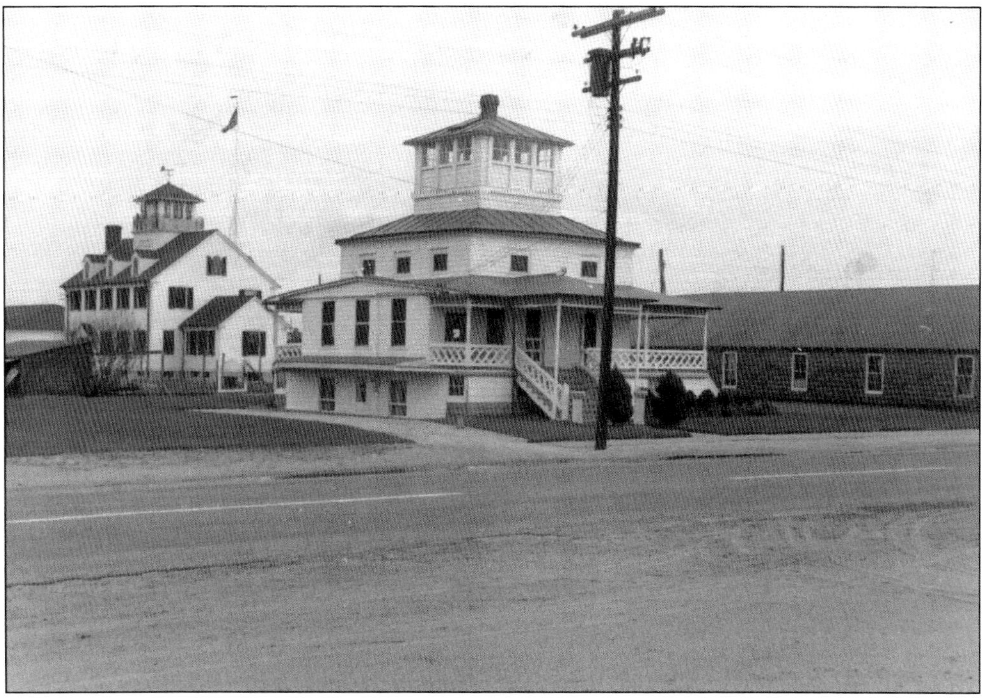

John Haddock died in 1918, leaving his eclectic home empty as the Atlantic advanced upon it. Another local, Dick Myers, bought it in 1920 and employed house movers to rescue it. First, it was slid to East Fifth Street. In time, another move to its final location on Central Avenue between East Sixth and Seventh Streets, seen here, was undertaken.

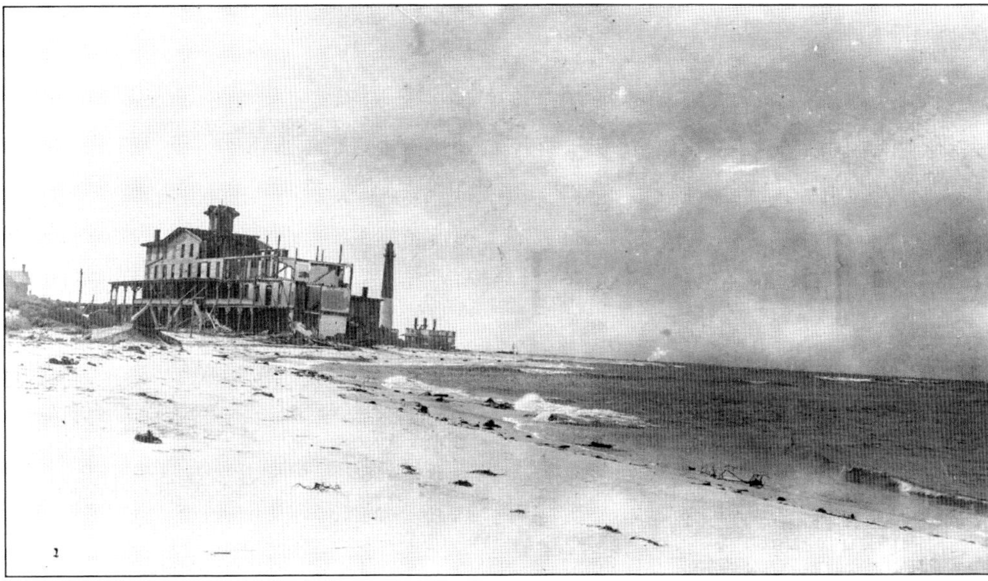

The Oceanic Hotel, almost 40 years old by 1920, was the next to fall victim to the sea. It began on the eastern end, claiming the porch and a few rooms from the first to fourth floors. However, demolition and salvage would claim much of the rest of the old crown jewel of the Barnegat City Beach Association, as pictured. (Courtesy of the National Archives and Records Administration.)

Tides and storms advanced through the winter and spring of 1920. Another column of floors went after this early April storm. The last owner salvaged what he could of value to lessen his loss. There had been hope in 1919 to open the Oceanic Hotel for the season, even though the crowds were long gone. (Courtesy of the National Archives and Records Administration.)

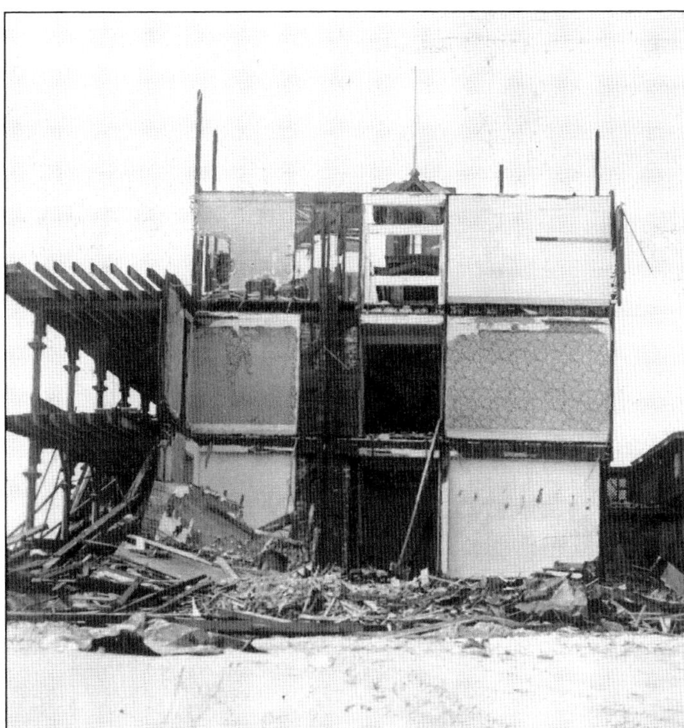

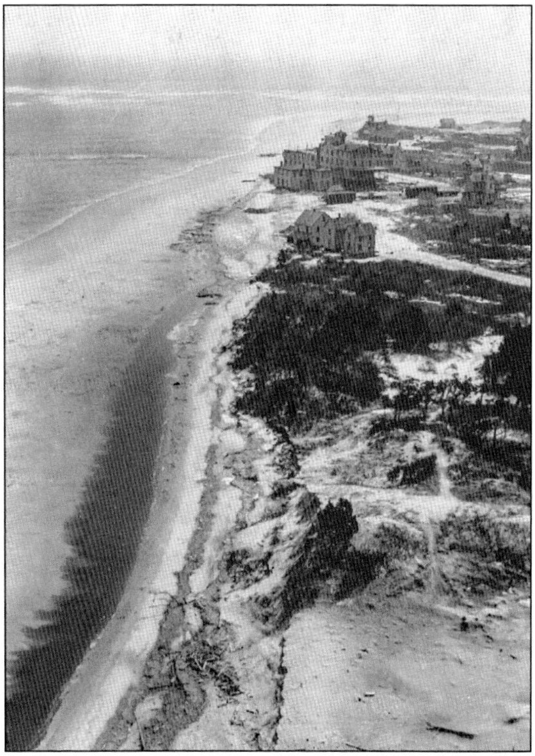

This 1920 view from the lighthouse, looking south along Barnegat City's beach, shows the extent of the encroaching tide's damage to that point. Where once there were hundreds of yards of sand between streets and ocean, the Atlantic was now perilously close. Here, the soon-to-be eroded houses of West Third Street and the remains of the Oceanic Hotel sit at the water's edge. (Courtesy of the National Archives and Records Administration.)

East Fifth Street would suffer next, although it got away with only one casualty. The old Life-Saving Station No. 17, pictured here, found itself undermined not long after the Oceanic Hotel began to crumble in 1920. The station, though, was an active and indispensable service building. Movers were called in and waited for a low tide to relocate the station to the south side of East Seventh Street.

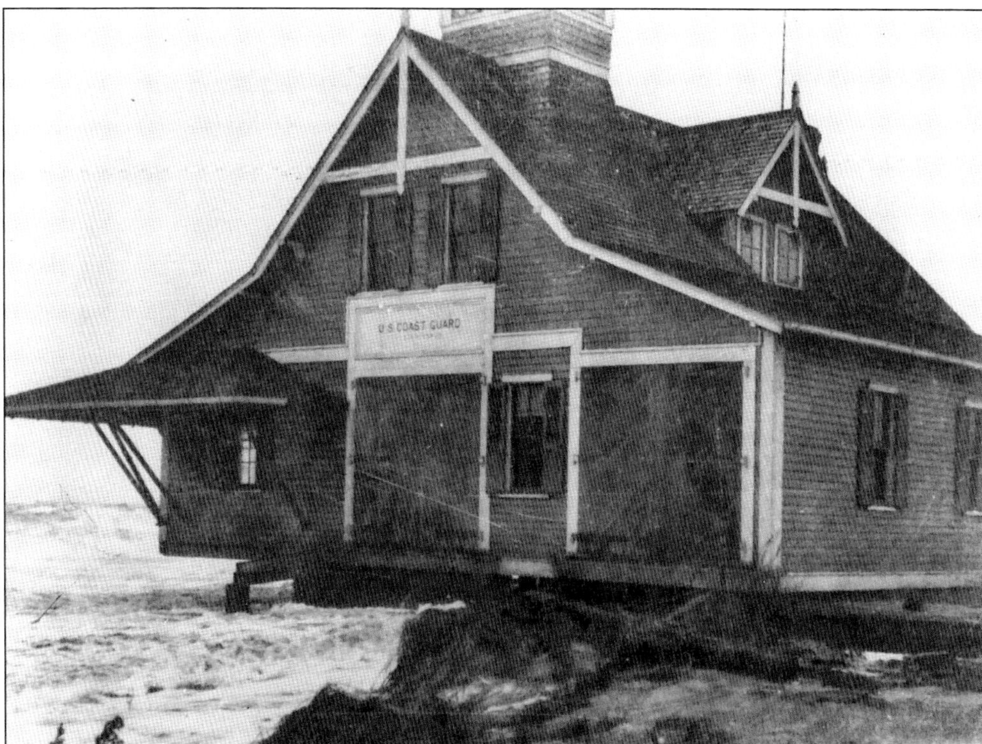

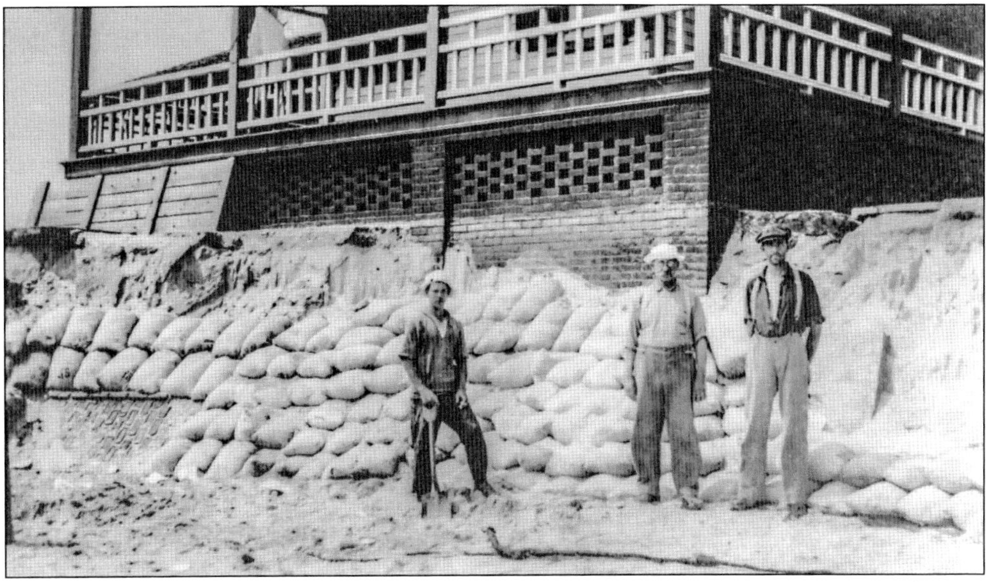

Heading into 1920, the situation was equally concerning at the lighthouse. Head keeper Clarence Cranmer and two unidentified men are busy sandbagging Cranmer's house in this photograph. The house was surrounded by a concrete wall embedded into the sand several feet down, but the water quickly and easily reduced that to piles of broken concrete.

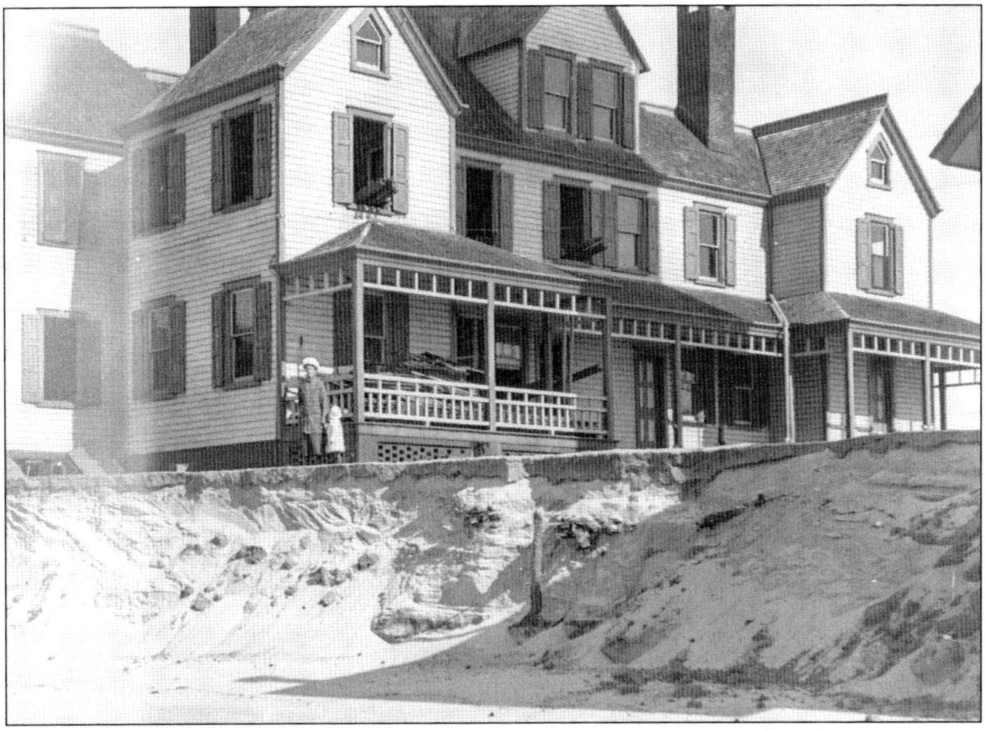

The threat to the keeper's house was not just from the east, but also the north and west, as seen in this view of Minnie Kelly and daughter standing on the inlet side of the grounds. Barnegat Inlet's powerful flows combined with the ocean's advance to eat away at the very tip of Long Beach Island for months. The keepers and locals held out hope the advance could be stemmed.

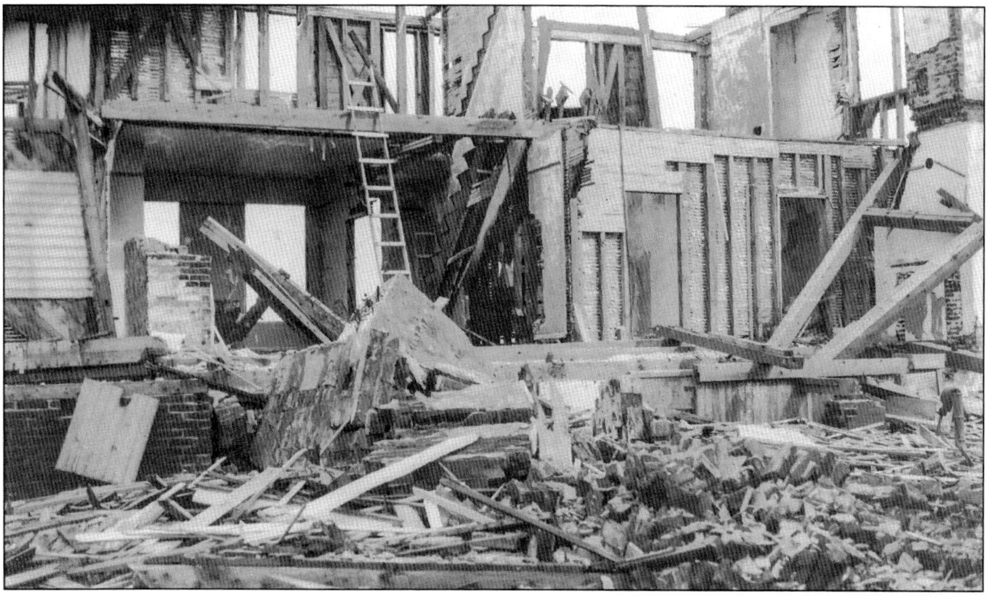

The end was apparent as 1920 wore on, and the government was quick to recoup expected losses. The house was sold, intact, at auction for a few dollars. Fittings turned a profit of a few hundred dollars for the buyer. Locals then gutted the house, as seen in this photograph, reusing the wood and brick on new houses and additions.

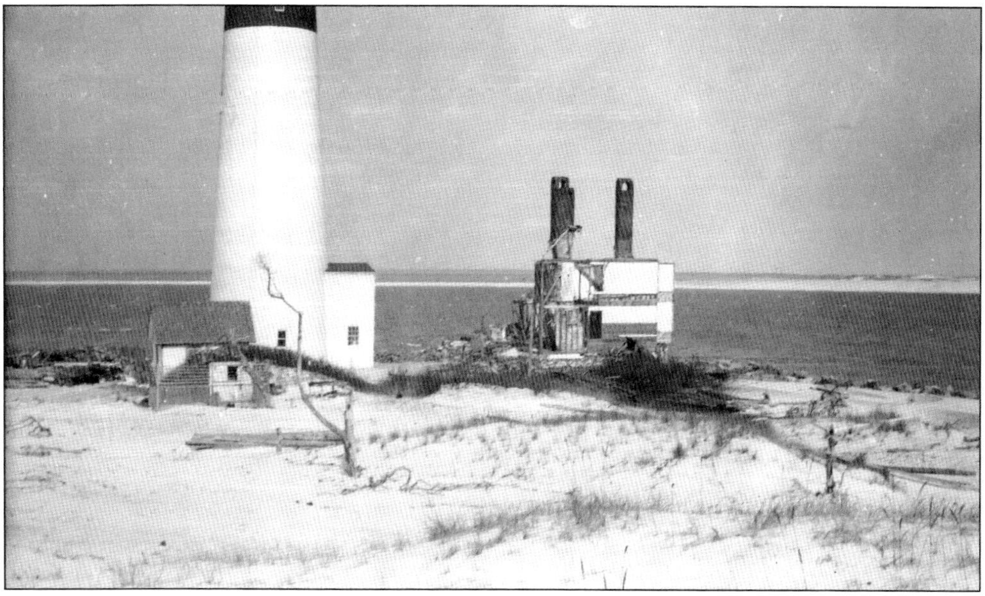

Before long, the sad ruin pictured here was all that remained of the once grand keeper's house. Ironically, the tide on the ocean side receded at the edge of the keeper's house shortly after, making it possible the house could have been left intact and survived. In town, other accommodations were made for the lightkeepers. (Courtesy of the National Archives and Records Administration.)

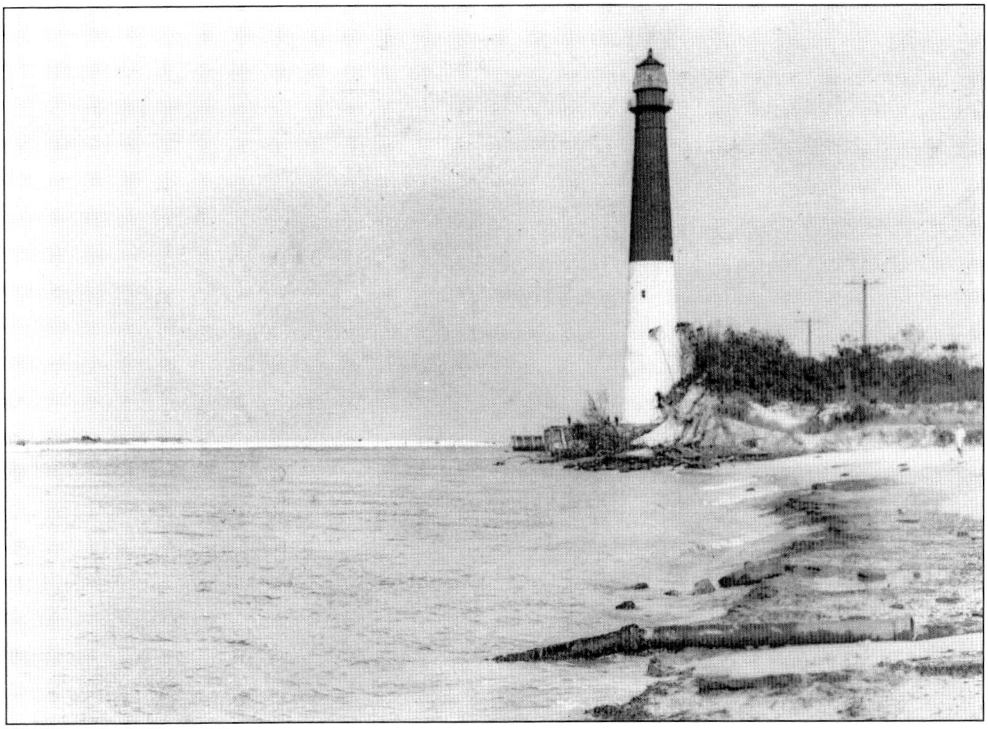

The threat to the lighthouse began in earnest once the waters had condemned the keeper's house. Danger to the landmark, though, came from Barnegat Inlet. A powerful current that ran along the contour of the bayside was eating away at Barnegat City's other coastline, seen here around 1925, long thought of as the protected part of town.

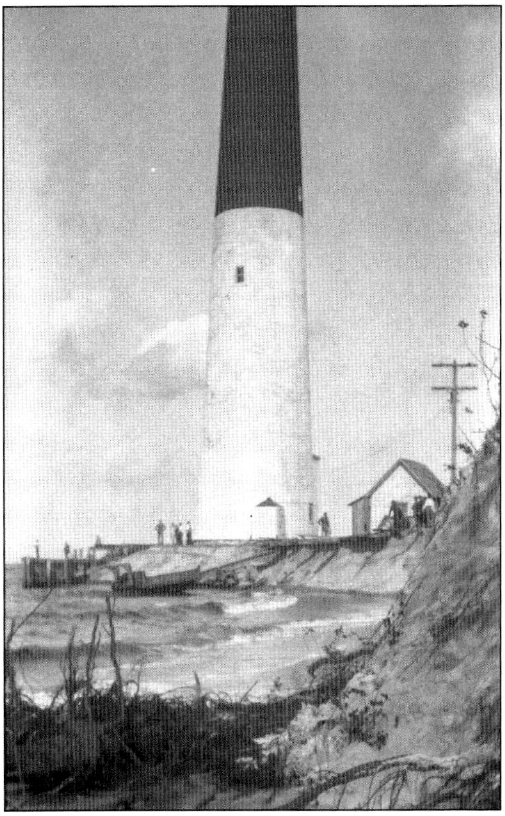

The currents struck with devastating and repeated force one year, carving away at the dunes on Barnegat Lighthouse's west side and exposing the tower to the full force of mighty Barnegat Inlet. The channel had become a big problem for Barnegat City. It was by then so volatile and riddled with shoals that fishermen could not take their boats through unless the tide was right, and many were hesitant even then.

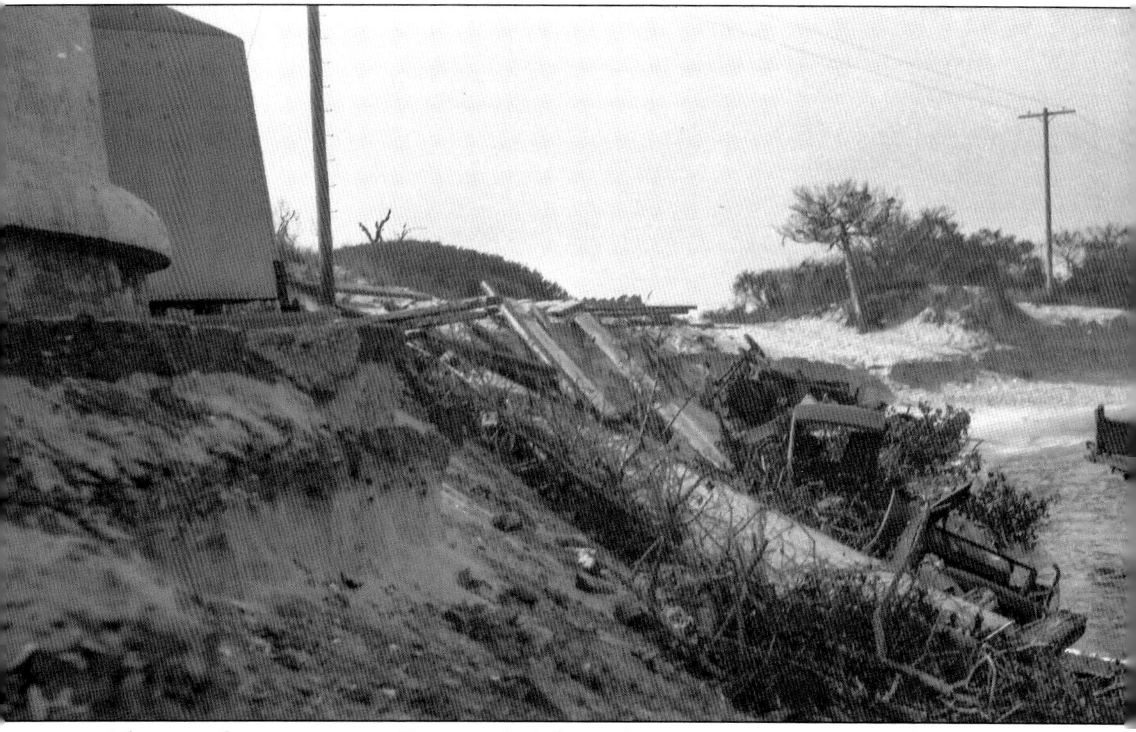

The saga of attempts to save Barnegat Lighthouse from a watery grave spanned much of the rest of the 20th century. From 1920 through the 1950s, Barnegat City, which renamed itself Barnegat Light in 1948 to further differentiate itself from Barnegat on the mainland and to capitalize on the famous lighthouse, achieved national fame at long last. All across New Jersey, and in New York and Philadelphia, repeated stories appeared chronicling the latest threat that would finally topple the tower at Barnegat Inlet. Numerous attempts and appeals for federal aid were recounted as the town fought to save its tourist attraction. Indeed, the danger was very real and imminent in the late 1920s. This photograph shows exactly how close the erosion came to claiming the lighthouse, the edge of which is at upper left. Some newspapers erroneously reported that during one storm, the landmark fell in or was leaning badly and was sure to go soon.

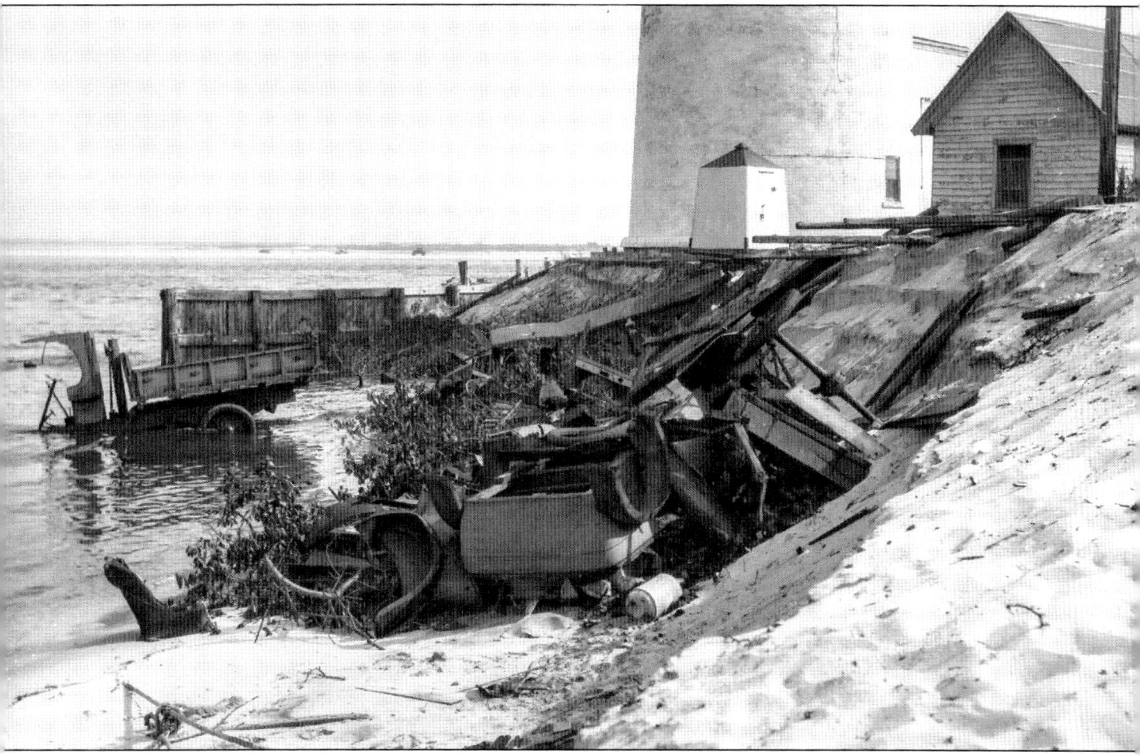

The people of Barnegat City were not about to let Capt. George Meade's creation go down without a fight. At the time, Barnegat Lighthouse was facing imminent danger, and the town was in a period of transition. The old development dreams of a resort had faded from view. What was now apparent was that "Old Barney," as advertisers began calling it, was the future, even though it predated the 1880s building boom by over 20 years. Barnegat City's path forward was not through speedy building and trainloads of day-trippers, but in maintaining a quiet, small-town charm anchored by the lighthouse. Through gradual construction of modest cottages and a marketing campaign targeting weekenders from the cities and growing suburban communities, the town saw a path to reasonable prosperity. To chart that course, though, the tower had to be saved. The town threw everything it had at the problem and went into debt when necessary to build jetties and groins when the federal government refused to use funds on a now obsolete and inactive piece of taxpayer property.

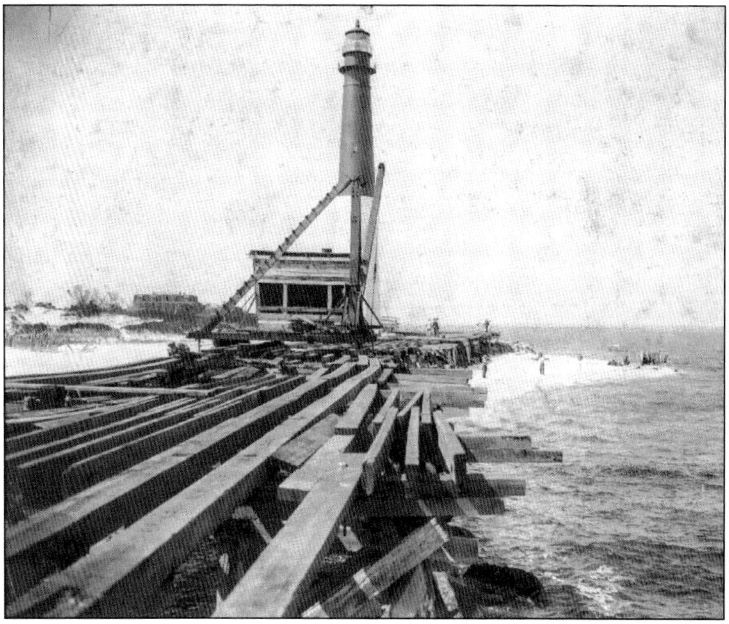

Some of the efforts by the people of Barnegat City are pictured here around 1930. Using their own labor and what was available locally, craftsmen got together to construct this platform and makeshift crane to hoist large boulders brought in to create crude but hopefully effective jetties. This practice was repeated many times over as Barnegat City battled the inlet for the fate of the Barnegat Lighthouse.

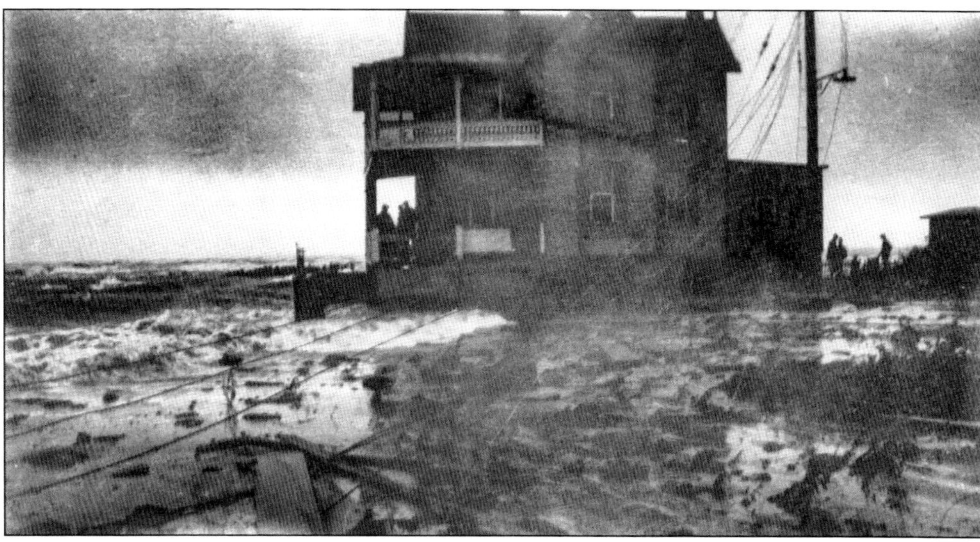

Erosion along the ocean side did not advance far after its gains in 1919 and 1920. Storms, though, often meant those spared earlier would be tested. This photograph of the old Whetstone cottage on the corner of East Fourth Street and Central Avenue was taken during the 1933 Chesapeake-Potomac hurricane that, although tracking inland through Maryland, still caused damage on the New Jersey coast.

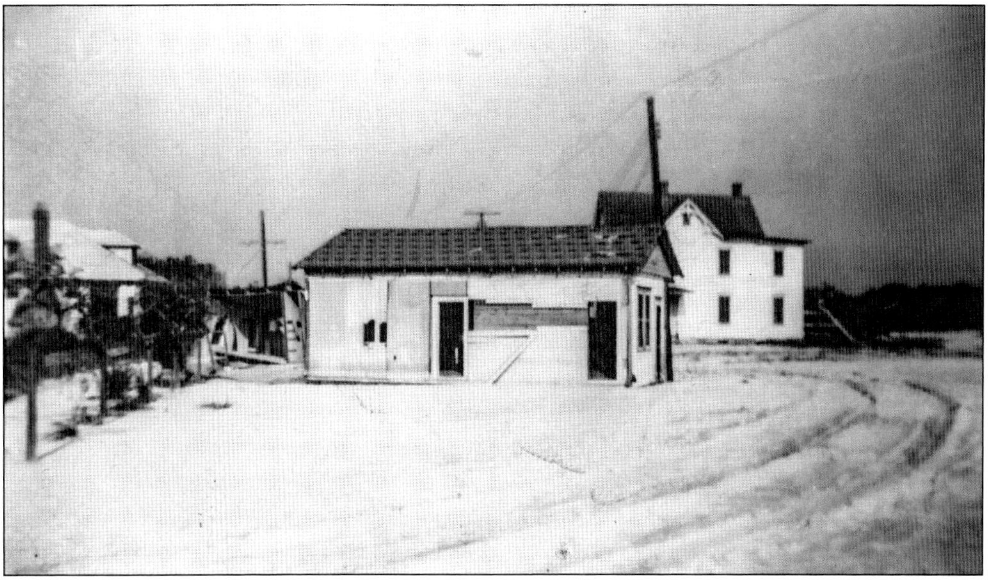

The Ash Wednesday storm of 1962 may be the most damaging storm to hit a populated Long Beach Island, but an earlier storm, the Great Atlantic hurricane of 1944, was equally powerful and nearly as damaging. The Category 4 storm weakened slightly when it grazed the New Jersey coast in mid-September. It dislodged a West Fourth Street ice-cream shop, pictured here, and deposited it in the road.

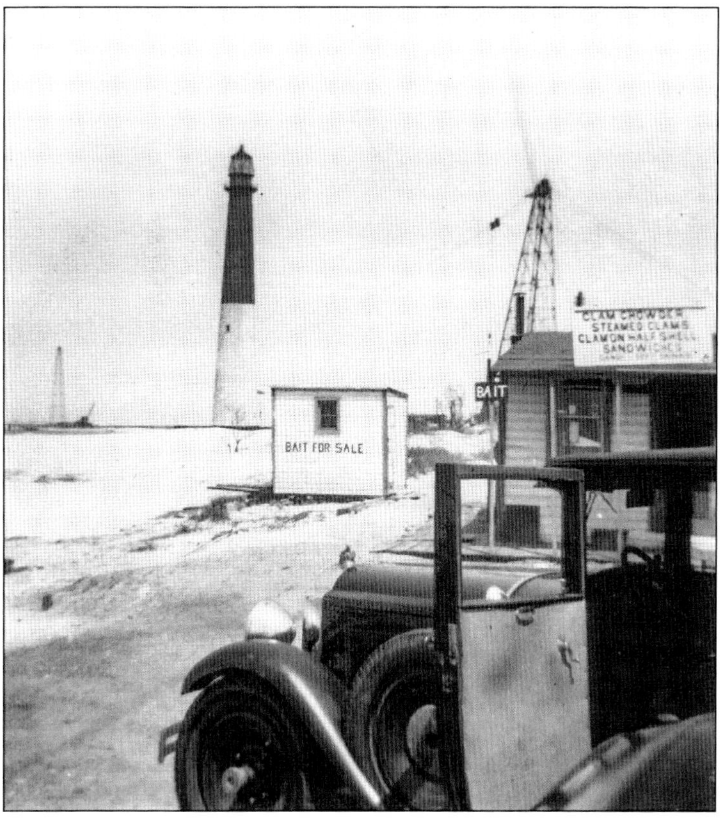

Appeals to Washington, DC, to save the lighthouse went unanswered for many years after the 1920 threat. As far as the government was concerned, once the lightship *Barnegat* was operational, the national interest was in the preservation of Barnegat Inlet as a navigational channel. To that end, in 1939, towers were erected to carry boulders across to stabilize the north side of the channel.

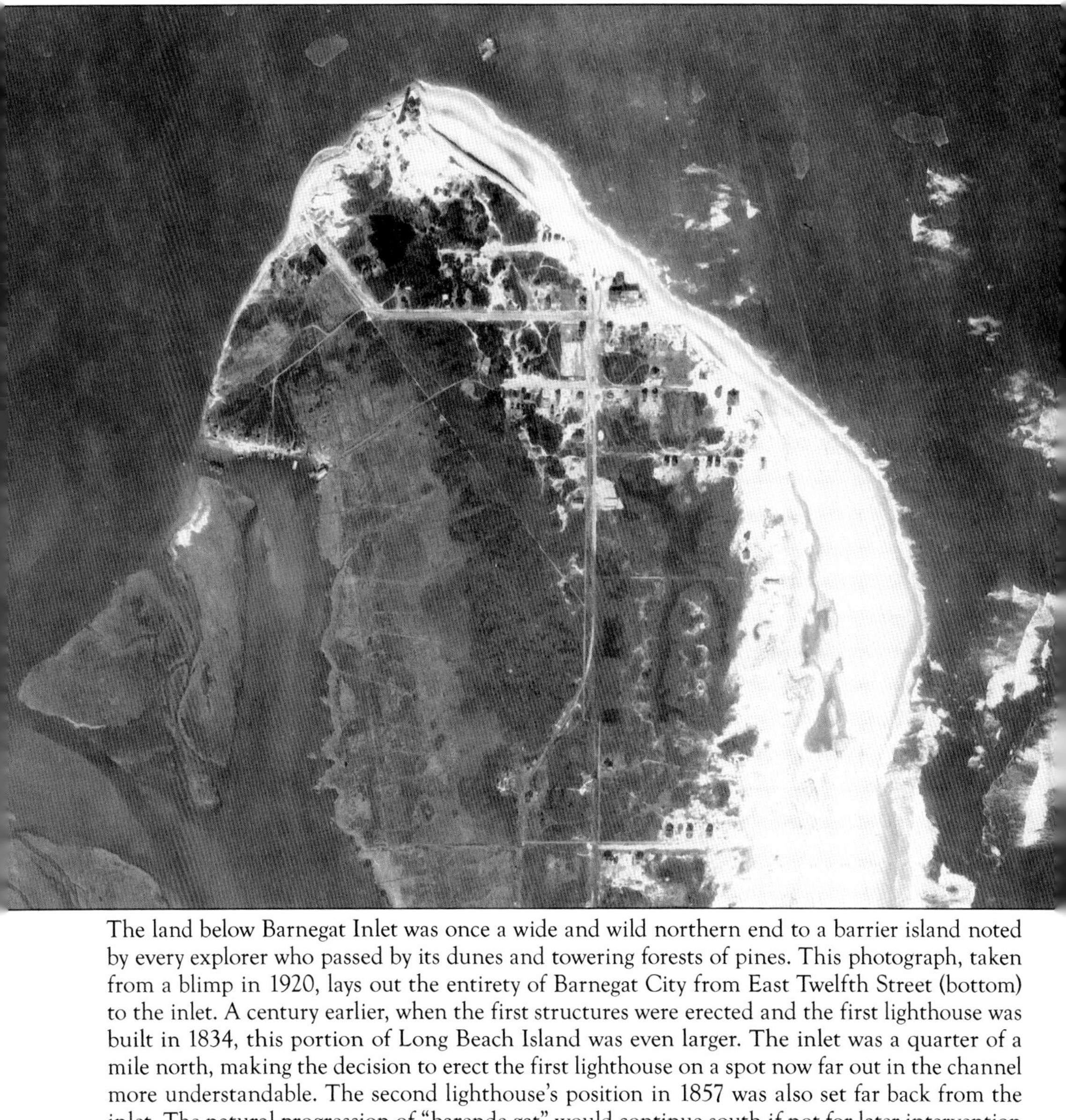

The land below Barnegat Inlet was once a wide and wild northern end to a barrier island noted by every explorer who passed by its dunes and towering forests of pines. This photograph, taken from a blimp in 1920, lays out the entirety of Barnegat City from East Twelfth Street (bottom) to the inlet. A century earlier, when the first structures were erected and the first lighthouse was built in 1834, this portion of Long Beach Island was even larger. The inlet was a quarter of a mile north, making the decision to erect the first lighthouse on a spot now far out in the channel more understandable. The second lighthouse's position in 1857 was also set far back from the inlet. The natural progression of "barende-gat" would continue south if not for later intervention by man. (Courtesy of the US Army, Coastal and Hydraulics Laboratory, Engineer Research and Development Center.)

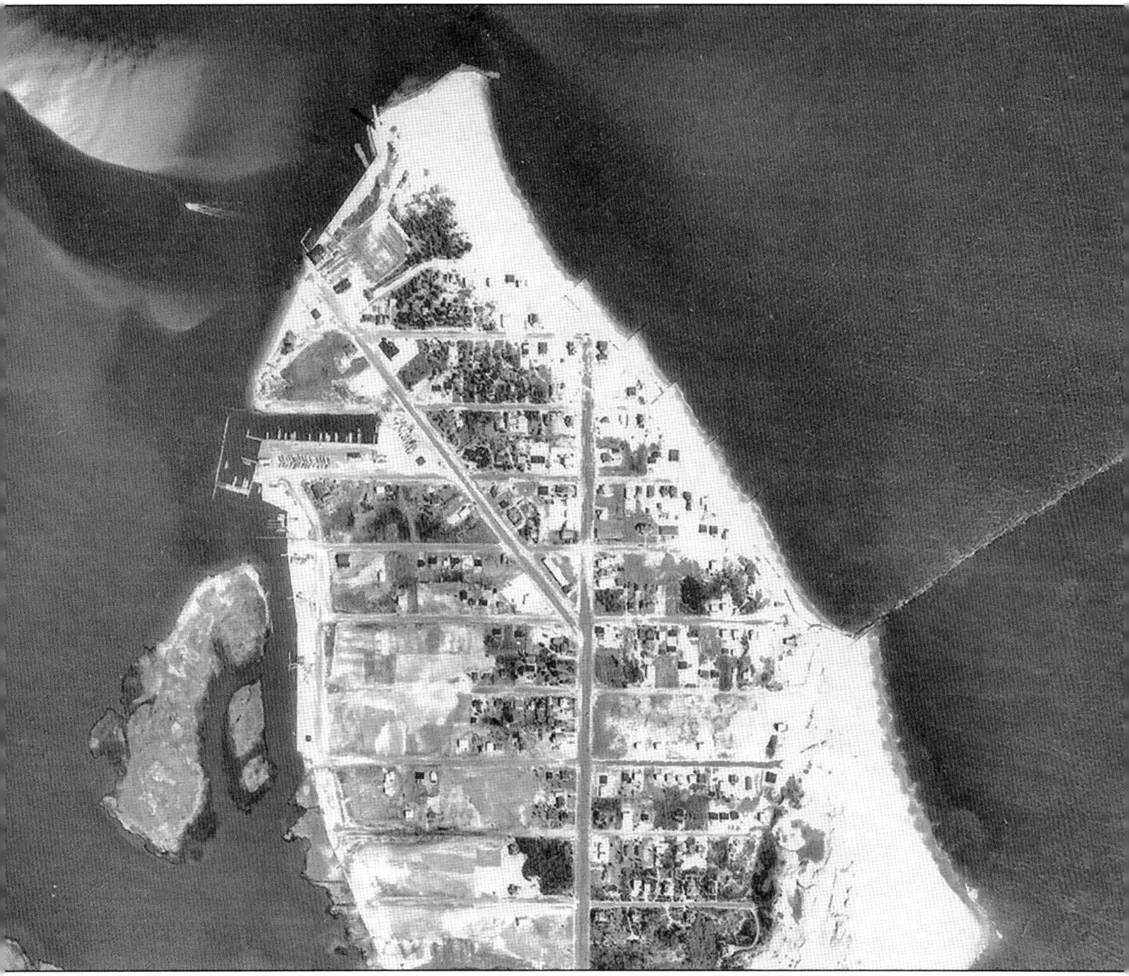

This 1962 aerial photograph following the Ash Wednesday storm shows the same view as the 1920 image on the facing page, yet the loss of land around the entire head of Long Beach Island is apparent. In the intervening years, the bayside was eroded to the point that the land on which the Sunset Hotel stood and the entire West Sixth Street harbor were lost to the channel that ran along the west side of town. The solution was to dam up the channel at West Twentieth Street across to the islands of High Bar and from High Bar across to another island west of the inlet. The bay shore was stabilized from then on. On the ocean side, the damaging 1919 and 1920 erosion was halted, though not reversed, by a 1940s jetty extending over 1,000 feet from East Eighth Street. The beaches, though, would take another 50 years, and further action from the Army Corps of Engineers, to finally recover. (Courtesy of the US Army, Coastal and Hydraulics Laboratory, Engineer Research and Development Center.)

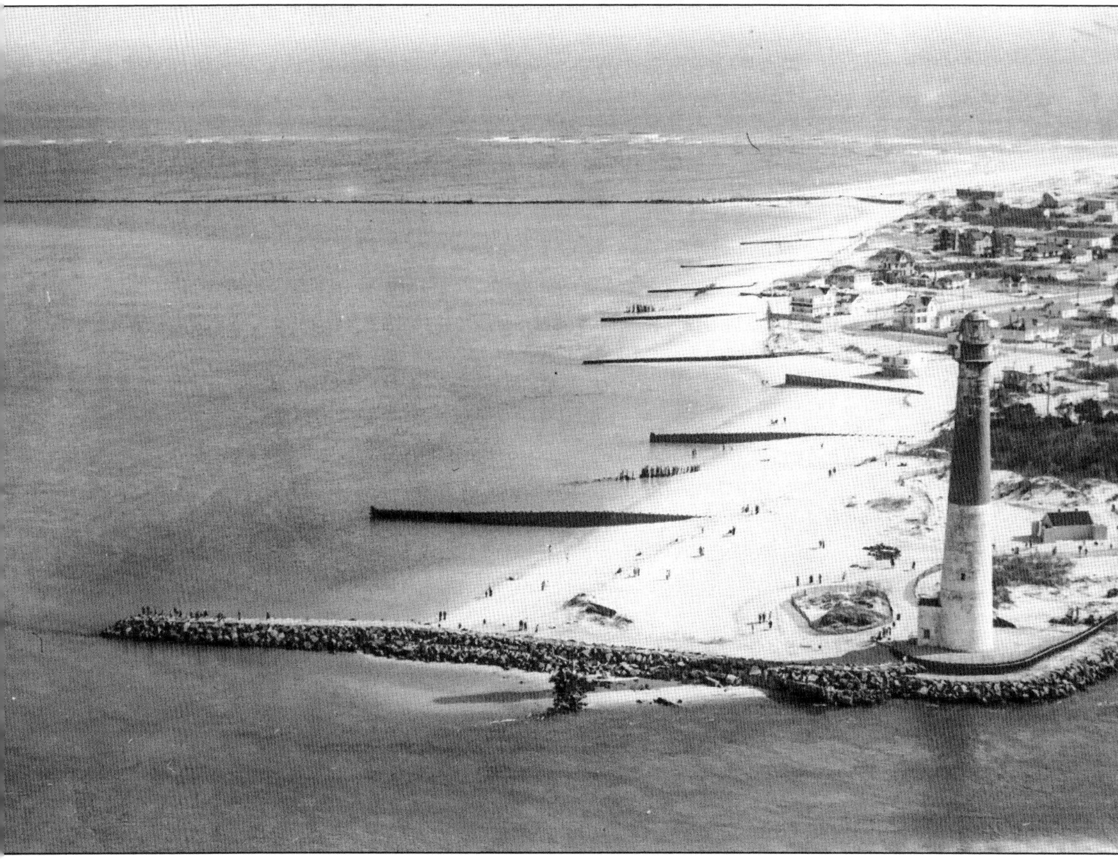

The goal of town, state, and federal efforts in and around Barnegat Inlet was to capture new sand moved around by the currents. Wooden groins, such as those in this 1950s aerial view, were built, then washed away or buried, and then rebuilt again over a period of years to build up the beaches. Often, the groins did little. Stone jetties proved the most successful, but a sufficiently long jetty using large enough boulders was expensive, and due to the necessity of state and federal funding, could take years to be realized. The massive jetty on the south side of the inlet extending east-northeast from the beach at Eighth Street was a much larger version of the same principle, among other aims in its design. It failed to restore the beaches from Seventh Street to the lighthouse, as some hoped, but it did help prevent additional significant erosion. If neither the town nor Barnegat Inlet channel were in imminent danger, requests for beach projects, such as those to shore up the lighthouse, were put on the back burner by the federal government.

Nine

Faces of Yesteryear

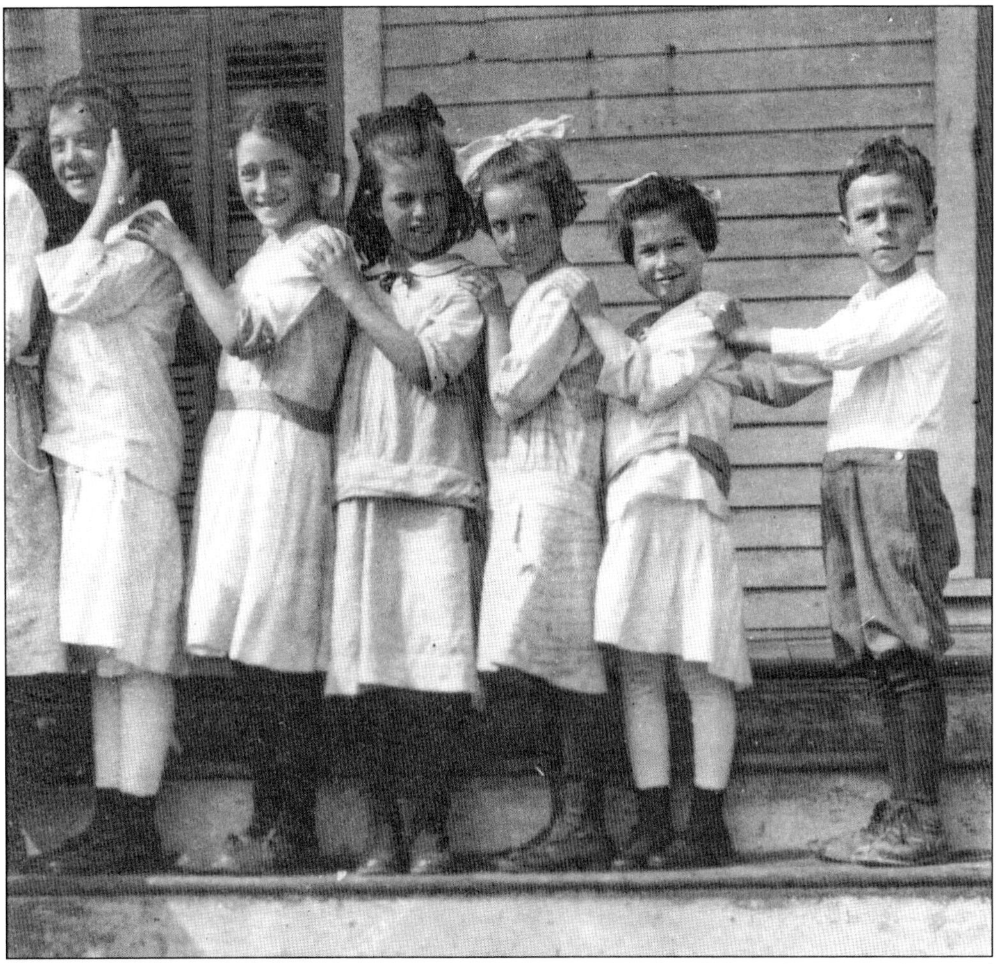

Schoolchildren from Barnegat City are, from left to right, ? Knox, ? Peer, ? Dingham, ? Dingham, and Ted Barber. Although real-world education was a fact of life for children of fishermen, lightkeepers, and lifesavers growing up on the edge of Barnegat Inlet, formal education was also encouraged and mandatory.

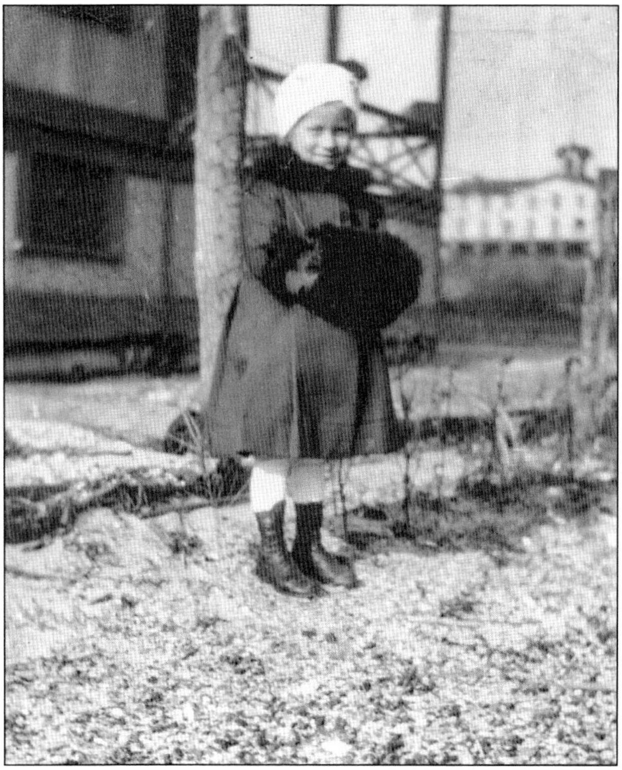

Barnegat City may have been regionally isolated to generations of mostly hardscrabble folks who made livings with their hands, but that did not mean fashion, refinement, and a worldly nature were foreign to these people. In this picture, young Alice Axelson stands in her finery warming her hands in a muff on East Sixth Street.

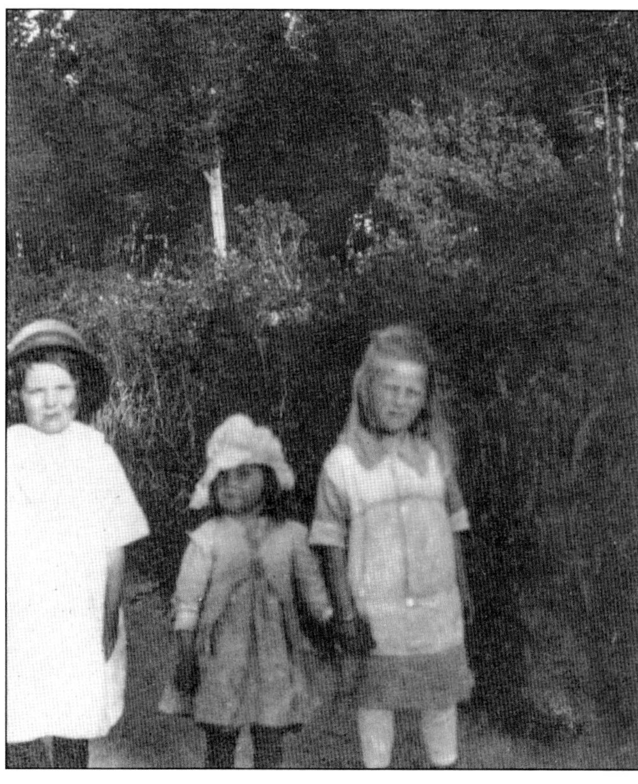

Around 1915, the times demanded that one always looked respectable. From left to right, Helen Sharp, Marie Bennett, and Evelyn Hoff demonstrate this. Not every local child, especially girls, would grow up and live their lives in Barnegat City. Some went off to college in one of the cities and started careers and families elsewhere. Some would return home to Barnegat Light for their golden years.

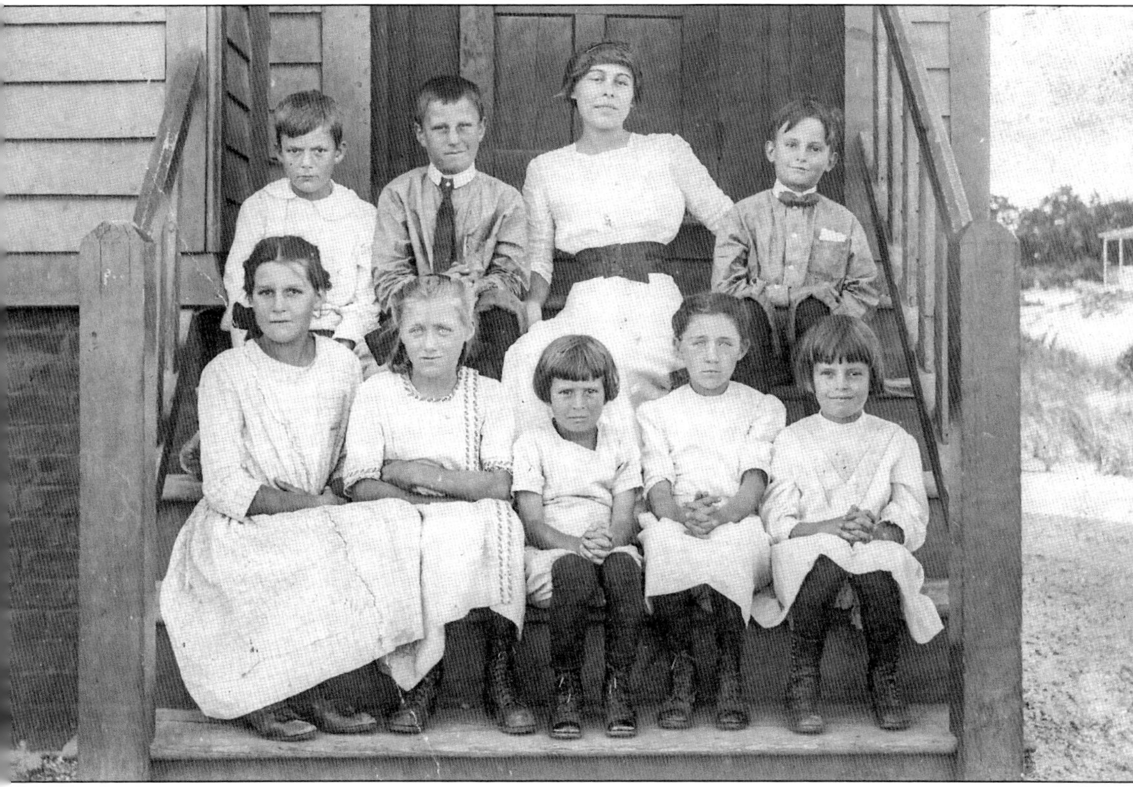

Class sizes at the Barnegat City School on East Fifth Street and Central Avenue varied over the years; in some years, only one student was enrolled. That was not the case in this 1912 photograph. From left to right are (first row) May Applegate, Edna Peer, Hazel Dugan, Clara Peer, and Mabel Dugan; (second row) Bob Applegate, George Camburn, teacher Vena Falkinburg, and Carnel Brown.

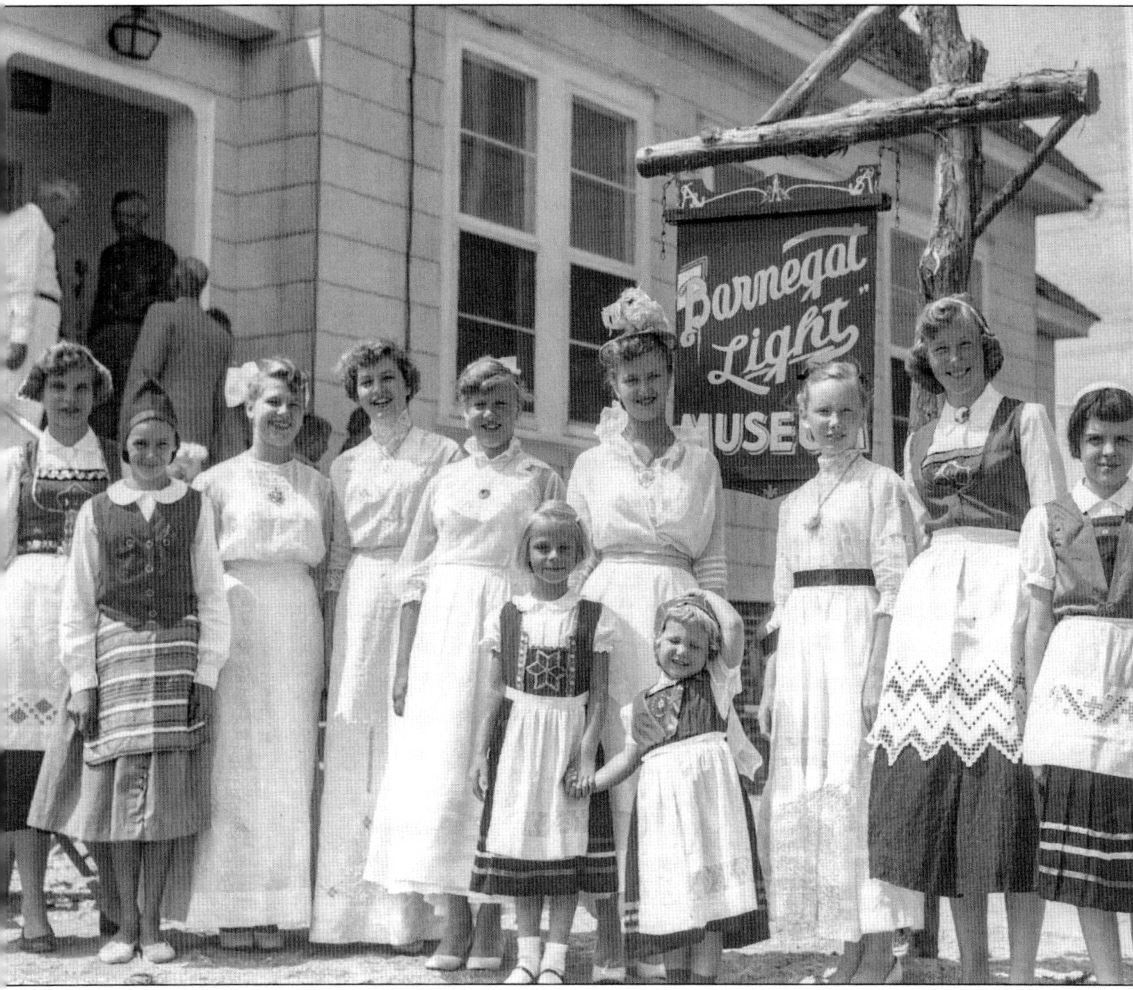

In the 1910s and 1920s, a wave of immigration from Scandinavian countries changed the makeup of the community. New traditions and languages were introduced. This led to frosty relations between some longtime fishermen and the foreign competition. Most welcomed the new arrivals. Many, in fact, were employed straight from the immigration docks and offices in New York. In this 1950s publicity photograph, children are honoring their Norwegian heritage.

The Barnegat City School taught first through fifth grade before students graduated to the Barnegat school on the mainland. One teacher was employed to handle all the classes. These women managed well, including keeping the school heated during the winter. Freda Cranmer, seen here in 1951 stoking the stove, was the last and one of the best-remembered teachers.

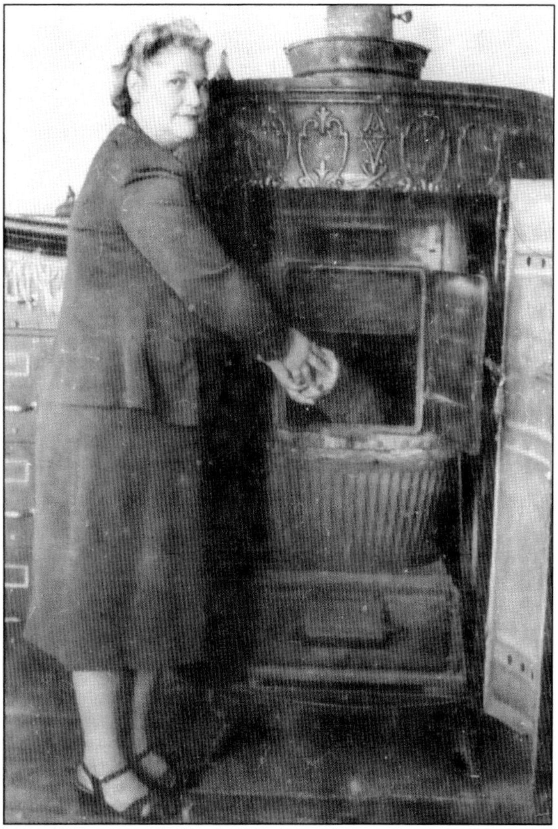

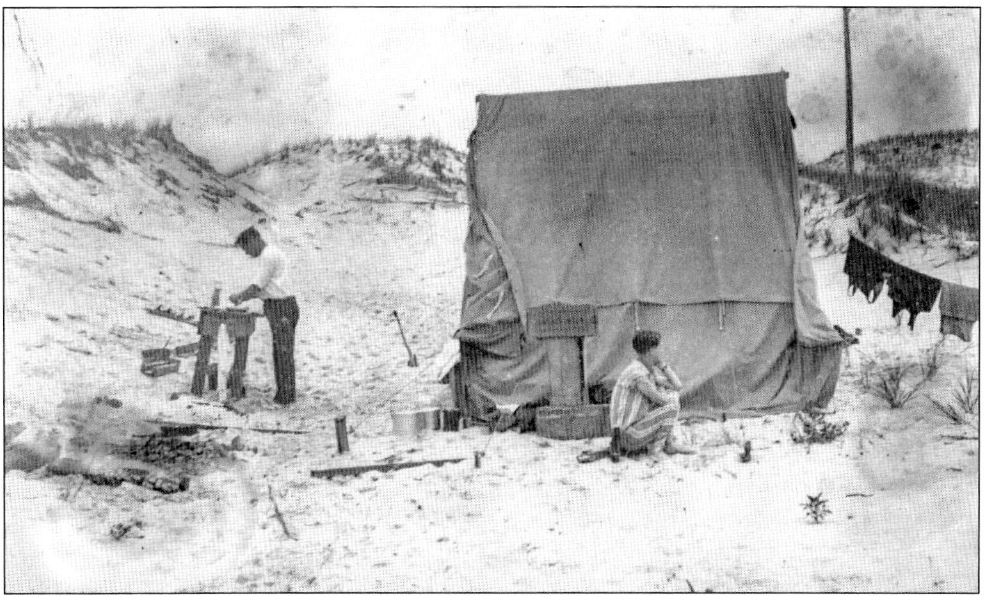

Sometimes, especially during the Depression, making ends meet just did not happen. Barnegat City and its mostly vacant, dune-filled blocks offered a pleasant respite from worldly troubles. This man drove his family into town and camped on the beach for a while in July 1927. With plentiful fishing and several freshwater springs, Barnegat City had a lot to offer those with limited means.

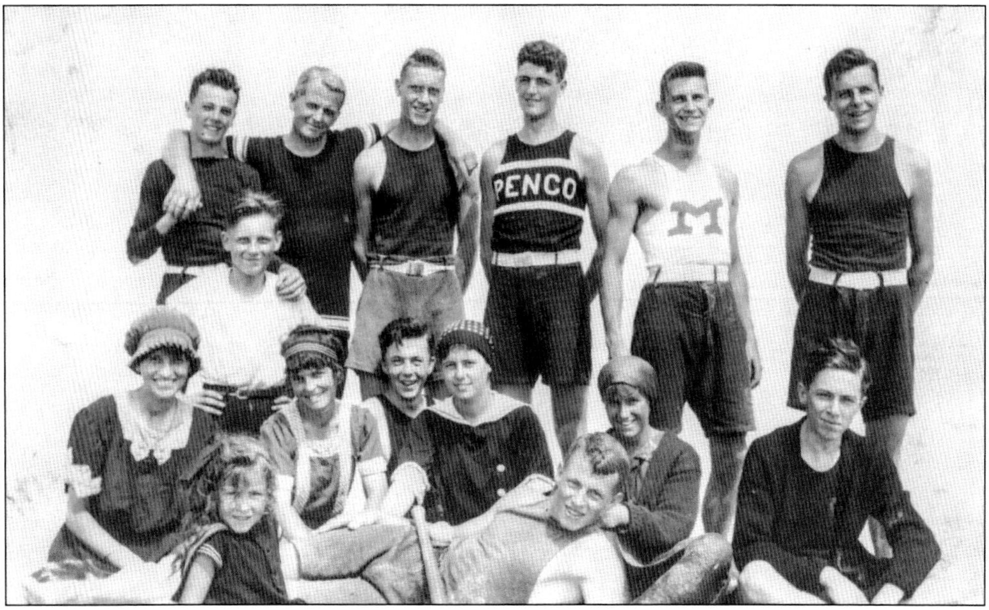

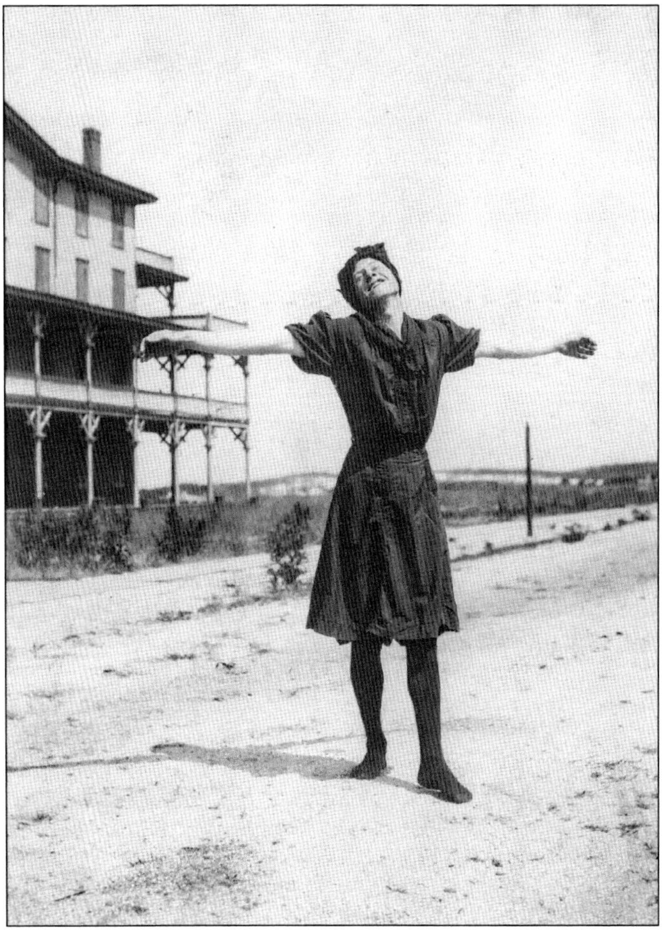

Barnegat Light and Long Beach Island became a beloved spot for bathers, especially once automobiles allowed for day-tripping by nearby college students. Some were strangers in town; others were children born and raised here returning home. Happy groups of bathers like those seen here became a more typical sight in the second half of the 20th century.

There were downsides to the respectable fashions of decades like the 1920s. Material could be light but layered, short-sleeved and short-legged, as Roberta Whetstone's dress is in this photograph on East Fourth Street. The bathing outfits of the time were black or navy blue and were made of wool, which was not only itchy, but also heavy when waterlogged.

Over at the old West Sixth Street harbor, Katherine Perrine is pictured standing behind the port gas station she helped run. Perrine's white middy shirt and skirt is an example of more sensible dress for beating the most sweltering heat. The lack of structures in Barnegat City in those days meant a refreshing sea breeze could reach every part of town.

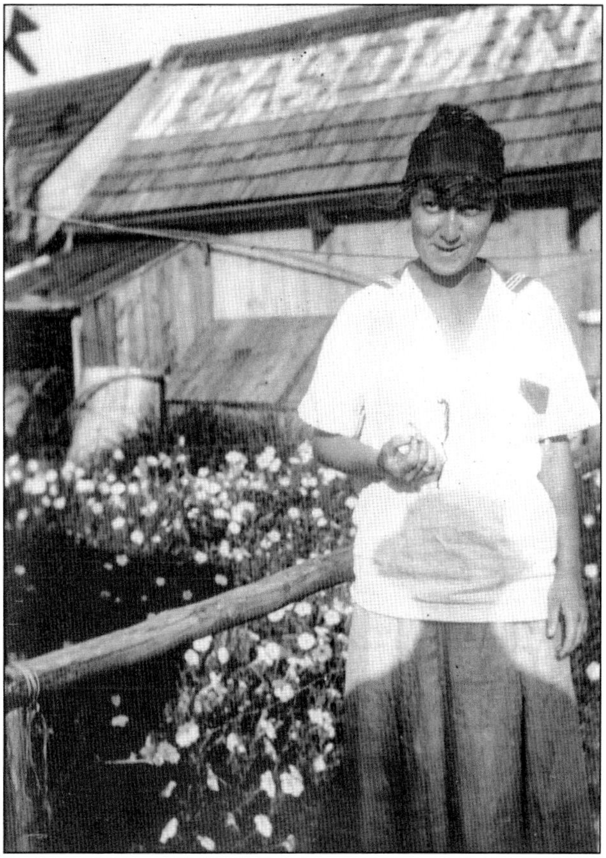

Haddock's boathouse stood at the east end of the dock, where John Haddock spent long hours convening with friends and neighbors. In this undated postcard, he sits in the shade at left with Barney the dog and his friend Dr. William Whetstone. Haddock was a beloved local character, whose house with the widow's peak on East Fourth Street was a necessary stop for all visitors.

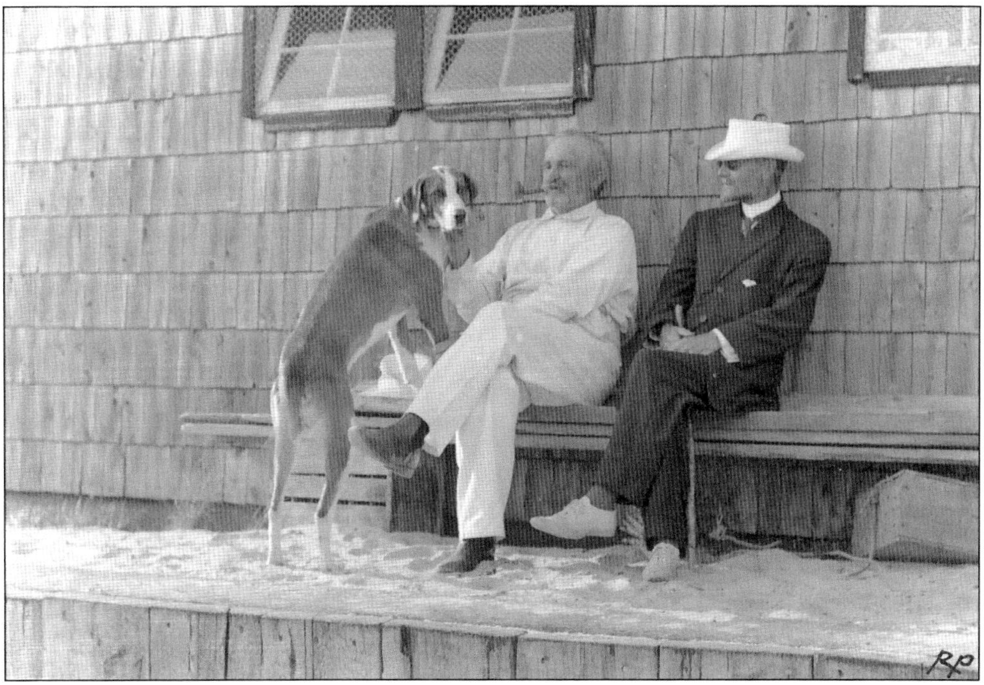

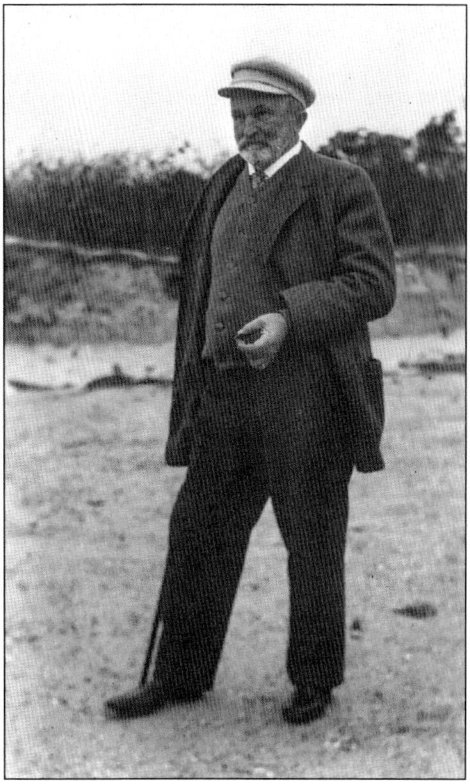

John Haddock, posing here as the trendsetter he was, achieved national notoriety in 1906 when his 1882 divorce reached the Supreme Court of the United States. The controversial Haddock v. Haddock 5-4 decision was a landmark ruling on the full faith and credit powers of the Constitution. In short, the court voided his divorce because he abandoned his wife, nullifying the act made in a neighboring state.

Baymen pose next to Haddock's boathouse in this c. 1915 photograph. From left to right are (first row) Lew Conklin, Harry Brown, and Axel Axelson; (second row) Bill Garland, Walter Perrine, Chris ?, ? Olsen, and unidentified. The descendants of several of these men still fish today.

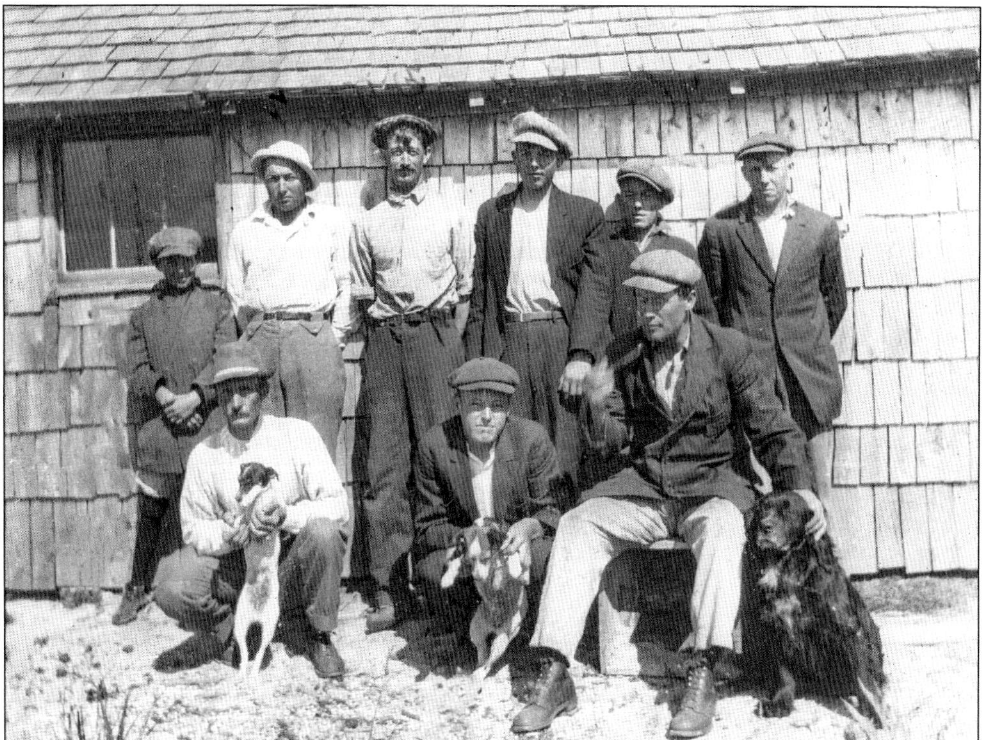

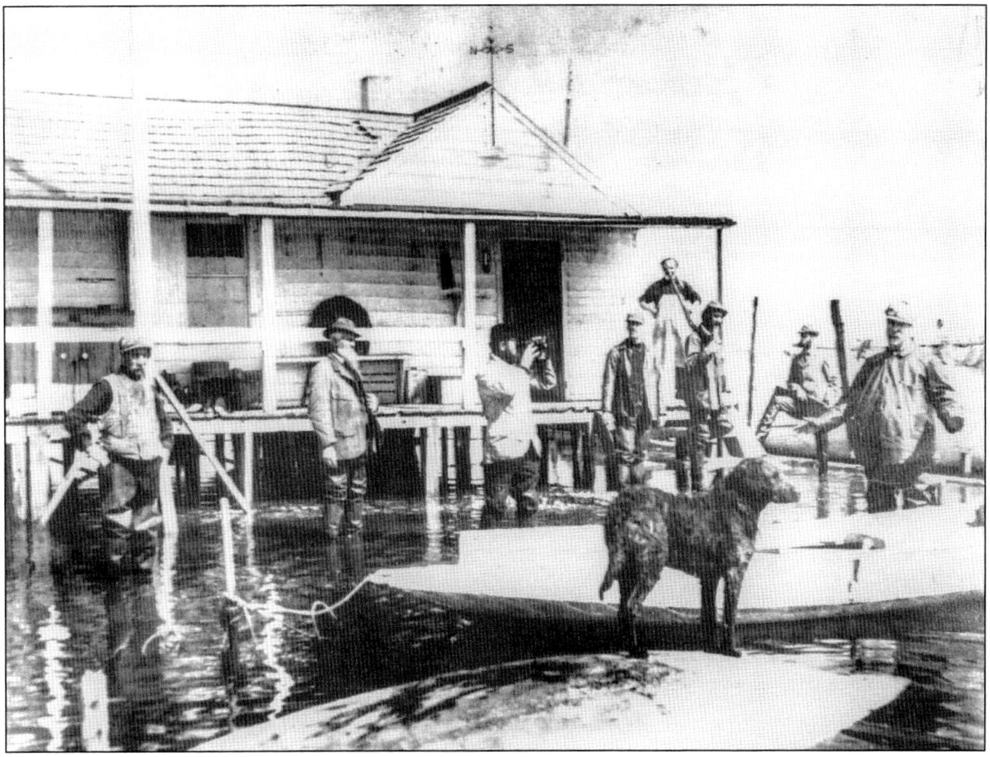

This 1890s image shows just how far word reached of some of the enviable attractions around Barnegat Inlet. The Sedge Island Gun Club was situated on a bar across the inlet from Barnegat City and behind the southern tip of Island Beach. This motley group of hunters includes, from left to right, Bart Clayton, Jess Birdsall, five unidentified, and Pres. Grover Cleveland. Chessie the dog stands in the foreground.

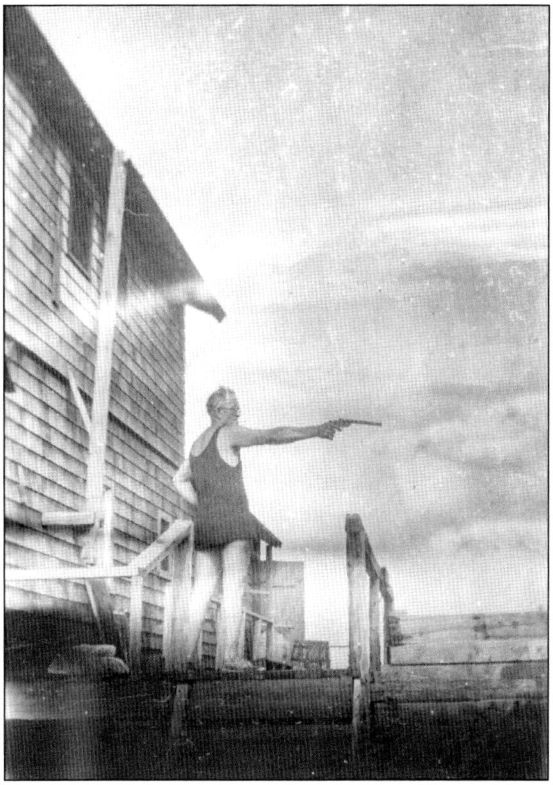

Other shooting clubs attracted groups from all over the East Coast. A Dr. Williams is pictured here in the 1930s practicing his shot with a pistol at the High Bar Gunning and Fishing Club on an island in the bay off Barnegat City. The sound of gunfire echoing over town was as common as ship horns and the breaking waves on the beach.

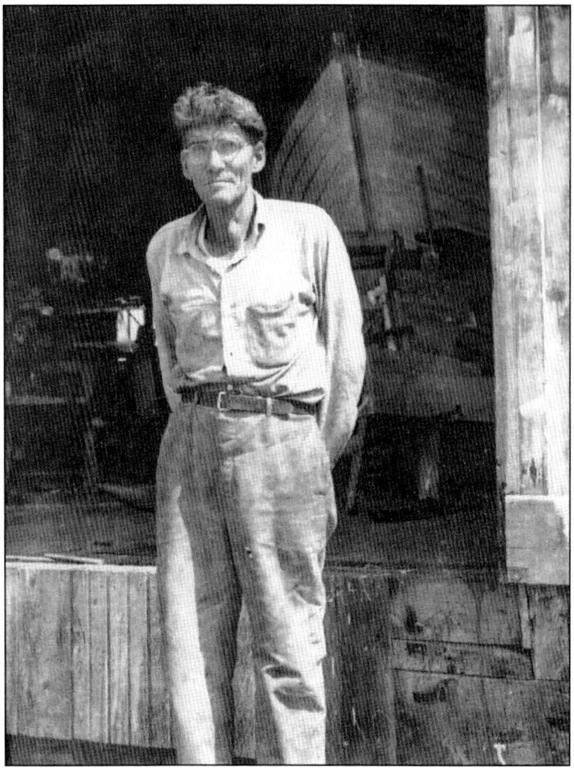

Pictured is Axel Sundquist, who worked on boats at the Brooklyn Navy Yard and even in China before he found himself in Barnegat City in the 1930s with a boat building business. Some said he was Finnish, but he hailed from Sweden. He was known as the man who could fix any boat. Quiet and kind, he toiled in his garage on West Sixth Street until his death in 1965.

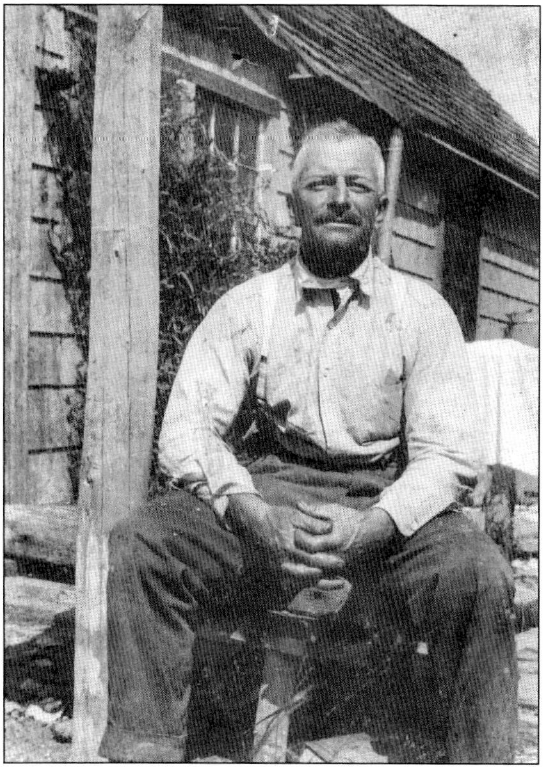

Prominent local Joe Peckworth, pictured here looking statuesque, was said by Morse Archer Jr. to have been the best fisherman in town. His house is still on West Fifth Street next to the schoolhouse. A shack in the rear used to hold ice for the fishermen, who sawed blocks from a frozen Barnegat Bay to keep their catch fresh.

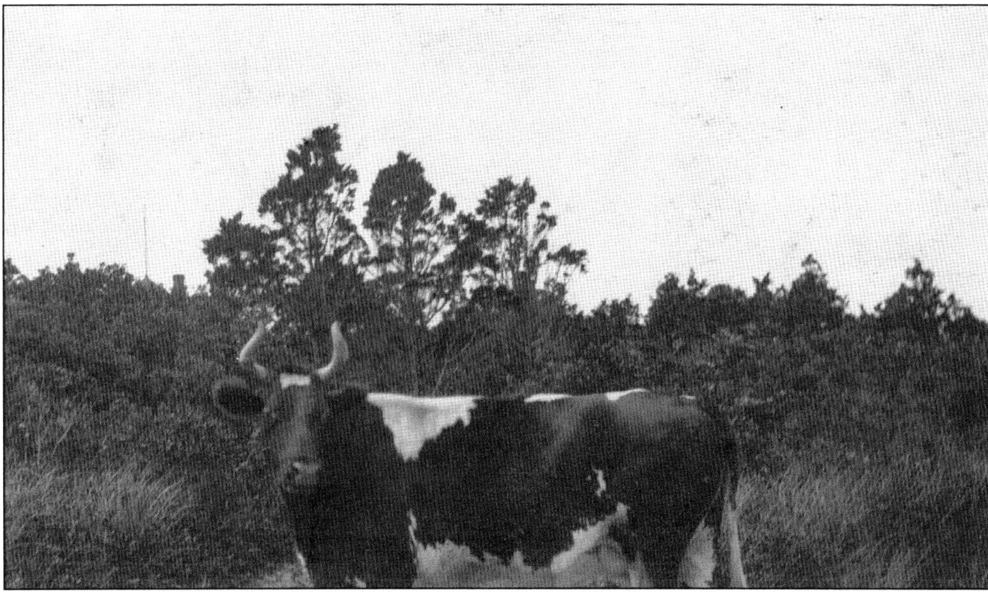

Joe Peckworth, like many locals, kept some sort of animal. Some had horses for pound fishing or for getting up and down Long Beach Island when necessary, some kept chickens, and one bred minks. Peckworth kept a cow named Mollie, seen here milling about in 1908. The plentiful berry bushes offered tasty grazing for some of the larger livestock.

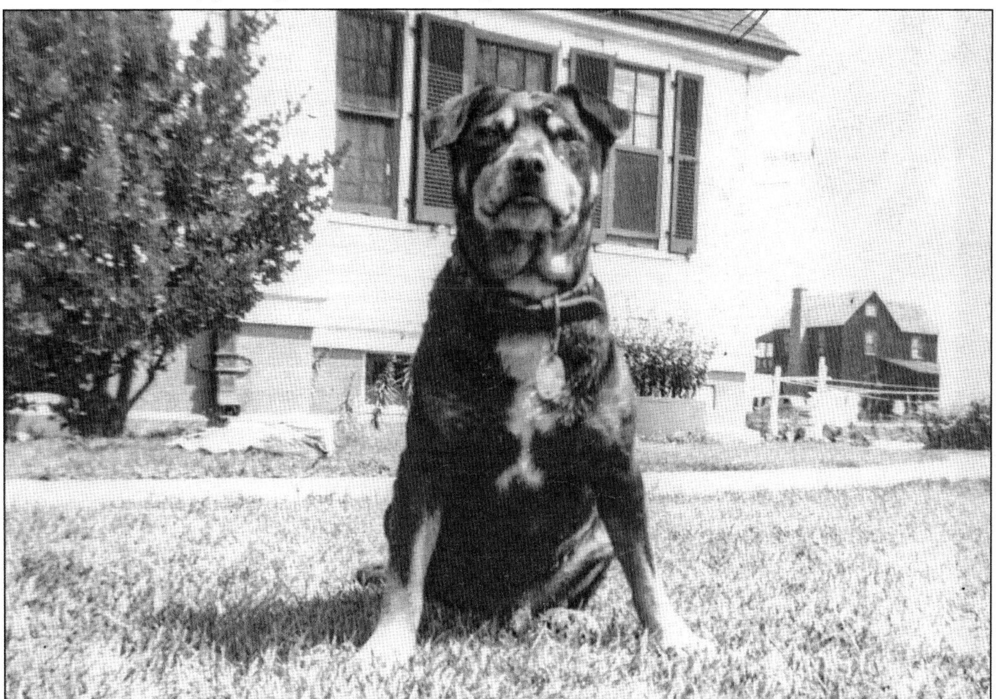

The most famous animal ever to live in Barnegat Light was this mixed breed pup named Sinbad. He was picked up by a sailor whose girlfriend could not keep him just before the Coast Guard cutter *Campbell* shoved off in 1937. Sinbad then served as the ship's mascot through World War II. A newsreel, comic book, and even his own biography of war stories publicized the canine.

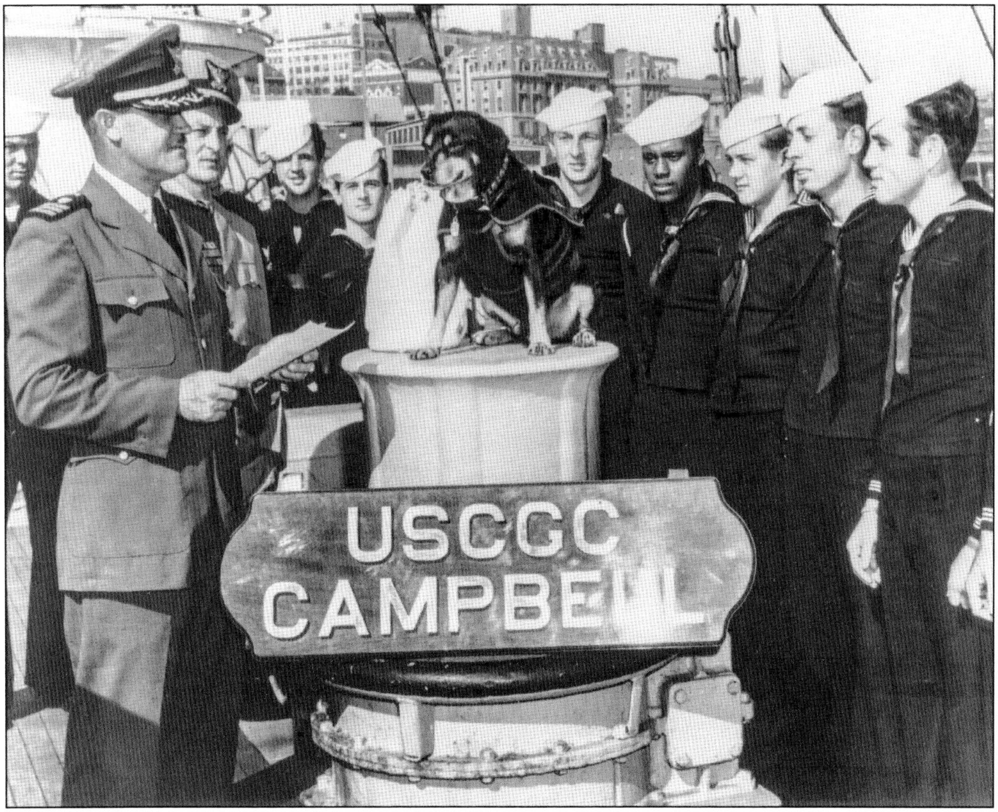

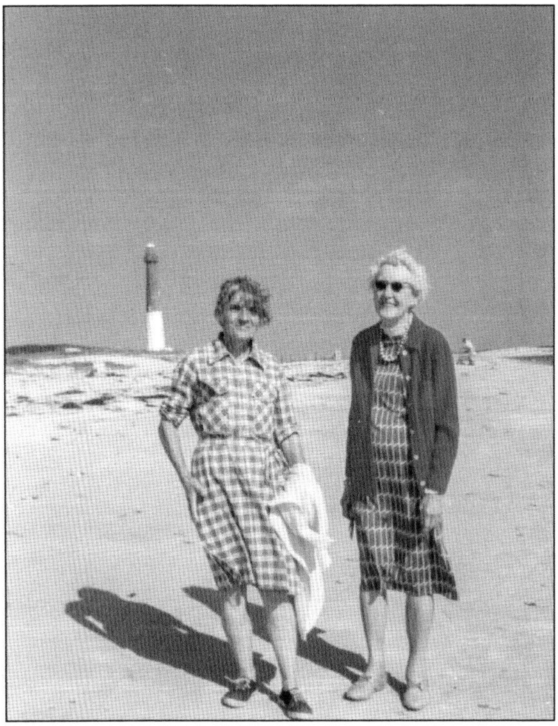

Pictured here being feted by the Navy, Sinbad was honorably discharged in 1948. He retired to Coast Guard Station Barnegat Light, where he kept the crew company and was free to go about town greeting locals, visitors, and children. When he died in 1951, Sinbad was buried beneath the flagpole of the East Seventh Street station, where he rests to this day.

After the Barnegat City School closed in 1953 and became a museum, a few enterprising women got the idea that they could do better than the barren grounds around the buildings. Frances Selover (left) and Edith Gwinn, pictured on the beach in 1973, worked with a team of volunteers beginning in the 1950s to create the Barnegat Light Museum Gardens, which have attracted horticultural tourists ever since.

Of the 26 captains who formed the Independent Fish Company in 1929, seven remained in the company by the 1960s. One of the charter members was John Larson Sr. His son, also John Larson, is seen here on the bridge of his excursion boat the *Miss Barnegat Light*. Like other locals, he and his father both fished and took tourists out on day trips. (Courtesy of Margaret Thomas Buchholz.)

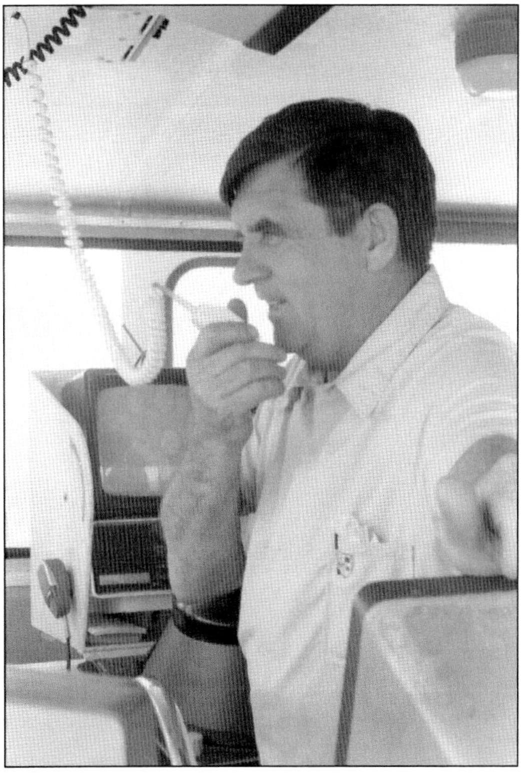

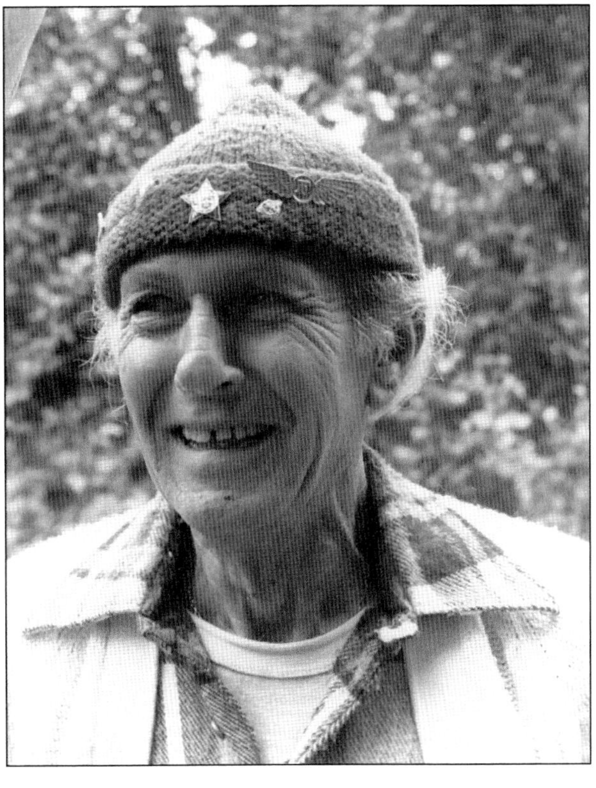

Sidney Rothman, pictured here, was another occasional summer visitor who fell in love with Barnegat Light and had a house built on Central Avenue between West Twenty-First and West Twenty-Second Streets, in which he opened a gallery, attracting figures such as Leon Kelly for showings. He volunteered at the Long Beach Island Foundation of the Arts and Sciences, started by Boris Blai in 1948. (Courtesy of Margaret Thomas Buchholz.)

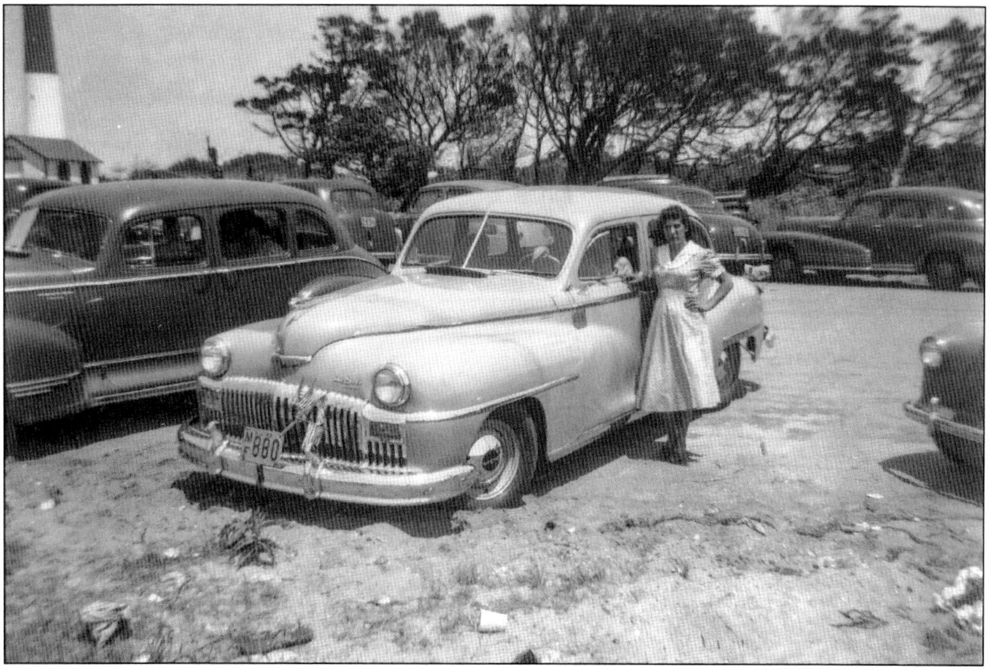

Anna Moser poses next to a DeSoto on a July day in 1948 near the end of Broadway in Barnegat City. The row of trees behind her would come down about a decade later for Kelly's Restaurant. The postwar prosperity driven by the GI Bill spawned a new age of tourism for the town, one that it hoped to foster with the name change to Barnegat Light that same year.

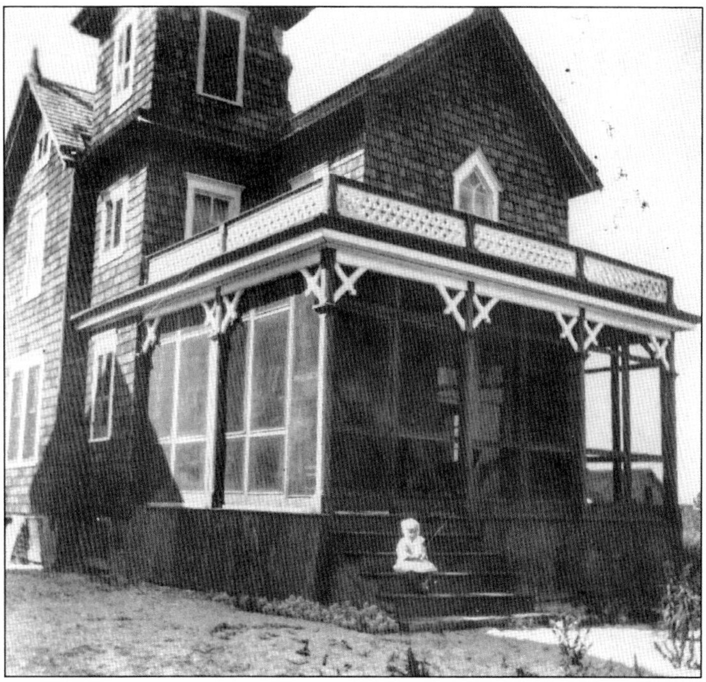

The name may have changed, but old Barnegat City's simple truths were still the foundation of the future. Families grew up in the shadow of the Barnegat Lighthouse. Children visited, even if their families did not live there. And all these children, such as Helen Johnson seen here on the steps of an East Sixth Street cottage in 1889, were given indelible memories of a place they would return to with their children.

Ten

OLD HAUNTS

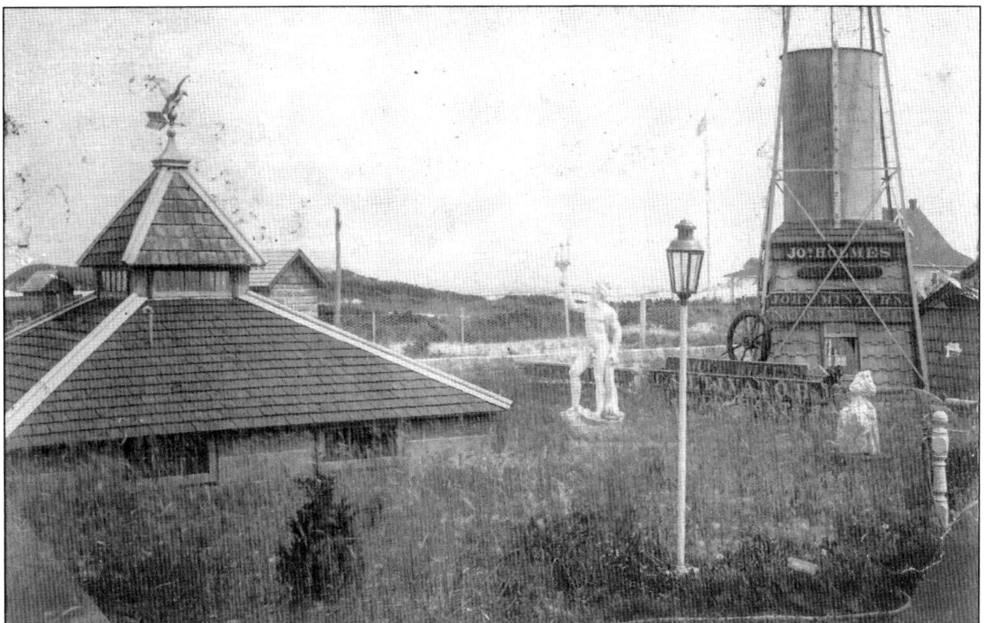

Towered over by the artesian well on the right, John Haddock's East Fourth Street yard was a hodgepodge of collected detritus from the beach. He even bought some artifacts from faraway places, like Malaysia; his appetite for nautical paraphernalia become insatiable. Guided tours were offered to friends and strangers alike. When the house was undermined and moved in 1920, virtually all of his collection was lost.

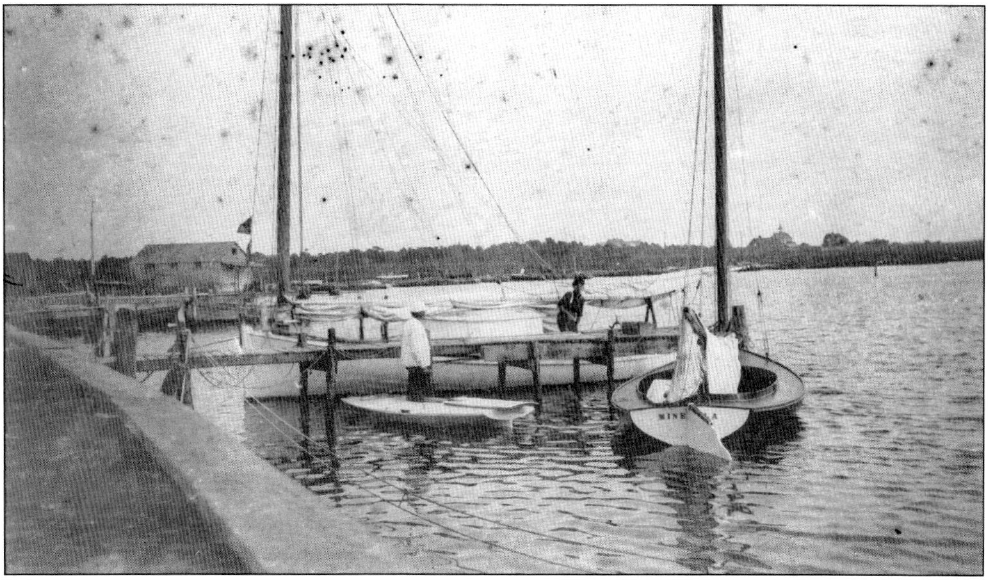

The West Sixth Street harbor was the hub of seagoing activity in old Barnegat City. Haddock's boathouse is in the distance in this turn-of-the-century postcard, while the Whetstone yacht *Aileen* is the large sailboat on the far side of the dock. This port would last until the land eroded in the late 1920s.

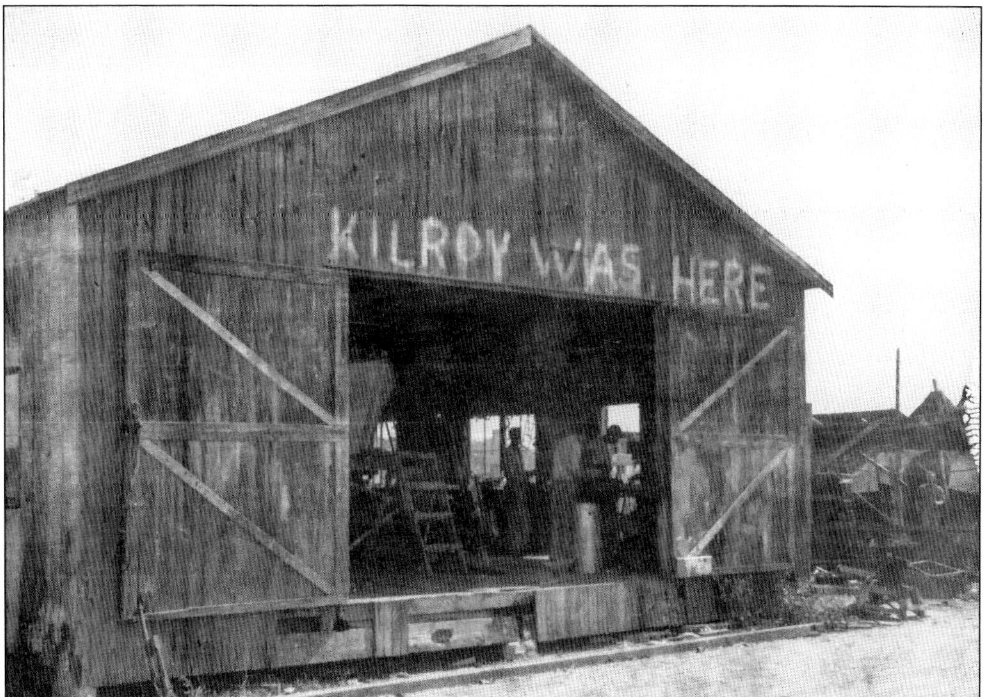

The Sundquist boatbuilding garage, pictured behind the West Sixth Street harbor in this undated photograph, was one of several that used to serve the fishermen at Barnegat City. During World War II, the "Kilroy was here" joke among soldiers found its way back from the battlefields and was scrawled atop his workshop.

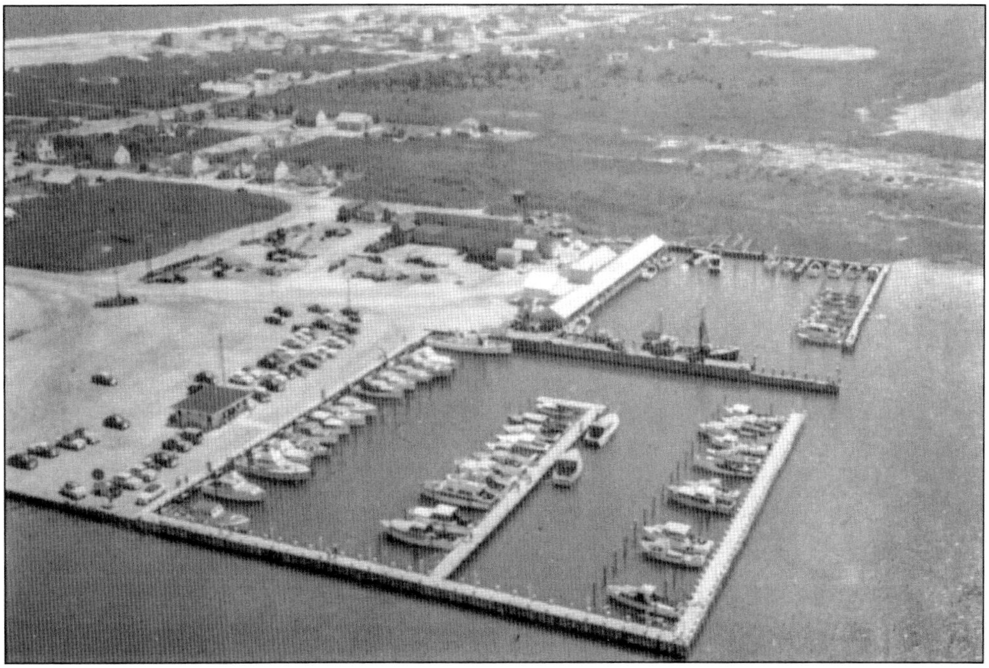

Construction of a dock at West Eighteenth Street was gradual at first, and used as many recycled materials as possible, including pieces of area bridges. After the Independent Fish Company bought the land in 1929, the site was transformed into a bustling port. A neighboring yacht basin was formalized in 1952. Both are pictured in this 1960s postcard.

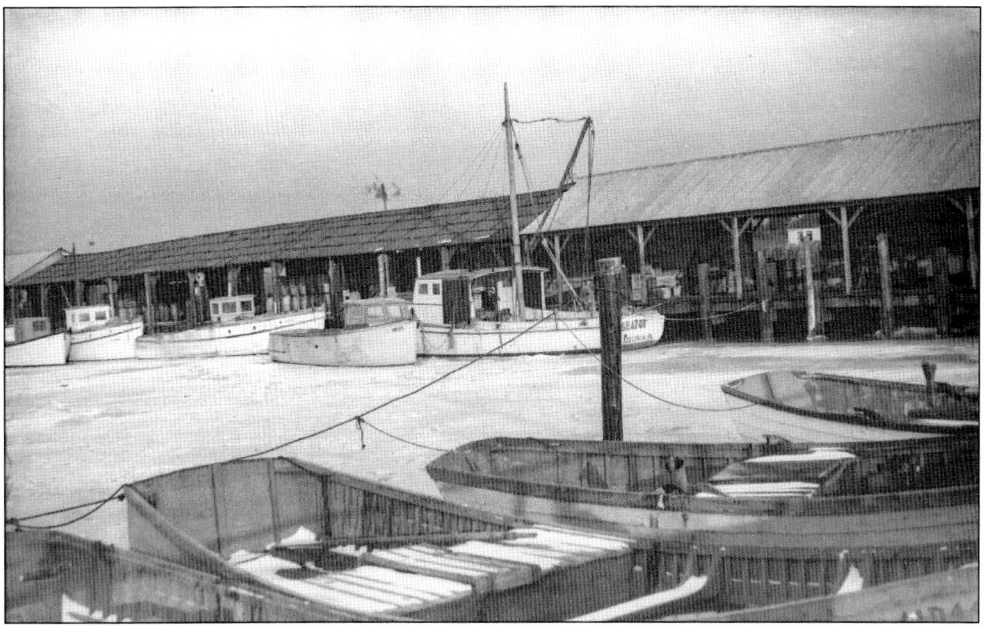

Independent Dock, seen here clogged by ice, was not an overnight success. It was the sons of the original investors who finally reached the promised land. The growth of the tilefish fishery, thanks to the dogged determination of local captains like John Larson Jr. and Lou Puskas, ushered in a new era for Barnegat Light that saw catches from its waters in demand around the world.

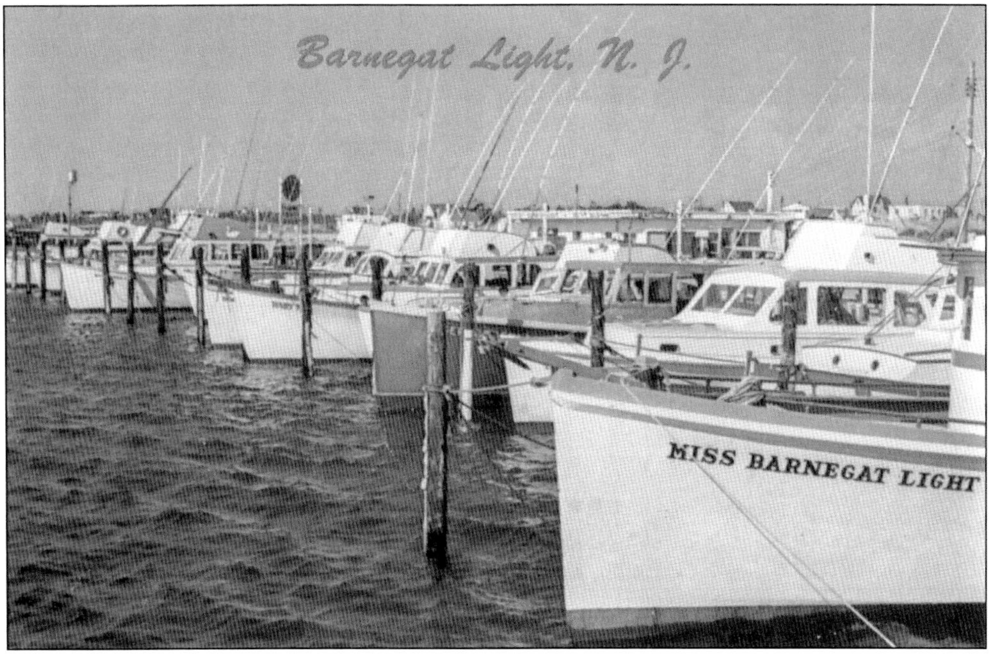

A rise in day-tripping and boat rentals helped the Barnegat Light Yacht Basin grow from its infancy in the 1950s. As the years passed, more and more fishermen bought second boats to take growing crowds eager to go out for an afternoon but who could not afford their own boat rental. Boats like the *Miss Doris Mae*, *Carolyn Ann*, and *Miss Barnegat Light* dominated the basin, pictured here.

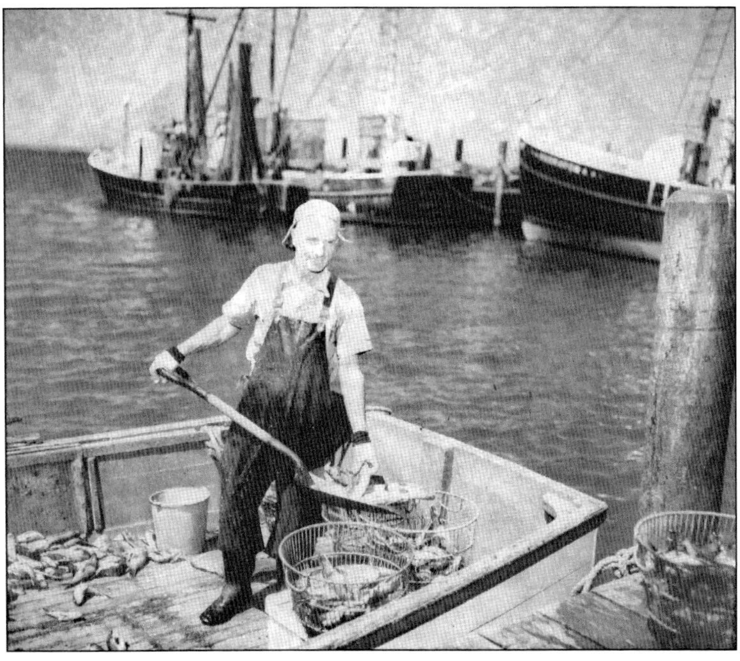

David Hansen shows off his catch in this undated photograph. The seven original members who remained in the 1960s were John Engelsen, David Hansen, Axel Jacobsen, Jens Jensen, John Larson Sr., Peder Nordstrand, and Otto Olsen. Many of their children carry on the fishing tradition today.

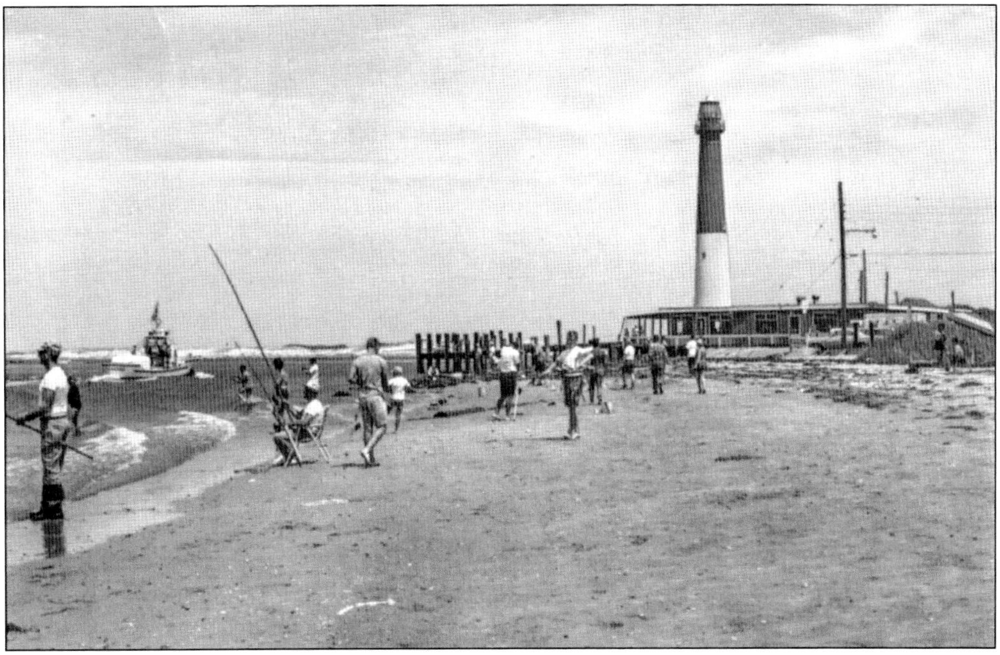

Among tourists, a favorite fishing spot was the shoreline next to Andy Bjornberg's bait and tackle shop at the end of Broadway, pictured here. After the demise of the Sunset Hotel, the area was frequented by even more fishermen eager to try for a record breaker. Even after the channel was redirected farther west in the 1940s, the fish kept biting in the usual spots.

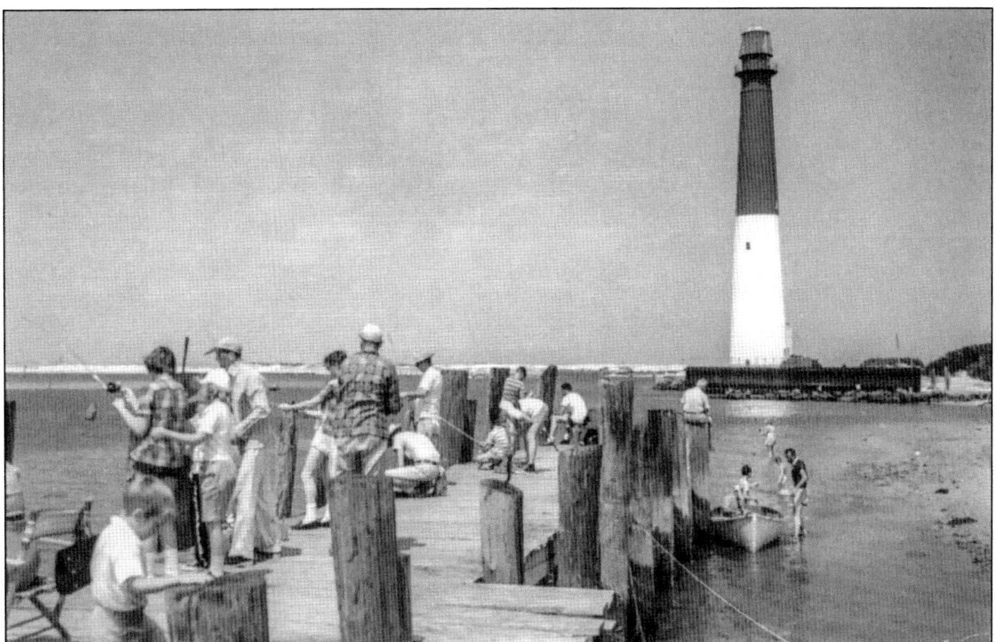

Andy Bjornberg's shop was also famous in the area for its dock, seen in this postcard, off of which people would cast and sit for hours on end. The rocky shore in this spot used to extend underneath Andy's, making it a true dockside location. This was later filled in and leveled, with a bulkhead affixing the bay shore in the 2000s.

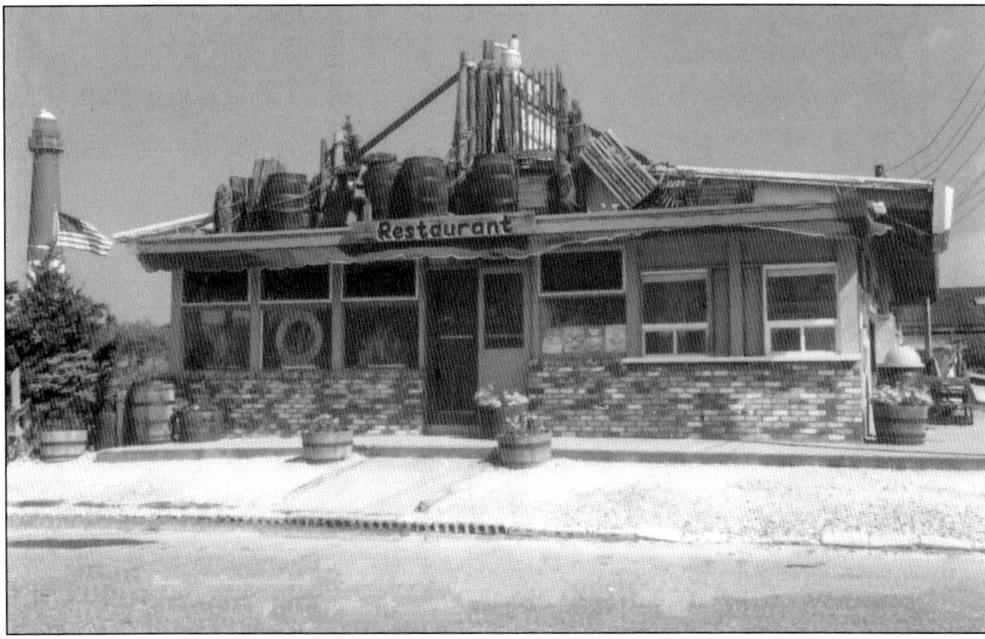

Built in the 1960s, another popular gathering spot along Broadway in Barnegat Light is Kelly's Restaurant, seen here with its maritime decor. Featuring a classic diner counter along with tables, everyone who visited during the summer would grab a meal here. The Dairy Queen that shared the space guaranteed long lines into the road were common on hot summer nights.

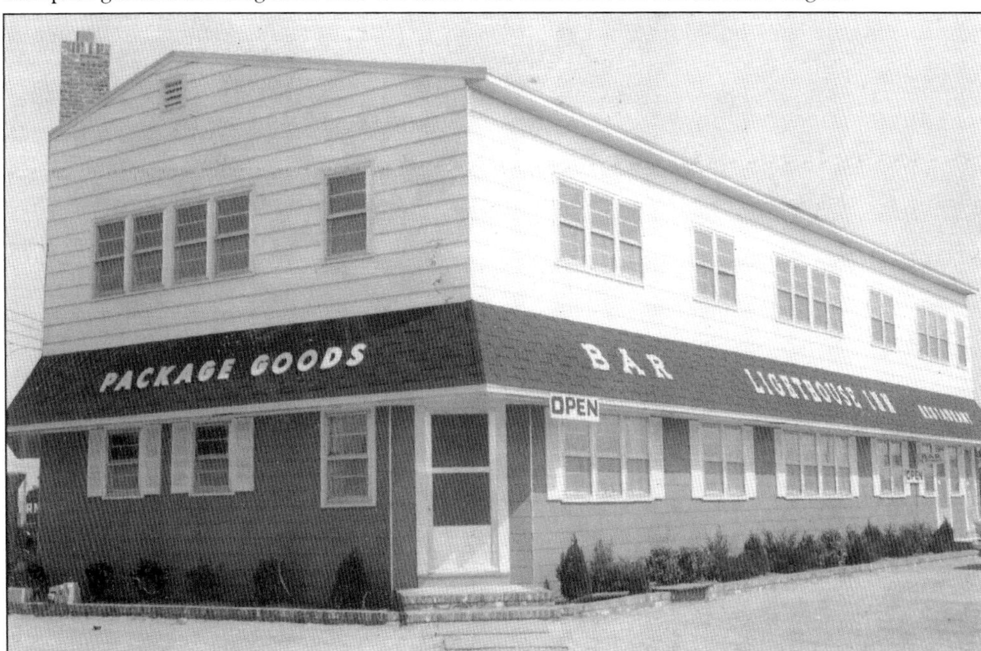

In the 1920s, a house and standalone garage on the corner of West Fourth Street and Broadway was built and run as a tavern called Hans'. It was a popular place among locals until it was torn down in 1960 and the Lighthouse Inn, pictured here, built. Later Rick's American Café, it was a regional hot spot for big musical acts such as Joan Jett. (Courtesy of Margaret Thomas Buchholz.)

Across from the West Sixth Street harbor was Kubel's, another popular watering hole. Named after its third owner, the 1920s-era bar was expanded several times as tourism brought more vacationers to Barnegat Light. Pictured here is one of its most famous visitors, Sinbad the Coast Guard dog. He would come in, hop onto a stool, and lap up a shot and a beer.

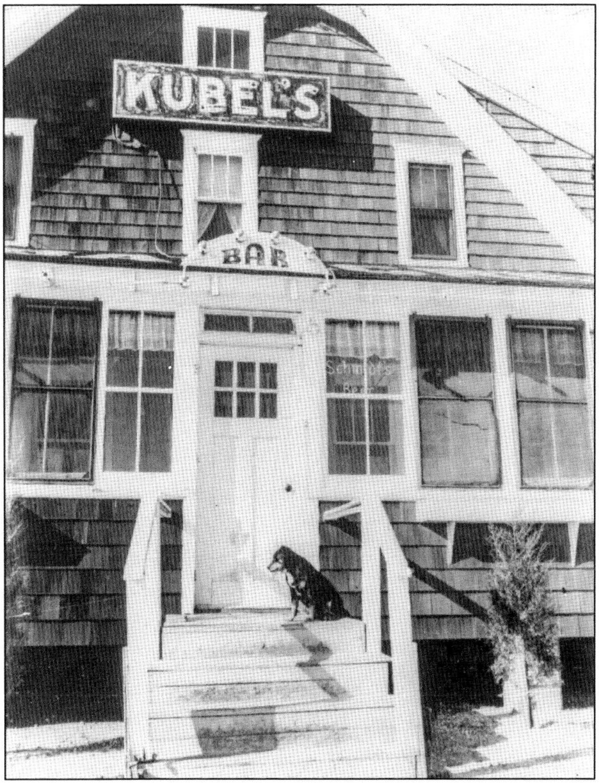

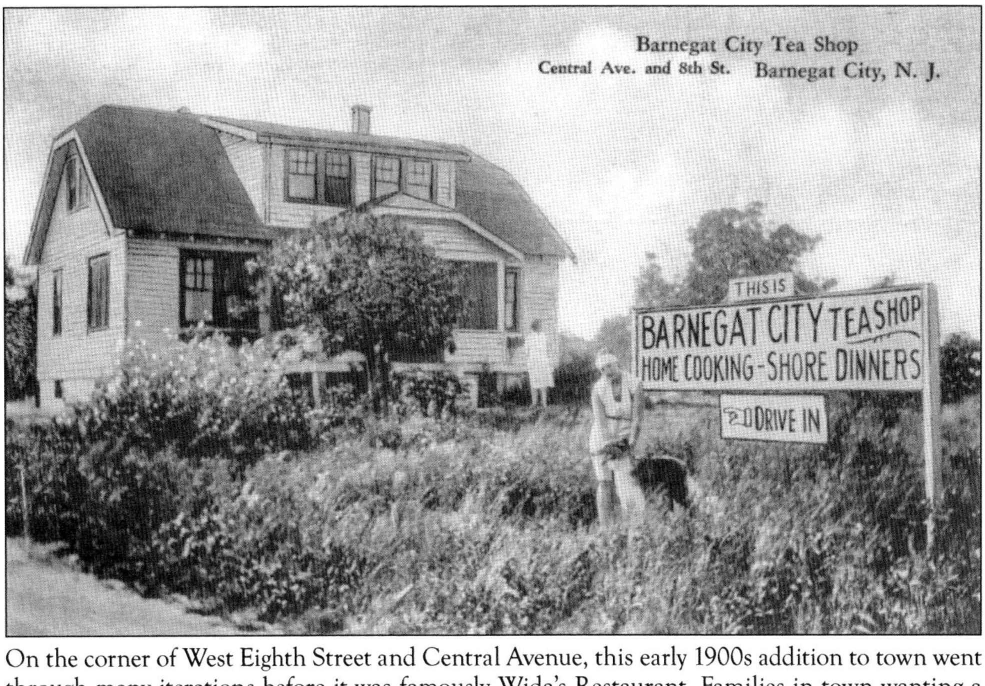

On the corner of West Eighth Street and Central Avenue, this early 1900s addition to town went through many iterations before it was famously Wida's Restaurant. Families in town wanting a meal would head to Wida's or Kelly's Restaurant for dinner. Breakfast was, and still is, usually had at Mustache Bill's Diner on the next corner. Wida's finally closed and was torn down in the 1990s.

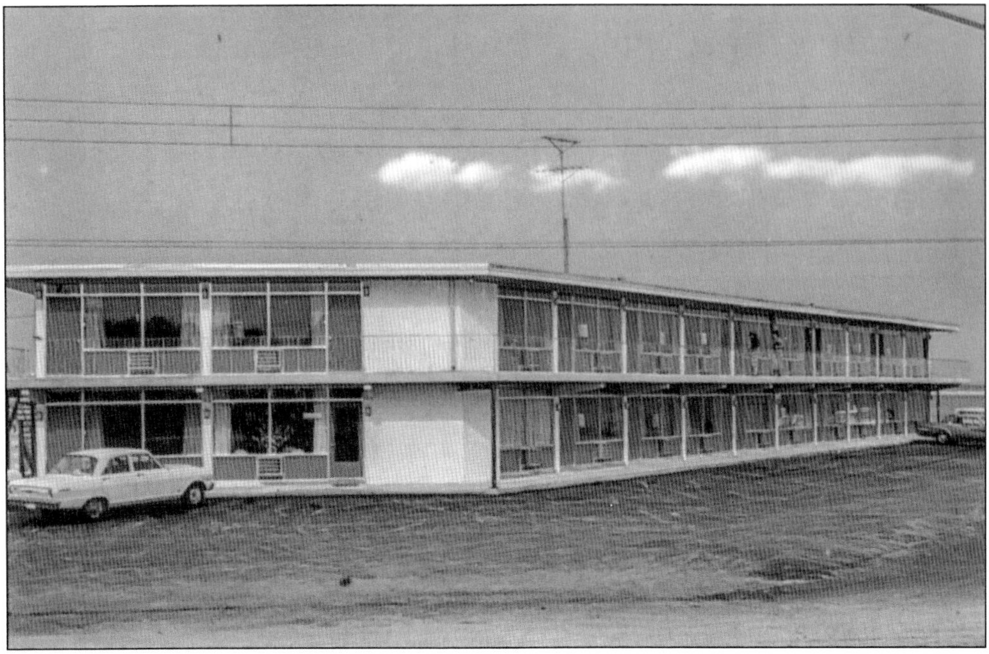

With the loss of the Oceanic, Sunset, and Social Hotels, lodging for those wanting to visit Barnegat Light but not rent or own a home became a need. That began to change in the 1950s with the arrival of motels. This one sprang up around 1960 on Broadway near the site of the Sunset. It was most well-known as Donovan's Reef and is now condominiums.

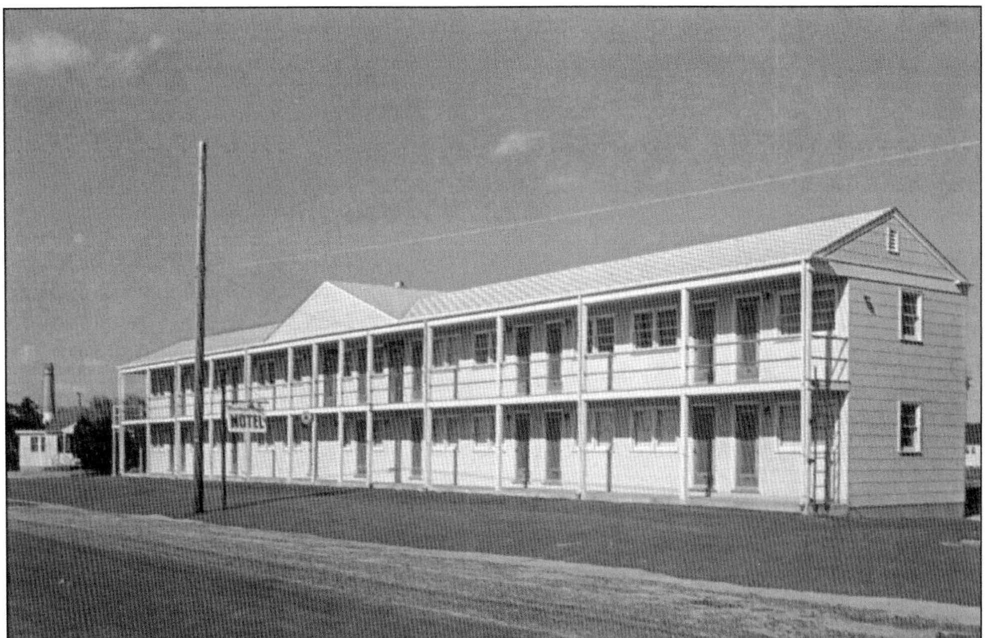

The 19-unit Barnegat Light Motel, pictured in this postcard, was built on Broadway between West Seventh and Eighth Streets in the 1950s. Built and owned by island fisherman Allan Anderson, it was the first new lodging in Barnegat Light since the Oceanic, Sunset, and Social Hotels were built in the 1880s.

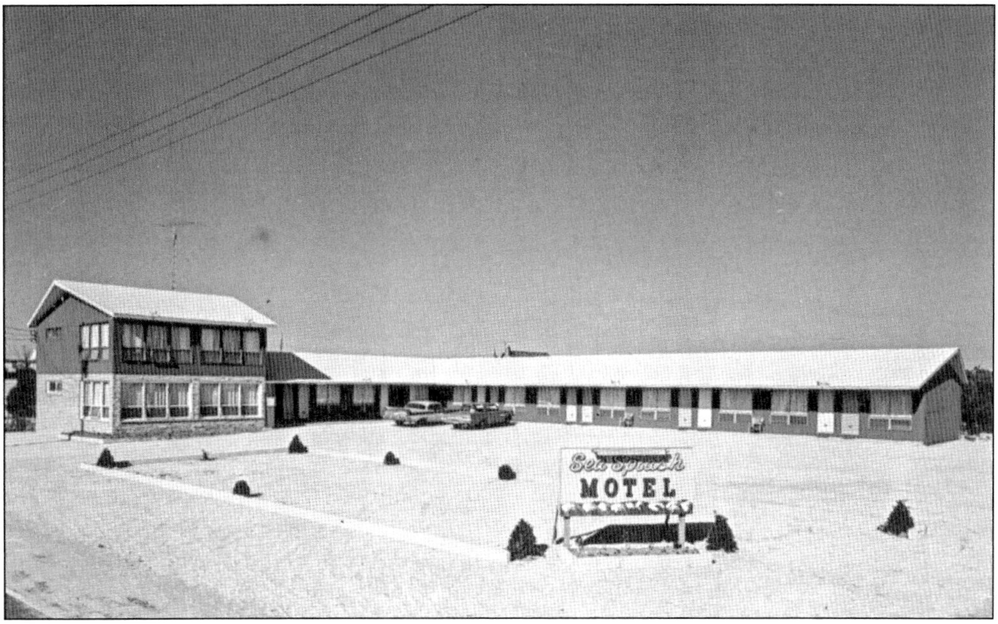

Seen in this postcard, the Sea Splash Motel, now the North Shore Inn, was built in the late 1960s by business partners Madeline Snesky and Helen Achren on the corner of East Ninth Street and Central Avenue. In 1971, the motel added a second story. Other local lodgings built around this time include Ella's Motel on West Eighteenth Street and the White Whale Motel on West Seventh Street.

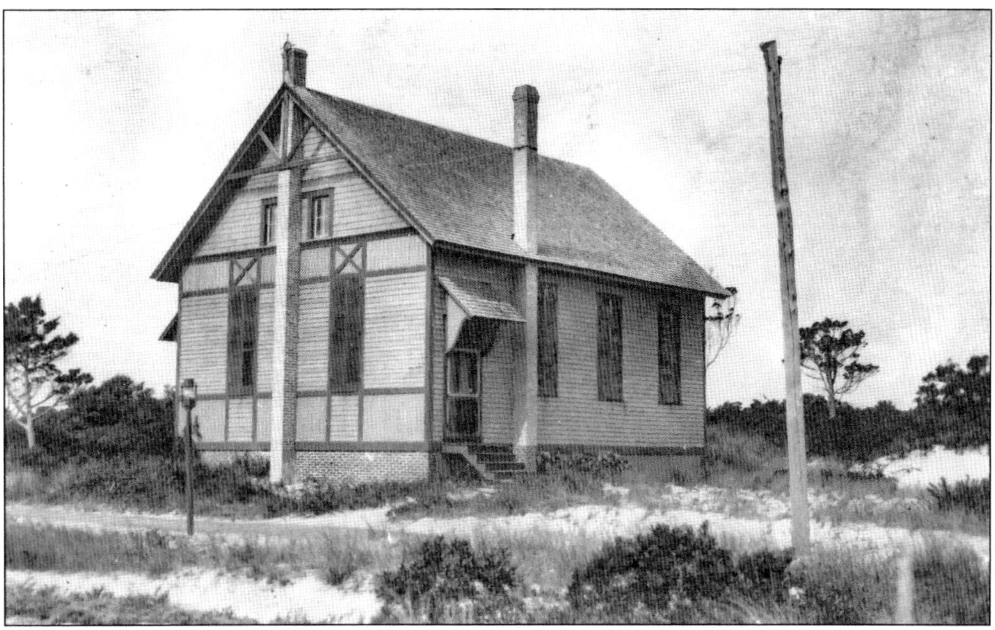

When William Bailey and Benjamin Archer built the Oceanic Hotel, they wanted to provide spiritual comfort to their guests along with everything else. To that end, they built this nondenominational church at the corner of West Seventh Street and Central Avenue. Over the years, it served as a theater and meetinghouse. In recent years, it became an Episcopal church, St. Peter's at the Light.

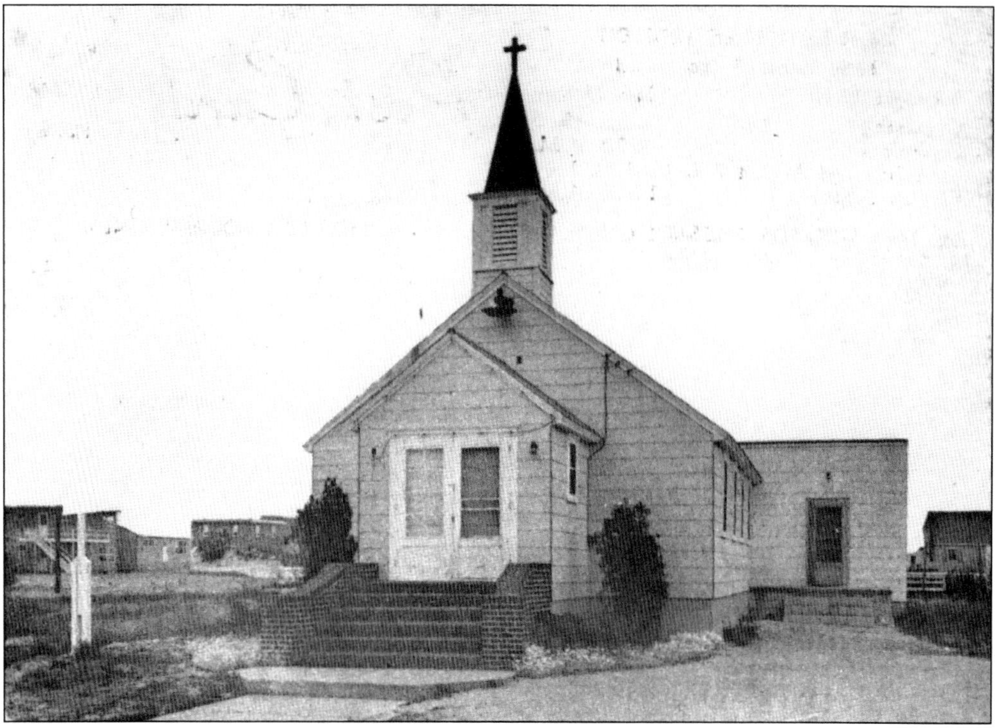

On the corner of East Eighteenth Street and Central Avenue, Zion Lutheran Church has served Barnegat Light for much of the 20th century. Seen here before it was attractively adorned with pines, the church was established in 1940 by local fishermen and has grown to become a part of town traditions, from its bake sales to its rummage sales, while attracting many summer vacationers as well.

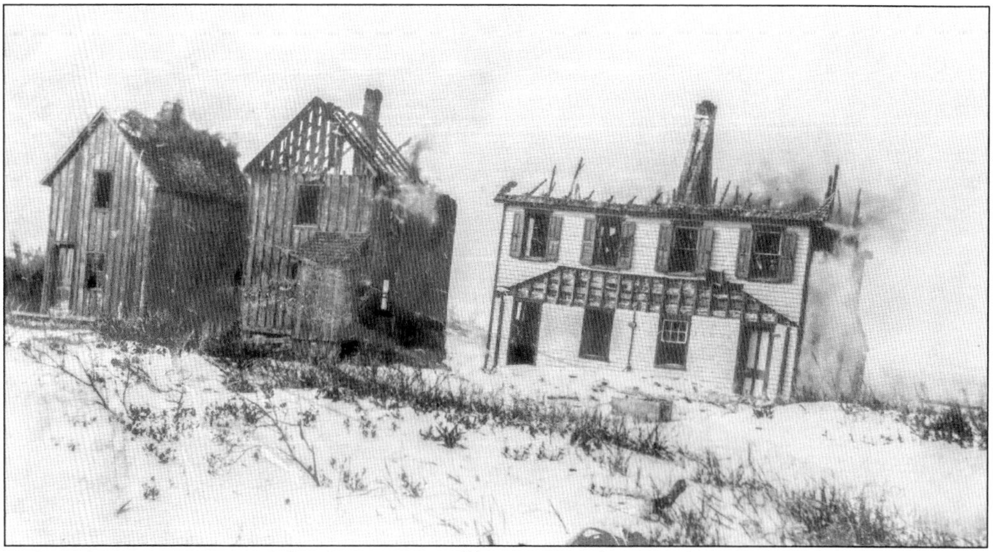

Before the Barnegat City School on West Fifth Street and Central Avenue was built in 1903, a cottage on West Third Street was used. It was decided in 1902 that a new, larger school was needed. Construction began in the summer of 1903, and the new school opened in November of the same year. Fortunately, it was only at this time that the old school caught fire, pictured here at center.

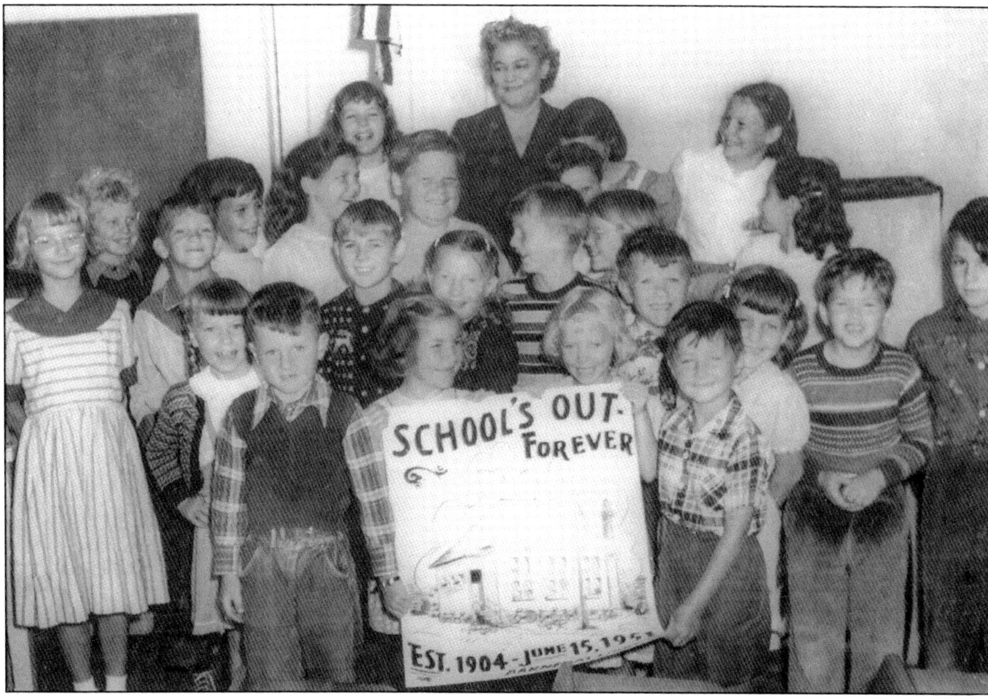

The Barnegat City schoolhouse taught children from Barnegat City and neighboring Harvey Cedars. Enrollment grew over the decades. The construction of the Long Beach Island Grade School in Ship Bottom in 1951 offered larger, more modern accommodations. The last class and last teacher, Freda Cranmer, are seen in this photograph commemorating the school's closing after 48 years.

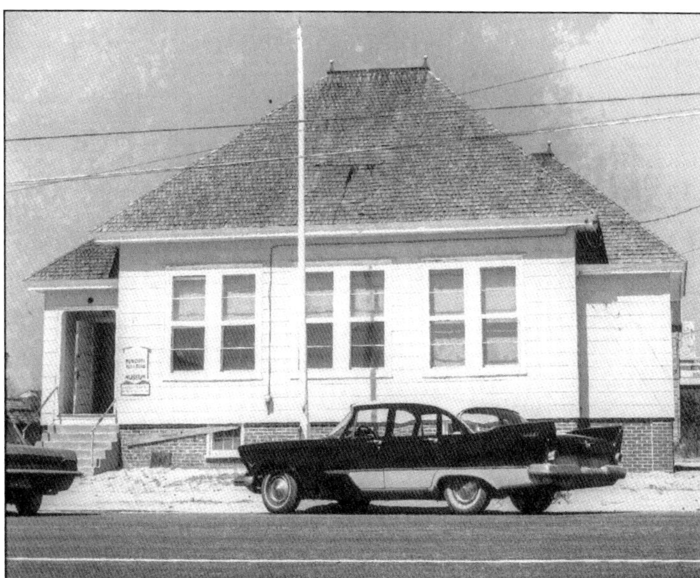

There were questions about what to do with the former schoolhouse after it closed. For a time, the town used it as meeting space. In 1954, a group of locals with the support of Ocean County's director of publicity, Jack Lamping, established the Barnegat Light Historical Society & Museum and filled it with family heirlooms and historical artifacts. In 1957, the original Barnegat Lighthouse lens was added as the centerpiece.